Ayrshire Echoes

Ayrshire Echoes

People, Places & Past Times

John Kellie

carn

© John Kellie, 2013.
First Published in Great Britain, 2013.

ISBN - 978 0 9567550 5 6

Published by Carn Publishing,
Lochnoran House,
Auchinleck,
Ayrshire, KA18 3JW.

www.carnpublishing.com

Printed by Bell & Bain Ltd,
Glasgow, G46 7UQ.

JOHN KELLIE

John Kellie was born in Ayrshire and educated at Pinmore, Kilmarnock and Glasgow. An enthusiastic outdoorsman and freelance writer, over the years his work has found its way into a variety of magazines on both sides of the Atlantic, as well as broadsheet and tabloid newspapers. He taught secondary school English for the best part of three decades, both in Scotland and Canada, until a brush with malaria in the jungles of New Guinea prompted a rethink and he is now writing and travelling full-time. *Ayrshire Echoes* is his first book.

For my late parents,
Marion Bryson of Galston and Robert Kellie of Pinmore.

Contents

Illustrations

Introduction

'You can always tell an Ayrshire man - but you can't tell him much!'
(as told to me by the late John McCulloch, Ballochtoul, Girvan.)

Ayrshire ceased to exist - at least in the official sense - during the 1970s when those and such as those decreed that the old county, in existence since the fourteenth century, should henceforth be abolished and absorbed within a new regional framework. The sprawling Strathclyde Region that they came up with stretched from the borderlands of Galloway, up through the central belt of Scotland as far as the mountains of Glen Coe, taking in as it did so roughly half of the entire Scottish population and yoking together communities and cultures as far-flung and disparate as the teeming city of Glasgow on the one hand and tiny Hebridean islands on the other. In no meaningful sense a 'local' authority, it should have come as no surprise to anyone that the behemoth, Strathclyde, proved unloved and unwanted and had to be dismantled little more than twenty years after its inception. The region's successor was an Ayrshire of sorts, divided along arbitrary lines and bureaucratically administered by three separate local authorities.

The failed attempt at regionalisation had demonstrated all too clearly that loyalty to the old county - centuries in the making - could not be so easily swept aside. That said, Ayrshire was not always a unified entity. During the Dark Ages a broad sweep of the county - the districts of Kyle and Cunninghame - formed an integral part of the ancient kingdom of Strathclyde (from which, of course, the unwieldy 1970s construct took its name) while the early history of the remaining southerly division of Ayrshire, Carrick, was by contrast bound up with the kingdom of Galloway to the south. The three territories became loosely unified with the establishment of a Sheriffdom of Ayr in the early years of the thirteenth century, but not until the coronation in 1371 of King Robert II - a Stewart of Kyle himself - did Cunninghame, Kyle and Carrick became properly amalgamated and a recognisable Ayrshire emerge.

With a coastline extending over 80 miles from tip to toe, Ayrshire formed the largest county in lowland Scotland, the shape of a crescent moon whose concave rim was washed by the waters of the Firth of Clyde and, in the far south, the North Channel between Scotland and Ireland. Almost without exception, the inland frontier followed lonely upland watersheds, effectively isolating Ayrshire from its neighbours and contributing perhaps to a highly-developed sense of local identity. As it worked its way south, the county's hilly backbone steadily increased in height and grandeur until finally it culminated in the airy summit of Shalloch on Minnoch, at 2,520 feet the highest hill wholly within Ayrshire's boundaries.

When it comes to producing national heroes, the county punched well above its weight. Many of William Wallace's celebrated exploits took place on Ayrshire soil, and the theory has gained ground in recent times that Wallace was born, not in neighbouring Renfrewshire - as was traditionally accepted - but rather at Ellerslie, near Kilmarnock. In 1274 Marjorie Bruce gave birth in Turnberry Castle to a son, Robert, who at eighteen years of age replaced his father as Earl of Carrick. Bruce's work, so decisively concluded on the field of Bannockburn, was begun seven years earlier in the shadow of Loudoun Hill. In a more settled age, the poetry of Robert Burns found a global audience that extended far and beyond the ranks of the literati.

But this Ayrshire of ours amounts to a good deal more than the sum total of its landscapes or, for that matter, its illustrious figures. On the farms and in the factories, ordinary folk too made their contribution: the tillers of the soil who over generations wrested fertility out of a sour earth; the men and women who declined to bend in the face of power and privilege, and all too often paid a heavy price; those brave souls who harvested fuel from the bowels of the earth to stoke the nation's furnaces and keep the wheels of industry turning. They too form vital threads in Ayrshire's tapestry and, alongside our great heroes, their stories deserve to be told.

In putting together this collection of Ayrshire stories I am indebted to a great many people, from shepherds in lonely places who have pointed me in the right direction, to those who have invited me into their homes and generously taken the time to share their knowledge and experiences. The following people deserve particular mention though, needless to say, any errors or inaccuracies are no-one's responsibility but my own:

Tom Barclay, Stewarton; Elizabeth Bicket, Fenwick; Keith Brown, Ballantrae; Roy Campbell, Glenluce; Alisdair Cochrane, Prestwick; Jean Dunlop, Ballantrae; Ken Harris, Glasgow; Hugh and Netta Hendry, Newmilns; David Hunter, Dailly; Ian Jones, Girvan; William Kyle, Cumnock; Tom Mackin, Muirkirk; Glenys McMillan, Prestwick; Paul and Julie Secord, Lendalfoot; Hugh Sloan, Colmonell; Frances Smith, Cumnock; Ken Wood, Mauchline. Also to the Staff of Carnegie Library, Ayr; Baird Institute, Cumnock; Dick Institute, Kilmarnock; Burns Monument Centre, Kilmarnock; and the North Ayrshire Heritage Centre, Saltcoats.

Laurienne's Cross, On Kilantringan Moor and *When Times Were Tough* were first published in *Scottish Home & Country*. *A Monumental Mystery, Flitting the Sow, In the Howe of Laggan, On Gallow Hill, Secret Stairs & Dungeons, The Coilus Enigma, The Minister's Curse* and *Wallace's Forgotten Tower* were first published in *Scottish Memories*. *Hugh's Pirlie-Pig* was first published in *The Countryman*. *The Drowning of John Gallon* was first published in the *Cumnock Chronicle*. *The Last Pigeon Post* was first published in *The Scots Magazine*. *Murder on Craigdow Moor, The Blacksmith's Boy, The Dalgig Martyrs* and *The Loudoun Burning* were first published in the USA in *The Highlander*.

LIFE & LORE

The Norsemen at Largs

An old legend recounts how, during the thirteenth century, one of the Hunters of Hunterston Castle foresaw the dramatic events of the Battle of Largs. By peering into a wishing well, apparently she was able to preview the entire progress of the battle as events played out on the surface of the water. For those Scots willing to go along with her story, the young lady's unusual vision must surely have provided a useful pre-battle morale-booster. For our part, we might lament the fact that she didn't have the presence of mind to jot down a few details for posterity since accounts of the battle itself, especially from a Scottish point of view, are thin on the ground.

By the autumn of 1263 trouble had been simmering for decades along Scotland's western seaboard. During the first half of the century, the Scots king, Alexander II, had made a number of unsuccessful attempts to consolidate his kingdom by wresting control of the Western Isles from Norse jurisdiction. Following the old king's death, his son, Alexander III, made efforts to settle the matter by negotiating a deal with Norway. When overtures to purchase the islands came to nothing, the Scots finally lost patience and invaded Skye, prompting King Haakon of Norway to assemble a mighty punitive force which departed from the city of Bergen during the summer of 1263, reputedly the most formidable fleet ever to set sail from Norwegian shores, comprising, so it is said, well over one hundred ships.

Things didn't go entirely to plan. Who knows whether King Haakon smelt a rat at the lukewarm reception he received from the Hebridean chiefs who undoubtedly sensed that power lay in the balance and hedged their bets accordingly? Whether or not he suffered a twinge of doubt, it was too late for second thoughts and he pressed on south, capturing castles and raiding coastal areas as he went, until finally his great fleet looped around the Mull of Kintyre and sailed into the waters of the Firth of Clyde where once again it turned north.

The Scottish king, of course, had been kept well informed of the Norwegians' movements and, in the absence of a fleet at his disposal, had set out to assemble a force of fighting men - a few miles inland, it is said, tucked away in a fold among the Kilbirnie hills. Mindful that the season was advancing, the wily Alexander played for time, negotiating at length with the Norwegians over sovereignty while he waited for the weather to break. Meanwhile his army continued to grow in numbers. As a diversionary tactic, Haakon dispatched forty of his ships to the head of Loch Long where their crews disembarked and portaged across the narrow neck of land to Loch Lomond. At Tarbet they took to the water once again and proceeded to travel up and down the loch, ravaging shoreside communities and terrorising their inhabitants.

But Alexander's stalling tactics soon paid off when nature most conveniently stepped in, prompted, the Norwegians were convinced, by Scottish witchcraft. A violent storm swept in during the night of 30 September, causing the ships of the Norwegian fleet to clash, one against the other, in the howling darkness and forcing a number of them, including a store-ship, on to the rocky shoreline. Some say that King Haakon retreated to the Isle of Cumbrae where, in an attempt to propitiate the elements, his priests conducted mass - to no avail, as it turned out, as the storm continued to rage unabated.

The Scots were quick to exploit this chance turn of events, energetically attacking the crews of the stranded ships, and forcing Haakon to send in reinforcements the following morning for the relief of their beleaguered compatriots. So ferocious was the Scottish onslaught, however, that, after a long day's fighting against the Scots - both Highland and Lowland foot soldiers and mounted knights - Haakon and his men found themselves with little option other than to re-embark and retreat. Rather than abandon supplies which would benefit the enemy, the Norwegians destroyed their beached store-ship by fire before they pulled back.

According to legend, Haakon requested and received leave to bury the Norse dead in a Christian burial-ground but where that might be located has never been ascertained. During the early nineteenth century, a number of cairns situated in the vicinity of the Chapel of St Vey on the Wee Cumbrae were excavated and found to contain not only bones but also steel helmets and other items, though the dead accommodated there would scarcely have accounted for the casualties incurred during the two-day

Battle of Largs Memorial

battle. Despite the fact that King Haakon left the battlefield in one piece, an ancient tumulus close to Largs became known as 'Haco's [sic] Tomb', while a retired local doctor, John Cairnie, took it upon himself in 1823 to affix a brass plaque to a standing stone in the garden of Curlinghall, identifying the site - in Latin, no less - as the resting-place of one Haco of Stein, a member of King Haakon's retinue. What evidence Dr Cairnie had is unclear, but it seems unlikely if, under the terms of the truce, the defeated Norsemen were granted sufficient time to erect hefty monoliths over the graves of their fallen countrymen. The reality is that both 'Haco's Tomb' and Dr Cairnie's stone predate the medieval period by a very substantial margin.

A few years after Dr Cairnie embellished his standing stone, an extraordinary find occurred just south of Largs which inevitably became linked with the famous battle. In autumn 1830 two labourers were digging ditches on the Hunterston estate on the narrow strip of land between the Hawking Craig, a western spur of Goldenberry Hill, and the sea, when they unearthed a remarkable artefact. Approximately five inches across, the 'Hunterston Brooch', as it came to be known, had been cast in silver, then decorated with gold filigree of astonishing intricacy and inlaid with pieces of amber. Undoubtedly the work of a highly-skilled jeweller, the item was judged to be of Scottish or Irish manufacture and dated to around AD 700. Intriguingly, two inscriptions on the reverse-side, probably added some time later, were written in Viking runes: *This brooch belongs to Malbritha* said one; and the second - *Olfriti owns this brooch*. The notion that those mentioned might have had an involvement in the Battle of Largs can be no more than speculative, though local folklore does record a skirmish between Scots and Norwegians which was said to have taken place in the vicinity of Goldenberry Hill.

Setting Dr Cairnie's plaque to one side, no-one could accuse the burghers of Largs of acting with undue haste when they finally got round to erecting a commemorative monument to the famous victory on their doorstep. The idea of constructing a pillar to mark the sixth centenary of the battle had been mooted in the mid-nineteenth century by the proprietor of Noddsdale House, just outside the town, but his idea met with little enthusiasm. When a similar scheme resurfaced in 1910, this time proposed by John Stewart, who ran a photographic business in the town, it is reasonable to suspect that profit as well as patriotism underpinned the suggestion. For some decades the Clyde coast had been feeling the commercial benefit of tourism, and probably it was thought that a new visitor attraction in Largs could hardly go amiss. A consensus emerged that whatever shape the memorial might take, for maximum exposure it should be clearly visible to those travelling both by land and sea.

The project gathered momentum as a number of heavyweights stepped aboard. The Provost and Corporation of Largs got behind the idea, with several organisations also expressing an interest, such as The Scottish Patriotic Society of Glasgow, The St Andrew's Society of Edinburgh and The Scottish Rights Association of Greenock. A local bigwig, the Earl of Glasgow, whose ancestors had been resident at nearby Kelburn Castle since the era of the Norse invasions, emerged as a willing figurehead. Addressing a meeting in Largs Public Hall, the elderly Earl veered slightly off-piste when he appeared to base his account of the battle on the Norwegian version of events which naturally highlighted the heroism of the invaders but he was tactfully repositioned in accordance with the party line and carried on to complete proceedings without further hitch. A committee was appointed to take charge of organisation and fund-raising.

Sadly, the consensus that had characterised the project's inception was to prove short-lived. Despite uncertainty as to where exactly the battle had taken place, the question of the proposed monument's location was settled fairly quickly - or, at least, appeared to be. After considering a number of possible sites, the committee accepted the offer of a gift of land on the foreshore from its wealthy owner, Otto Ernst Phillipi of Warren Park, Largs - a German-born managing director of J. & P. Coats, the Paisley thread-manufacturer. The site was the rocky peninsula known as the first Bowen Craig, the place where - in popular imagination at least - a number of King Haakon's ships had been blown ashore. It was deemed a suitable location whose solid rock foundations would make it unlikely that the proposed memorial would ever be undermined by the sea. Largs Town Council duly set about making necessary arrangements to extend the burgh boundaries so as to incorporate the site within its jurisdiction.

Next to be settled was the form that the proposed monument might take. Initial suggestions that an obelisk possessed the virtues of being both visually impressive and also inexpensive were countered by the argument that, Egyptian in origin, it was an alien form in Scotland. A native Celtic cross was put forward as an alternative, impartially decorated with both Celtic and Norse engravings. As a means of resolving matters, it was decided to initiate a competition, inviting ideas for the proposed monument, which attracted in the event a total of 59 entries, one of the most popular being a bronze statue of King Alexander III, mounted on a natural rock pedestal and - unnecessarily - shielding his eyes from the sun as he gazed manfully out to sea. When push came to shove, the idea was rejected, largely on grounds of cost, as was Otto Phillipi's preferred submission.

On concluding their study of the entries, the committee plumped for the design submitted by a Glasgow architect, J. Sanderson Kay, whose idea had gained the approval of the Earl of Glasgow, as well as the public at large. One dissenting voice was Otto Ernst Phillipi who took the hump when his favourite design failed to gain approval and promptly withdrew his offer of land. A potentially tricky situation was averted when the Earl of Glasgow stepped in and donated a similar coastal plot, a short distance from the original location and in what many considered a superior spot. Not perhaps highly original, Kay's winning design was based on an indigenous Scottish edifice - the Pictish round tower - such as could be seen at Abernethy and Brechin and which some believed, probably erroneously, to have been constructed as a place of refuge from marauding Vikings. In addition to its native Scottish credentials, one advantage of building a tower, it was noted, was that building work could be halted whenever funds looked like drying up. A local contractor, James Hunter, submitted a tender of £290 and was duly awarded the contract, his first action to dispatch his foreman to Brechin to ascertain the dimensions of the town's ancient tower.

By summer 1912 the west coast version of Brechin's Pictish tower was complete and an inauguration ceremony was planned for Wednesday, 10 July. On the day a sizeable crowd assembled on the Bowen Craig in spite of weather that old King Haakon would undoubtedly have found familiar. (The Earl of Glasgow was later most indignant that both his and his wife's hats were ruined beyond repair by the rain.) Cutting a dash in full Highland regalia, in spite of wind and weather, was Theodore Napier, a somewhat eccentric Australian-born Jacobite who had founded the Victorian Scottish Home Rule Association in 1891. Speeches were made and flags flown - Scottish, British and Norwegian - though no Norwegian visitor is known to have been present at the ceremony. The Earl of Glasgow was presented with a silver model of the monument, but sadly the weather dampened proceedings, putting paid to the day's planned musical programme.

It didn't take long for the Battle of Largs monument to acquire a nickname. The Earl of Glasgow was more than a little put out, apparently, when he learned how the irreverent local populace referred to the monument he had worked so hard to establish. With its dark whinstone walls and pointed red sandstone cap, the memorial had apparently become known as 'The caunle' - the candle - though this pithy Scots nickname was destined not to last. Who it was who first dubbed the Largs memorial 'the Pencil' is now forgotten but within a few years of its inauguration the name was in general use. Today the monument is seldom referred to in any other way.

At the end of the day, it doesn't really matter whether events commemorated by 'the Pencil' constituted a monumental Scots victory or were, as is widely thought today, something more akin to a prolonged series of skirmishes. The Battle of Largs' significance rests in its position at a turning-point in Scottish history. Possibly already a sick man, the Norwegian king, Haakon, retreated round the Mull of Kintyre and turned north to Orkney where he intended to spend the winter, but before the year was out he died there in Kirkwall. Magnus VI followed in his father's footsteps but, sensing a palpable shift in power, the Hebridean chiefs switched sides and swore allegiance to Alexander III and to Scotland. When the Treaty of Perth was finalised in 1266, the era of Norse invasions was officially brought to a close. With the sole exception of our southern neighbours, King Haakon and his Norwegian forces at Largs were the last foreign invaders ever to set foot on Scottish soil.

The Blacksmith's Boy

In a half-forgotten corner of an Ayrshire country churchyard lies the seventeenth century tombstone of a local blacksmith. Surprisingly grand, the stone is adorned with a shield and cross, with the motto, 'Virtue Through Struggle', inscribed in Latin beneath. In the quaint spelling of the time, the accompanying legend commemorates one 'Andro Snell [who] died March 10, 1663 aged 72,' and records that his memorial stone was erected by 'Mr. Johne Snell onely son of the forenamed in filial respect to the memory of his parents.' At the time of his father's death, John was in his mid-thirties - wealthy, educated and moving in influential London circles. The path that led him from a lowly boyhood in the Ayrshire countryside to a position of rank and status was one that few perhaps might have predicted.

Little is known of John Snell's early life. Even the supposed year of his birth – 1629 – is no better than an approximation since his home parish of Colmonell did not maintain formal records until a century and a half later.

Snell Monument

What is certain is that in 1642 he matriculated at Glasgow University, aged about 13, signing himself in Latin: *Johannes Snell*. The University record describes him as 'the son of Andrew Snell in McCalanstone' - a name no longer recognised in the Colmonell district. Of his 72 fellow freshmen, the majority sprang from influential and landowning backgrounds, making the presence among them of a blacksmith's son perhaps a little unusual.

Snell's career at Glasgow University corresponded with unsettled times. Conflict raged south of the border between Parliament and King, and the fall-out inevitably spilled into Scotland. In common with many of his fellow students, Snell appended his signature to a copy of *The Solemn League and Covenant* (now preserved in Glasgow's Hunterian Museum), contesting King Charles' right to meddle in the Scottish Kirk. His decision to sign appears puzzling in the light of subsequent events, as the next time his name surfaces the young Snell has departed for England and enlisted in the Royalist army. No record exists of him having completed his studies at Glasgow.

The years that followed saw John Snell's involvement in a number of Civil War engagements, including the Royalist defeat at Worcester in September 1651 from which he narrowly escaped with his life – a turn of events which paradoxically he appears to have used to his advantage. In the aftermath of the battle, he is believed to have sought refuge at the home of the Archdeacon of Chester, Sir George Snell, where he was introduced to the churchman's nephew by marriage, Sir Orlando Bridgeman. For Snell this was to prove a fateful encounter.

That John and George Snell were related has never been established, though the Archdeacon, born around 1582, was of an age that might plausibly have made him John's uncle. This might go some way to explaining the young Scot's curious fervour for the English Royalist cause, not to mention the Archdeacon's eagerness to place his young guest in the service of a rich and powerful nobleman such as Orlando Bridgeman. But a tentative solution to one mystery trails a second puzzle in its wake: why, we might wonder, would the younger brother of an English Archdeacon have chosen to seclude himself as a humble labouring man in a quiet Scottish parish? Andrew Snell's motive will probably never be known.

When Bridgeman engaged Snell as his clerk it signalled the beginning of the young Scot's rise to fortune. Son of the Lord Bishop of Chester, Sir Orlando was an eminent London lawyer whose Royalist credentials paid off at the Restoration of King Charles II in 1660 when he was made Lord Chief Baron of the Exchequer and, later that same year, Lord Chief Justice. On both occasions he was accompanied by his clerk, and as his star rose yet higher when he was promoted to Lord Keeper of the Great Seal in 1667, Snell duly followed as Seal-Bearer, an exalted position that he retained even under Bridgeman's successor, the Earl of Shaftesbury. When Shaftesbury in turn left office, he recommended Snell to the attention of the Duke of Monmouth who engaged him as secretary and commissioner of his extensive Scottish estates, acquired through a judicious marriage with a Buccleuch heiress.

Sadly our picture of Snell during this illustrious period remains rather two-dimensional, with private and domestic details notably lacking. We do know that he married, but the date and place of the wedding ceremony are uncertain, as is even his bride, Johanna's, maiden-name. The manor and lands of Ufton in Warwickshire became the couple's family home where, in due course, Johanna gave birth to an only child, Dorothy, who in the fullness of time made a favourable match when she wedded William Guise of Winterborough in neighbouring Gloucestershire. The blacksmith's boy, it would appear, had successfully scaled the social ladder and, secure in his position as a pillar of the establishment, he might have been tempted to cast off memories of his humble birth.

But not so. In 1661 Snell travelled back to Scotland where he visited his elderly father, probably for the last time, contributing on the same occasion 100 merks for poor-relief in Colmonell parish. In June of that same year he presented a six-volume *Great Bible in the Orientall* [*sic*] *Languages* to the library at Glasgow University, where he graduated M.A. the following year. There are records of further book donations, and Snell was active at this time in gaining places at Oxford University for Scottish students. But these were relatively minor acts of generosity when compared with the full extent of his philanthropy which would only become apparent after his death.

On 6 August 1679 Snell died at Oxford of causes unknown, probably not long before his fiftieth birthday. For the most part the terms of his will offer no surprises. His wife and daughter were well provided for, Johanna being granted lifetime tenure of the Warwickshire estates. From the will we discover, somewhat late in the day, that Snell had two sisters – Silvester, wife of the Oxford University Registrar, and a second sister who remains unnamed. More distant relations are not overlooked, with one nephew,

Robert Steward, receiving a supplementary £20 as a kindly nudge 'to binde him to a trade.' Servants at Ufton were to receive a full year's wages over and above their due, and money has been set aside for poor-relief. A further sum is earmarked for the repair of Ufton parish church. At first glance it might seem unexceptional, the will of a prosperous, community-minded citizen with an eye to his immortal soul.

But there is more. The residue of John Snell's estate was to be devoted to financing Scottish scholars, formerly students of Glasgow University, in furthering their studies at Oxford, an act of philanthropy, however, which was not without strings attached. Each subsidised student would be obliged to enter into Church of England holy orders, 'it being the testator's will and desire that every such scholar should return into Scotland.' Snell's intention is clear: to advance the cause of Anglicanism in Scotland. But before his wishes could be carried out, history intervened.

When the Glorious Revolution of 1688 placed William of Orange on the British throne, Scots Presbyterians found themselves once again in the driving-seat. As a result, the requirement for Snell scholars to take Anglican orders was revoked, as well as the injunction to return to Scotland. In 1693 Balliol was nominated as host college - an appropriate choice, perhaps, having been founded five centuries earlier by Devorgilla, Lady of Galloway, the mother of John Balliol, King of Scots. In 1699 the first Snell 'Exhibitioners', as they were known, commenced their studies at Balliol, and the three centuries since then have thrown up a variety of illustrious and otherwise interesting beneficiaries.

A number of Snell Exhibitioners were noteworthy less for their own achievements than through association. One of the earliest, Charles Gregory (Exhibitioner in 1699), was a kinsman and contemporary of Rob Roy MacGregor, the Scottish Robin Hood as some would have it. John Gibson Lockhart (1809) found fame when he married Sophia Charlotte, the daughter of Sir Walter Scott, while the young wife of David Scott Meikleham (1822), was Septima Randolph, a grand-daughter of US President, Thomas Jefferson. John MacCunn (1872) was the uncle of the romantic composer, Hamish MacCunn, while, continuing the musical theme, William Douglas Veitch (1819) was a descendant of none other than Annie Laurie of Maxwelton, heroine of the much-loved song that bears her name. Less well-connected, however, was William Young Sellar (1842) whose father, Patrick Sellar, factor to the infamous Duke of Sutherland, was guilty of some of the Highland Clearances' most dreadful atrocities.

Not every Exhibitioner had a career that went entirely without hitch. Robert Stirling (Exhibitioner in 1710) lost his place at Oxford because of his Jacobite leanings. Following a literary disagreement, Jonathan Henry Christie (1808) fought and won a duel after which he stood trial for murder and was subsequently acquitted. Christie's 'second', as it happened, was fellow-Exhibitioner, James Traill (1810).

But the vast majority of Snell Exhibitioners went on to pursue successful careers while a select few scaled the heights in their respective fields. Doubtless his benefactor would have been gratified to know that Archibald Campbell Tait (1829) rose through Church of England ranks to become Archbishop of Canterbury in 1869. At the time of the Indian Mutiny, Robert Blair (1852), Lieutenant of the 9th Lancers, was awarded the Victoria Cross for an act of heroism during which he was gravely wounded. Sadly he died soon after. (Remarkably his cousin, James Blair, was similarly decorated during the same conflict.) John Gibson Lockhart (1809) became the celebrated biographer of his father-in-law, the Waverley novelist, while folklorist Andrew Lang (1864), though largely neglected now, was one of the most popular and prolific writers of his day. With the publication in 1901 of his uncompromising novel, *The House with the Green Shutters*, George Douglas Brown (1891) diverted the entire course of Scottish fiction and set the tone for a new century.

In more recent times Neil MacCormick (1963), son of one of the Scottish National Party's founding members, rose to be an influential legal philosopher and sat for five years as an SNP Member of the European Parliament. But undoubtedly the most distinguished Exhibitioner to date was born in March 1723 at Kirkcaldy, gained a Snell scholarship at the age of 16, and with the publication of *The Wealth of Nations* in 1776 claimed his place as the foremost political thinker of his day and one of the key figures of the Scottish eighteenth century Enlightenment. John Snell's legacy may not have turned out exactly as he had envisaged, but with an Exhibitioner of Adam Smith's stature, it proved considerable nonetheless. What future Exhibitioners may achieve, time alone will tell.

The Cost of Coal

The use of coal has a lengthy pedigree in Scotland, though exactly how long no-one can say for sure. It is possible that *sea-coal* may have been the starting-point, harvested along the tide-line by our distant ancestors, but records show that by the twelfth and thirteenth centuries early colliers had started to exploit accessible coal seams, often by tunnelling horizontally to form an early drift-mine, known in the Scots language as an 'ingaun e'e'. Despite the efforts of those early miners, peat, turf and wood remained for some considerable time the most readily available sources of fuel for a population that was small in number and still predominantly rural. Even in locations where coal was available, an early prejudice - based on what were believed to be its unhealthy smoke and fumes - took time to fade.

Early mining was a seasonal activity, carried out for the most part during the winter months when work on the land had eased and the need for fuel was at its greatest. Initially the industrial use of coal was fairly limited - in Ayrshire mostly used in salt production, a fairly small-scale coastal industry, and in limestone burning to produce agricultural fertiliser. But, as roads and communications picked up and people congregated increasingly in towns, the Scottish lowlands became virtually denuded of trees and conditions became right for coal. Demand went up and shortages followed, prompting the Scottish parliament in 1563 and once again in 1579 to pass legislation which banned the export of coal.

The growing importance of the coal industry was further highlighted in 1592 when an act was passed which placed the malicious burning of coal-pits on a par with treason, no less. An East Lothian miner named John Henrie fell foul of the legislation after setting fire to the coal-heugh of Mungo McCall at Little Fawside. Henrie, it seems, had built up 'ane deadlie rancour and evill will' against his employer and over a period of weeks had caused underground fires to break out, ensuring beforehand that the air-vents had been stuffed with straw, thus making the pit unsafe to enter and effectively halting coal production. After his malicious ploy was rumbled, Henrie was convicted and sentenced to be hanged at the Mercat Cross in

Edinburgh. The dead man's head was later removed and displayed on a pole at Little Fawside as a grisly example to others.

The harsh conditions that early Scottish colliers laboured under can only be guessed at, but a miner's status at least was crystal clear, laid down by statute in 1606. Making for shocking reading today, an act passed that year was calculated to prevent new coal-owners from poaching employees from existing workforces by binding miners irrevocably to their workplaces. Even worse, if a collier's son or daughter took up employment in his or her parent's place of work – even for a single day – then the child too became tied to the pit for life. Almost unbelievably, the act went so far as to empower coal-owners to waylay passing tramps and beggars and press-gang such unfortunate souls into working underground.

Thirty or so years later parliament went even further, extending the terms of the act to include all colliery workers, not just the miners themselves. Effectively enslaved from cradle to grave - men hewing, women and children lugging – pit-workers were obliged to struggle through a twelve-hour shift at the very least, six days a week, with no holidays of any kind to look forward to other than their statutory Sundays. It should be no surprise then that colliers and their families quickly became a community apart, a stigmatised underclass with its own customs, superstitions and even forms of speech - 'a separate or avoided tribe,' wrote a young advocate, Henry Cockburn, in 1800. That many of their number sank into lives of drinking and debauchery is hardly surprising. The colliers' apartness was underscored in 1701 when the Scottish parliament passed a Habeas Corpus Act, outlawing wrongful imprisonment and undue delay in trial, but exempting mine-workers. Not until the tail end of the eighteenth century was the law enslaving Scottish colliers and their families repealed, and a colossal, two-hundred old year injustice brought finally to an end.

In the early years of the eighteenth century the Scottish coalfield found itself in the doldrums, with one geographical area alone standing out as an exception. Responding to a rising population in Ireland, in particular Dublin's growing urban market, at the turn of the new century Sir George Cunninghame of Auchenharvie funded construction of a new harbour at Saltcoats and what had been a relatively small-scale trade for the previous couple of centuries suddenly boomed. Pits in the immediate vicinity were first to benefit, but as time went on railways and waggonways were constructed which linked Ayrshire's inland areas with developing ports at

Ayr and Irvine, soon to be followed by Ardrossan and Troon, and enabled a large part of the Ayrshire coalfield also to benefit. The final decade of the century saw an annual Scottish export to Ireland of over 40,000 tons of coal, an estimated 85% of which was sourced from Ayrshire collieries.

While Ayrshire's coal-owners devoted themselves to servicing the Irish market, domestic demand experienced a major upturn during the second half of the eighteenth century with coal increasingly valuable as a means of powering Scotland's growing industrial sector. Not everyone, of course, would benefit: as coal production shot up, Ayrshire's remaining peat-diggers saw their age-old business dwindle. But inescapably coal was the future and meeting the upsurge in demand meant sinking more and deeper pit-shafts as well as excavating coal from less accessible and trickier seams - with all the added risk that this involved.

Who can have any idea of how many unfortunate souls there were who lost their lives during the early days of Ayrshire mining? Health and safety considerations, we may be sure, were not of the highest priority and, as statutory registration of mining fatalities was not established until 1855, surviving facts and figures are likely to represent only the tip of the iceberg.

A number of early recorded accidents took place in collieries located within easy reach of Sir George Cunninghame's new harbour. In February 1751 two Stevenston miners – James Hume and John Taylor – died underground and, in the years that followed, fatal accidents occurred right across the Ayrshire coalfield - from Beith and Dalry in the north, east across the moors to Muirkirk, and south to pits around Dailly. In September 1786, Janet Merrie died in a mining accident at Birnieknowe, Auchinleck, and less than six months later William Merry [sic], also of Auchinleck, was killed under similar circumstances, raising the suspicion perhaps that the slip of a scribe's pen had masked a grievous family tragedy. In the early nineteenth century Newton-on-Ayr appeared to have a particularly bad safety record with a total of thirty fatalities listed between 1812 and 1838. There is always the possibility, of course, that this may simply be down to more zealous record-keeping than elsewhere.

As time went on, accounts of accidents began to appear in newspapers, both local and national, many of which made it clear that, as pit-shafts probed deeper underground, colliers found themselves increasingly at risk from the hazards posed by flammable gas. In October 1847 four workers at the Black Diamond Pit at Auchincruive were seriously injured in an explosion caused by 'foul air' which was reckoned to have been ignited by one of the miners' lamps. One boy, James Vance, was thought unlikely to survive. A few years later, a firedamp explosion killed four Hurlford miners, their bodies recovered from under a weight of debris fifteen hours later. A naturally arising methane-based gas, firedamp presented a constant danger, viewed in an earlier age as the work of the devil himself to halt the invasion of his infernal kingdom. 'Firemen' were employed in mines whose unenviable task it was to burn out pockets of gas using lighted torches, having taken the precaution beforehand of soaking their clothing with water. It seems more than likely that the casualty rate would have been considerable.

As well as gas, of course, there was gravity. In December 1804 two Kilmarnock colliers, Adam Miller and Peter Stewart, were plunged to their deaths when a rope supporting the bucket in which they were descending snapped as a result, it was believed, of frost-damage. Tragically, Stewart's father had died in the same pit some fourteen years earlier. In November 1815 Alexander Brown experienced an extremely close call when he misjudged his way in darkness and tumbled headlong into a 300 feet pit-shaft near Ayr. In all probability the miner's life was saved by a coal-bucket, dangling 150 feet below, which broke his fall and where he lay for some six hours until he was discovered. Amazingly, despite a broken thigh-bone and severe bruising, Brown was expected to recover. Less fortunate was James Grier of Hurlford whose badly broken body was discovered on the morning of 28 January 1855 at the foot of a 400 feet shaft. The 25-year-old collier was known to have been drinking heavily the previous evening, and the fact that he had become embroiled in a quarrel in a local public-house added perhaps a degree of spice to his mysterious fate.

Other casualties were caused by falling objects. A week before Christmas 1845, a 14 year-old boy was killed in Dalquharran pit, Dailly, when a large lump of coal - which miners were in the habit of placing for their own use on the top of their final load - fell from the ascending creel and struck him so hard as to cause his instant death. Eighteen months later two men lost their lives in a pit near Kilbirnie when a barrel of earth and stones plummeted down the shaft and crushed them, the result, it was alleged, of the engine-driver having fallen asleep. The man believed responsible had fled, it was reported in the press, and was being sought by police. In November 1855 a boy was gravely injured in the Craigie pit, Ayr, when a pick-axe fell from an ascending tub and struck him forcibly on the head. He was carried home but died within the hour.

In September 1841 an unusual case came before Ayr Circuit Court when the charge of culpable homicide was brought against John McCulloch, a ploughman on Wheatpark Farm, close to the hamlet of St Quivox. Two months earlier, in unexplained circumstances, McCulloch had thrown a dog – whether dead or alive is unspecified – into a pit-shaft situated close to Wheatpark. At that precise moment, a miner named David Steel was ascending the shaft and was struck by the falling animal, dislodged from the bucket, whereupon he fell to his immediate death. After hearing the testimony of witnesses, members of the jury passed a guilty verdict and McCulloch was subsequently sentenced by the Lord Justice Clerk – with what seems like remarkable leniency – to three months' imprisonment. What the convicted man's motivation might have been for his bizarre and reckless act is not on record.

That the death or serious injury of a collier dealt a grievous blow - financial as well as emotional - to his family goes without saying. In March 1850 a case came to court when a bereaved woman refused simply to accept without question the loss of her husband. Some years previously James Wark had been employed as a coal-hewer by Messrs' Russell and Wardrop at their Langbar pit near Beith. When a pit-prop collapsed on 27 October 1846, the ceiling came down and Wark was crushed under a weight of coal, his injuries so severe that he died some two hours later. It came out in court that managers at Langbar had been alerted more than once to the dangerous condition of various pit workings, and this particular prop was alleged to have been affected by a noticeable crack. Whilst expressing conventional sympathy, the defence countered that the miner had lost his life through a 'pure accident such as every worker in a coal mine is at all times inevitably subject to.' Clearly the jury was not convinced, taking a mere fifteen minutes to find in the widow's favour. Mary Anne Wark was awarded the sum of £100 in respect of damages for the loss of her husband, and each of her six children received an additional £50.

James Wark's fate was far from unique. Roof-falls presented a perennial threat to mine safety, and instances of injury to life and limb were by no means uncommon. One of the most extraordinary cases related to John Brown, a 60 year-old native of Midlothian who in 1835 had been working for a number of years as a collier at Kilgrammie, near Dailly. During

Brown's shift on the morning of 8 October a roof-fall took place, and the miner found himself trapped alone behind the debris. With nothing to sustain him other than a day's supply of tobacco and two small flasks of lamp oil (which he sampled and found entirely unpalatable) he was driven to drink the foul water had that accumulated in his underground cell. Brown would later recall that his pangs of hunger had subsided surprisingly quickly.

During his first week of captivity the trapped man set about exploring his small underground chamber, fumbling in total darkness in search of any possible escape route. He found that he was able to keep tabs on the passage of time from the sounds of other miners, coming and going from their shifts. Despite having eaten nothing, he was still strong enough to move around during his second week underground, his main concern, he later stated, being for his work colleague, Thomas Wilson, who had also been at work at the time of the accident and whose family Brown had lodged with for the previous two years. His mind remained entirely clear, he said, and never at any point did he abandon hope of being rescued.

By week three, the starving man's strength had ebbed away and he found himself unable even to access his source of water. When rescuers finally broke through, they found Brown lying face-down, still conscious but apparently close to death, his voice, it was reported, little more than a whisper when he breathed his first words, 'Boys, oh, but you were long in coming.' From his emaciated condition and unshaven, hollow cheeks, it would later be said of poor John Brown that he had 'an unearthly appearance' – the comment harking back perhaps to the superstitions of an earlier age. Small wonder if the unfortunate collier looked a little ghostly - he had survived a total of twenty-three days underground without either food or clean water.

Those tending Brown were fully aware of the danger of over-feeding a famished man, so they were careful to moisten his mouth with a little butter before proffering tiny spoonfuls of sherry, arrowroot and milk at regular intervals. To their surprise, the rescued man was able to recount his underground experiences, and to shake the hand of the parish minister, Dr Hill, requesting that thanks be offered up for his safe deliverance. But it appeared that his ordeal had been too much for him. Three days after being pulled from his lonely prison John Brown passed away – peacefully, it was said - an hour or two before midnight on Tuesday 3 November. In the ensuing days it emerged in the press that during an earlier mining accident – no mention of where or when - Brown had been rescued after a three-day spell underground, and that in a previous phase of his life he had even survived a shipwreck. But in the depths of Kilgrammie, at a time when possibly he least expected it, fate finally caught up with John Brown.

Despite mining's appalling safety record, the industry remained entirely unregulated in the early years of the nineteenth century. It took a tragic accident in South Yorkshire in 1838, during the course of which 26 child-workers lost their lives, to finally galvanise parliament into action, and the resulting Mines and Collieries Act of 1842 crossed a watershed when it took the first tentative steps towards improving the lot of the nation's colliery workers. Further regulation followed, but even when coupled with the onward march of technology, the human cost of mining remained stubbornly high, as continued loss of life through the nineteenth and twentieth centuries showed only too clearly.

The Fate of Monthraw

There is an old adage about the farm of Monthraw, the name of whose author is long forgotten. So isolated was *lone Monthraw*, the unknown poet tells us, that *man never heard/ His neighbour's cock craw.*

It was no exaggeration. Situated at the top end of Glen Afton in Ayrshire, the lonely farmstead was decidedly out on a limb, nearly 1,500 feet above sea-level and two miles adrift of its nearest neighbour. From Craigdarroch a cart-track wound its way along the hillsides, traversing numerous burns and bogs until it dipped down to ford the Afton at its broadest stretch. After the crossing, there was still the best part of a mile to cover - possibly in wet feet - before the welcome sight of Monthraw came into view among its tiny shelter-belts and drystone enclosures. In wet or snowy weather, the journey must have been well-nigh impossible.

Yet, in spite of the glen's remoteness, over the centuries several eminent Scots have linked their fortunes with its woods and hills. In the eighteenth century Robert Burns composed his poem, *Afton Water*, as a literary compliment to a local landowner, Catherine Stewart, but highlighting in the process the natural beauty of the glen. The fifteenth century makar, Blind Harry, states that William Wallace maintained a residence at 'Black Crag' whose location in the glen remains uncertain though the name survives in the farm of Blackcraig and its rock-strewn hill above. A craggy outcrop nearby has long been known as Castle William, though its rocky battlements are the work of nature, not of man – despite the claims of an early mapmaker.

Wallace's successor in the quest for Scottish freedom is also thought to have spent time in Glen Afton. Dogged by enemy soldiers using bloodhounds, Robert the Bruce hid out among the surrounding woods and hills, and if one of his pursuers was Sir Henry de Bohun, then the Englishman surely got his comeuppance in the fullness of time, slain by King Robert himself on the banks of the Bannock Burn. A rocky defile to the west of Glen Afton, the Craig of Bohun, is claimed – without much evidence – to be named for the ill-fated English knight.

Strange though it may seem, history even came knocking on the lonely front-door at Monthraw. Two centuries and more after Bruce had departed, a second sovereign rode up the glen - Mary, Queen of Scots, in retreat following her defeat at Langside and making for the hill passes into Galloway. A cairn near the farm of Dalhanna was reputed to have marked the spot where her party halted for refreshment but its stones were removed long ago for the construction of dykes and farm buildings. Perhaps it was one of Mary's followers who was the source of the gold and silver coins that surfaced some three hundred years later beneath the feet of a disbelieving local shepherd, Peter Murdoch. At the head of the glen, the royal entourage must have forded the Afton and passed by the lonely homestead at Monthraw, where it is tempting to believe that the herd and his family would always have remembered the spring day in 1568 when they marvelled as they watched a queen ride by.

Glen Afton

Monthraw; Mounthraw; Montraw; Monquhra, Montquharow: the name has a variety of spellings depending on what source you choose to consult. Most probably it derives from the Gaelic *monadh*, signifying a hill or moor, and *airbhe* - a border or boundary. Barely a mile from the summit of Blacklorg Hill where Ayrshire, Dumfriesshire and Kirkcudbrightshire all converge, the farm was an obvious meeting-point for those crossing the hills, either on lawful business or otherwise. Probably the herd of Monthraw barely turned in his sleep when the brandy-smugglers and their strings of pack-ponies passed by, ferrying their goods into Galloway by moonlight. And, given its strategic location, it was perhaps inevitable that Monthraw would become caught up in turbulent events during the Covenanting years of the seventeenth century.

When Andrew Forsyth appeared without warning on the doorstep, there was no doubt about where the shepherd of Monthraw's loyalties lay. A late convert to the Covenanting cause, Forsyth had left his father's home at Kirkcowan, Wigtownshire, for the safety of the other members of his family and had found employment as a shepherd at Glenlee, a remote farm on the banks of the Water of Deugh. Glenlee was situated in an area routinely patrolled by the king's dragoons and, despite a bold attempt to outwit them, Forsyth was finally captured, escaping only by sheer good fortune when the horse on which he was mounted stumbled in the dark and fell, enabling him to break free of his bonds and melt away into the night.

When he turned up at Monthraw, Forsyth must have cut a sorry figure, having slept in the open for some weeks and subsisting, it is said, on the raw eggs of wild birds. One version of the tale relates how the tenant of Monthraw, whose name is not on record, convoyed Forsyth over the hills into Dumfriesshire where he was passed into the hands of another Covenanting sympathiser by the name of Kerr at his secluded home by the Scar Water. Happily, the story goes on to say that when the Glorious Revolution of 1688 brought *The Killing Time* to an end, Forsyth was still alive and able to return to his family home in Wigtownshire.

A story dating from *The Killing Times* that presents the king's soldiery in anything other than a negative light is a rarity indeed. Yet such a tale exists - even if it contains events that might not stand too close a scrutiny - and it has as its setting the lonely farmstead of Monthraw.

One winter evening, wet and stormy, the herd of Monthraw and his family were settled by their fireside, the day's work done. The mood apparently was one of contentment since earlier that day the shepherd had received a useful sum of money, some say from the sale of a cow. All at once, however, the peace was shattered by a violent knocking at the door and by the sound of a gruff voice demanding admittance.

Despite his trepidation, the shepherd unbarred the door and saw before him one of the king's moss-troopers, dejected and weary, who declared that he had become lost in the storm and had been drawn by the light in the shepherd's window. In spite of his support for the Covenant, the rules of hospitality were clear, requiring the goodman of Monthraw to provide his enemy with food and accommodation and to find a corner of the byre to stable his worn-out horse.

There is no record of what conversation took place between the shepherd's family and their unexpected guest, but sometime later the trooper retired for the night, through habit keeping his weapons close at hand. Exhausted by his wanderings, he was quick to fall asleep but soon was roused by a faint creaking sound which he identified as coming from the window-shutter (the window being glassless) as it moved gently on its hinges. The dragoon leapt to his feet and demanded loudly to know who was there but his words went unheeded, lost perhaps in the storm. Fearing for his safely, he took careful aim and discharged his pistol through the narrow gap that had opened up between the shutter and the window-frame.

The deafening report of the gun roused the shepherd and his family but inexplicably it was daylight before the two men stepped outside to investigate. When they did so, to their horror they found beneath the soldier's window the bloodied body of an armed man which the shepherd quickly identified as belonging to the farmer to whom he had sold his cow the previous day. Why, he mused, had this man travelled the lonely miles to Monthraw under cover of darkness on such a wild and windy night?

It didn't take long to piece the story together. Having paid for the cow, the farmer knew full well that a considerable sum of money was now to be found at Monthraw and his intention, the shepherd surmised, had been to steal back the money that he himself had paid over less than twenty-four hours before - if necessary resorting to violence in the process. What he had not, of course, foreseen was the presence of an armed dragoon - at first sight an enemy at Monthraw but who, as things turned out, was to prove the shepherd and his family's salvation.

Being located in an area of proven high rainfall – close to 100 inches in an average year - was ultimately what would prove Monthraw's undoing. When Ayr County Council took the decision to flood the upper reaches of the Afton, the old house's history and folklore were obliged to step aside to make way for the modern world. Over 2,000 acres of hill-land were purchased as catchment for a new reservoir whose rising waters would eventually lap to within a stone's throw of the threshold of Monthraw. Several hundred labourers, many of them Irishmen, were brought in to construct a mighty dam half a mile upstream from Craigdarroch that, when complete, would rise nearly eighty feet from the valley-floor.

Predictably a hitch or two cropped up along the way, but after six years of hard labour the project was complete, and on the back of three successive dry summers the reservoir's provision of four million additional gallons of water per day seemed more significant than ever. On a sunny first Wednesday in September of 1935 the Afton Reservoir's official opening ceremony took place with two hundred guests in attendance, Sir John Gimour MP being granted the honour of opening the new water-valve for the first time. To general hilarity, one of the speakers claimed that the reservoir's total capacity of 638 million gallons was sufficient to fill a 12-inch pipe circling the entire globe, or alternatively a 4-inch pipe that ran all the way from Glen Afton to the moon. And if that wasn't whimsical enough, it was further stated that there was enough water stored up behind the dam to form one gigantic drop, 580 feet in diameter or the height of several church steeples. No-one, it seems, contested the calculations. Instead, local dignitaries and contractors spent their day applauding speeches and presenting one another with commemorative gifts – a gold wristwatch, a silver entrée dish, a silver inkstand, and - less predictably - a replica Ayrshire bull on an onyx base.

Significantly there was no presentation made to any of the squads of men who had toiled and strained and sweated during the previous six years as they excavated nearly 3,000 tons of rock and barrowed in excess of 35,000 tons of clay, concrete and masonry. Nor does the sacrifice of Martin Atkinson, the sole fatality during construction, appear to have merited a mention.

Amid the razzmatazz, no-one thought either of the fate of 'lone Monthraw', marooned at the far end of the reservoir. The last shepherd, Gideon Pringle, had moved out some time earlier, carting his goods down to Craigdarroch before rising waters obliterated the old hill-track for ever and left Monthraw more isolated now than at any time in its past.

The Lost Ayrshires

My father always slowed down for the bend at Bargower - or slowed down even more than usual, I suppose. Dad had reached his fifties by the time I started primary school and it was clear that by then he'd lost any taste for speed. As we rounded the looping bend there was plenty of time to take in our surroundings, including the sign by the roadside that announced to the passing world: *Bargower Ayrshires*.

I can still picture those red and white cattle, grazing purposefully in fields lush with summer growth or else lying with their hooves tucked neatly under them whilst they worked over the cud. But the half-century since then has seen some startling changes. First, the cattle around Bargower have lost their noble horns. Worse still, the rich tones of their markings have been reduced to black and white. And to cap it all, there is no longer any need to slow down at Bargower, since its long, curling bend has been made soulless and straight.

The surrounding fieldscape with its neatly-hedged meadows and sheltering bands of trees is not one that Robert Burns would have been likely to recognise, however often he must have passed during his time at nearby Mossgiel. In the eighteenth century, agricultural improvement was only just getting off the ground in Ayrshire and much of what is now productive land remained in Burns's day wet, sour and depleted for want of drainage and manuring.

The native cattle were no more impressive. Stocky, dark-coloured creatures, they were weakened by inadequate winter feeding and further debilitated by the process of bleeding, the drawn blood to be mixed with oatmeal for human consumption. Shortage of fodder meant that many animals were slaughtered in the autumn and their meat preserved by salting against leaner times to come. The chances of building up and maintaining a reasonable-sized herd were slim, and milk production for the most part was at little more than domestic levels.

For centuries little had changed, despite contributions to the bovine gene-pool alleged to have been made by beasts that had struggled ashore from foundering Viking longboats during the Battle of Largs, or from storm-blown remnants of the Spanish Armada some three centuries later. Change only came about when an influx of new, more scientific ideas persuaded eighteenth century landowners of the benefits of manuring and the need to rotate their crops. Dykes were constructed at this time and hedges planted, thus for the first time regulating the breeding of livestock, and copses of trees were put in place to act as shelter-belts. Greater efficiency led to a higher number of cattle being overwintered which were therefore available for breeding the following spring. Interest grew up in how these animals might be made healthier and more profitable.

It was around this time that dairy cows in the northern part of Ayrshire started to acquire their distinctive brown and white livery, the consequence, it is thought, of the importation of Dutch bulls, brought to Scotland by drovers returning from southern markets. The resulting progeny were initially named Dunlop cattle, and when Robert Burns married Jean Armour in August 1788 it is reasonable to suppose that the cow he received as a wedding gift from Major Andrew Dunlop of Dunlop was one of the new breed. It has even been suggested that it was Burns who first introduced Dunlop cattle into Dumfriesshire when he took up the lease of Ellisland that same year.

As the Dunlop cattle spread out from their place of origin, they gradually became known as Cunningham cattle, and then subsequently as Ayrshires, the name, of course, which ultimately stuck. In the early years of the nineteenth century animals of the new breed were to be found across a substantial swathe of the west of Scotland, and by mid-century their reputation had crossed international boundaries. A commemorative book entitled *Les Races Bovines*, issued for the World Agricultural Congress held

Ayrshire Cattle

in Paris in 1856, contained an illustration of an Ayrshire cow - the only dairy breed, then or since, truly native to the British Isles.

Ironically perhaps it was an Englishman who first attempted to compile a herd book of Britain's Ayrshire cattle. Cumbrian dialect poet and ardent agriculturalist, Thomas Farrall published his volume in 1877 in which details were listed of 59 Ayrshire cows and 17 bulls. Perhaps Farrall's efforts were what spurred Scottish breeders to take action, around 90 of whom assembled in Ayr's County Buildings on Tuesday, 26 June 1877, where they agreed to set up The Ayrshire Cattle Herd Book Society of Great Britain and Ireland.

The Society's first herd book appeared the following year, 1878 – several years after the equivalent North American volume. 'Better late than never' wrote its defensive compiler, G. R. Vernon, but he quickly warmed to his theme. 'The Ayrshire breed of Cattle [is] now universally admitted to be the best for dairy purposes in Great Britain and North America,' he crowed in his introduction to listings for nearly 600 purebred Ayrshires, the breed's status clear from the fact that the breeder with the highest number of entries was none other than Scotland's largest landowner, the Duke of Buccleuch, with more than twenty bulls and one hundred cows to his name.

In the interests of accurate record-keeping, Vernon highlighted the need for each animal to be given a specific name which would not subsequently change. A certain predictability, it must be said, runs through the 1878 herd book's cow and heifer section which features more than one *Ayrshire Lass*, as well as several *Blossoms* and no fewer than nine *Daisies*. *Duchess* also proves highly popular, gaining a grand total of sixteen entries, but why *Too Late* has been so-named we can merely speculate. Even more puzzling perhaps is *Pea Soup*, the property of Mr Ivie Campbell of Craigman, New Cumnock.

Bulls vary just as much, from the couthy *Heather Jock* to a more romantic *Prince Charlie*. *Stonewall Jackson* has imported his name from across the Atlantic, while a dash of the exotic is added by *Osman Pasha*, the namesake of a Turkish hero of the Crimean War. Less flamboyant is a beast owned by the Hon. Grenville Vernon of Auchans, Kilmarnock - the herd book editor – who has listed his bull simply as *Zero*.

By the turn of the twentieth century the herd book had expanded considerably with well over a thousand entries for pedigree Ayrshires. Such was the breed's growth in popularity that life members of the Society were to be found in various far-flung corners of the globe – Sweden, Cape Town, and Australia. Of the rank and file members, barely more than half were resident within Ayrshire itself. By the 1920s there were an estimated 200,000 breeding Ayrshire cows across Scotland, and consignments of animals were routinely being exported to countries as varied as Sweden, Finland, South Africa, Australia, New Zealand, USA, Canada and Japan, all of which had established breed societies of their own. Ayrshire bulls were even put to work in the hill country of India, helping to improve the quality of the native cattle.

The Ayrshire's expansion out of her traditional heartland was based on a number of key strengths. Much of the ground where her breed had evolved was poor and high-lying, enabling her to subsist on relatively meagre grazing and in exposed locations. Long-lived and notably resistant to disease, she presented in addition few difficulties during calving. The Ayrshire's trump-card, however, was her ability to produce a copious amount of high-quality milk under astonishingly varied geographical and climatic conditions.

None of that success, however, prevented the Ayrshire Cattle Society from becoming bogged down from time to time in a spot of controversy. During the 1940s and '50s the thorny question cropped up periodically of dehorning - the removal, normally for safety reasons, of an animal's horns – a subject guaranteed to divide opinion amongst the breeders of the day. It was suggested that dairy farmers in the east of Scotland were deterred from working with Ayrshires because of the breed's perceived quarrelsome nature, and that these men might be won over if dehorning became standard. Traditionalists, however, objected on the grounds that an Ayrshire's magnificent horns were an essential part of its character.

When Highland Games enthusiast and collector of WWII aircraft, Sir James Roberts of Strathallan Castle imported a number of naturally hornless Ayrshires from the USA whose semen subsequently became available for artificial insemination, there was a move by the Society old guard to have the resulting calves excluded from the herd book. Trends, however, were moving in exactly the opposite direction and their motion was roundly defeated. In 1956 the first ever cup for a hornless Ayrshire heifer was awarded at Castle Douglas agricultural show, and there was by now an inescapable sense that the writing was on the wall for traditional horned Ayrshires.

While the Society chewed over the dehorning issue and minutiae such as the preferred size of teats, a dark cloud was building for all Ayrshire cattle, horned or otherwise. For millennia the grasslands of northern Holland had bred large quantities of cattle, a fact clearly demonstrated by the ancient Friesian people's practice of paying taxes to their Roman governor in the form of ox-hides and horns. In the 2,000 or so years since, Friesian black and white cattle continued to be bred in the area for both milk and beef production - though, despite imports from Holland, the breed's expansion in Great Britain was initially sluggish. All that changed during the 1970s when Friesians experienced a boom in popularity, based not only on their prodigious milk-yield but also on their ability to generate as a by-product good quality beef.

The spread of black and white cattle – Friesians and related Holsteins – turned out to be less rapid in Scotland than elsewhere in the United Kingdom, probably due to entrenched loyalties to the Ayrshire. When the Ayrshire Cattle Society celebrated its centenary year in 1977, the native breed still formed the majority at its showcase Ayr Show, though Friesian cattle were seen to be mounting a growing challenge. Some farmers hedged their bets, maintaining what amounted to a cosmetic loyalty to Ayrshires by introducing to their herds only Dutch cattle which happened to be brown and white – a colouring, incidentally, widely frowned upon by Friesian-Holstein purists. But as time went on the rise of the black and white breeds proved inexorable until finally the Ayrshire cow was toppled from her position of supremacy.

So, what hope today for the remaining Ayrshires, something of a rarity even in their own heartland? Well, there are signs that the pendulum may yet turn in their favour as a reaction sets in against high-yield, high-maintenance breeds that are less suited to the Scottish climate, less resistant to disease and which incur higher veterinary bills than our hardy, home-grown Ayrshire whose rugged constitution and ability to forage are exciting renewed interest and whose robust health and proven longer lifespan sit well with the current drive for sustainability. It is not inconceivable that the years ahead may see a second red and white revolution that will restore the Ayrshire to something approaching her former glory and transform in the process the colour-scheme of our countryside.

The Case of Mungo Campbell

When Alexander Montgomerie, 10th Earl of Eglinton, went head to head with a suspected poacher, Mungo Campbell, on the Ardrossan sands on 24 October 1769 the contest must have seemed a fairly unequal one. Assuredly the Earl had all the power and influence of the British aristocracy at his disposal, whereas Mungo by contrast was an old soldier, his health damaged by war, who gleaned a modest living as a public servant. On the other hand, Mungo was wielding a loaded firearm while Lord Eglinton went unarmed. Whatever the balance of power, before many minutes had elapsed a shot was fired, Lord Eglinton was mortally wounded, and Mungo Campbell found himself arrested, bound in chains and facing the prospect of a murder trial.

Probably the 10th Earl had felt fairly confident of his chances of dying comfortably in old age, unlike some of his more bellicose forebears. In 1388 Sir Hugh of Eglinton fell at the Battle of Otterburn, transfixed by an English arrow, and just over a century later the eldest son of the family died during a violent fracas on the High Street of Edinburgh. In 1586 the 4th Earl perished on the banks of the Annick Water, ambushed by a band of Cunninghames during a century-long vendetta between North Ayrshire's two pre-eminent families. Some Eglintons, however, did manage to emerge unscathed from the scrapes they got into. Fighting under the banner of Mary, Queen of Scots, the 3rd Earl survived the Battle of Langside and lived on for the best part of another twenty years. The Covenanting 6th Earl attracted the nickname 'Greysteel' for his readiness to indulge in swordplay, yet for all his belligerence he survived into his seventies and died at home in Eglinton Castle. The 10th Earl - the one who encountered Mungo Campbell - had it pretty easy by comparison, dividing his time between improving his Scottish estates and networking on the London social scene where he is credited with having introduced a young James Boswell (to whom he was related by marriage) to the cream of metropolitan society.

Mungo Campbell too was not without connections, though his story reads rather differently from Lord Eglinton's. For all that his father had been the Provost of Ayr, a blood-relation of the illustrious Campbells of Cessnock, Loudoun and Argyll, life for young Mungo did not pan out entirely smoothly. When a ship carrying trade goods went down, his father incurred grievous financial losses and further problems were quick to follow. Following his father's untimely death, a number of Mungo's twenty-three siblings had to be farmed out to be raised by relatives, in his own case to his Uncle Mungo at Netherplace near Mauchline.

On completing his education aged eighteen, Mungo enlisted in the Scots Greys, a regiment commanded by another of his relations, General Campbell. Over the next twelve years, he participated in active service throughout two European campaigns during which he took part in the Battle of Dettingen - the occasion in 1743 when Sir Andrew Agnew of Lochnaw famously warned the men of the Royal Scots Fusiliers not to open fire on the enemy until they could 'see the whites o' their een.' Disheartened at his inability to secure promotion through lack of funds, and suffering from ill-health associated with his years of tough campaigning, Mungo obtained a discharge in December 1744. His parting testimonial, penned by Major Alexander Forbes, stated that he had 'served […] for the space of twelve years, honestly and faithfully.'

Arriving back in Scotland, Mungo found the '45 Jacobite Rising in full swing and the country in uproar as a result. Like most other Ayrshire men, he came down on the government side and enlisted in his kinsman, the Earl of Loudoun's, regiment. Following the Jacobite defeat at Culloden, he returned to Ayrshire where his commander, Lord Loudoun, procured for him the post of exciseman, based initially at Newmilns before moving on to Stewarton, then Irvine and finally to Saltcoats. Mungo was said to have been sociable and well-liked in the communities where he served but, given his years of military hardening, it would not be surprising if he were regarded as a man not to be trifled with.

When Mungo came face to face with Lord Eglinton on the Ardrossan north shore, it wasn't as though the two men's paths hadn't crossed previously. At one point they were on sufficiently cordial terms for Mungo to have lent the Earl a dog - probably a gun-dog - but in the autumn of 1768 relations took a marked turn for the worse. Scouring the shoreline for contraband, Mungo and two companions were returning along the edge of Lord Eglinton's fields when a hare darted from cover directly in front of the three men. In what Mungo would later claim to have been a reflex action, he raised his rifle and promptly shot the creature. Unfortunately for him, it happened that Lord Eglinton was at the time visiting his nearby farm at Parkhouse, and on hearing the sound of gunfire he sent an employee, an Englishman named Alexander Bartleymore, to investigate. Summoned to account for his actions, Mungo would recall later that he found the Earl in a vicious temper and, although he made a clean breast of matters and apologised for his rash action, he was 'accosted [...] with many harsh and injurious expressions, accompanied with many oaths.' In spite of his dressing-down, before leaving the Earl's company Mungo gave a solemn undertaking that the offence would not be repeated.

A year or so later, Alexander Bartleymore was instrumental once again in the next - fatal - encounter between the Earl of Eglinton and Mungo Campbell, exciseman. At around ten o'clock in the morning of 29 October 1769, Mungo and John Brown, a local 'tide-waiter' - or customs officer - left Saltcoats to walk to Montfode Bank, a wooded slope running parallel to the sea, after which they planned to return along the shore. As he often did, Mungo carried a gun, partly in the hope of taking a pot-shot if any opportunity should arise on the estate of Montfode where he had the landowner, Dr Hunter's, permission to shoot. On their way, the two men passed through fields belonging to Lord Eglinton, following an established footpath equipped with styles to enable walkers to pass. A little further north, they spent some time searching Montfode Bank for woodcock, but finding none they climbed to high ground in order to obtain an outlook over Horse Island, a spot frequently used by smuggling vessels for cover. With nothing to be seen, they made their way down towards the shore where they turned south, stopping off at intervals to investigate locations which were known to be popular with smugglers. They hoped that as a bonus they might perhaps be able to surprise some plover along the shoreline.

That same morning Lord Eglinton happened to be travelling by coach from Eglinton Castle to Southannan, near Fairlie, accompanied by five servants on horseback. The party was joined along the way by the Englishman, Alexander Bartleymore. Despite recently having taken out newspaper advertisements with the specific object of deterring poaching on his estates, already that morning the Earl had sighted suspected poachers and he was not in the best of moods. A short distance north of Parkhouse farm one of his employees drew the Earl's attention to two men he had spotted in the fields and whom he believed to be poachers. When the Earl inquired whether any of his staff recognised either of the men, Alexander Bartleymore was quick to identify Mungo Campbell.

There was a history of bad blood between Mungo and the Englishman. Four months earlier, local customs had received intelligence to the effect that a large consignment of smuggled goods was due to be brought ashore at Castlecraigs, a notorious smuggling haunt near Ardrossan. Early the following morning, Mungo and two fellow-officers had intercepted Bartleymore who was driving a horse and cart near the shore which, on closer inspection, they found to be loaded with casks of rum containing eighty gallons in all. The spirits were confiscated as a matter of course and Bartleymore consigned to the tolbooth in Irvine, and apparently only through Lord Eglinton's intervention did he escape deportation to the colonies. No suspicion was voiced at the time - at least not officially - that Lord Eglinton might have had an interest in his employee's illicit activities. What Mungo did strongly suspect, however, was that from that day forth Alexander Bartleymore became his sworn enemy, seizing every available opportunity to blacken his name in the eyes of Lord Eglinton.

Perhaps, as Mungo firmly believed, it was Bartleymore's baneful influence that fuelled the tragic events that unfolded on 24 October. After the Englishman had identified the exciseman, Lord Eglinton immediately stepped down from his coach, mounted an available horse and approached the two suspected poachers. 'Mr Campbell, I did not expect to have found you so soon upon my grounds, after the promise you made me when I last catched you, when you had shot a hare,' was His Lordship's opening salvo. Not having fired a shot all morning, naturally Mungo protested his innocence but to no avail. Hostilities escalated as the Earl urged his horse forward, demanding that Mungo deliver up his firearm, a step too far for the old army man who stated that he would not under any circumstances surrender his weapon. Mungo cautioned Lord Eglinton against attempting to use force, backing off steadily as he spoke, his gun held firmly at his side with the barrel pointing directly towards the Earl. In subsequent court proceedings Mungo's action would be portrayed by the prosecution as an act of aggression, but it seems just as possible that it followed the form of an orderly retreat such as might have been effected by a trained and disciplined soldier.

Dismounting from his horse, an irate Lord Eglinton was heard to declare that he too could 'shoot pretty well' and he sent his servant, John Hazle, to fetch a gun from his carriage. At this disturbing development, Mungo's companion, John Brown, took fright and beetled off along the shoreline while Mungo himself continued to retreat, exhorting Lord Eglinton to keep his distance. He would later claim that when he heard the Earl call for his gun he had feared for his own life, believing that it 'was as good as Lord Eglinton's.' This was the point where fate intervened. Continuing to retreat, Mungo tripped on a jutting stone and crashed headlong to the ground. Whatever took place during the seconds that followed, the upshot was that his firearm was discharged and the Earl of Eglinton, a few yards in front, took the full force of the shot in his lower body. In spite of undergoing treatment from Dr John Cumming, physician in Irvine, and John Moore, a surgeon summoned from Glasgow later that evening, the Earl passed away at Eglinton Castle shortly after midnight. By that time Mungo was under lock and key in the Irvine tolbooth.

When, several months later, the case reached the High Court of Justiciary in Edinburgh questions were raised regarding the court's legitimacy on the grounds that the alleged crime had taken place between high and low water marks on the Ardrossan sands, and that consequently jurisdiction rightly lay with the office of the Vice Admiral of Scotland - William Douglas, 4th Duke of Queensberry. The objection was over-ruled, as was a suggestion by Mungo's counsel that improper efforts had been made to tilt the jury with a preponderance of 'landed gentlemen'.

During court proceedings Lord Eglinton's servants did their best to back up their late employer and to depict him as a blameless victim. Their continued employment, of course, may have depended on it. None would admit to having heard the Earl threaten or verbally abuse Mungo, though he himself asserted that 'Lord Eglinton used several harsh expressions' such as 'scoundrel' and 'rascal.' Andrew Wilson claimed that, in spite of the Earl's deliberate efforts to evade the line of fire, Mungo had kept his gun firmly trained on him. He also let slip, however, that his employer appeared to be 'in a passion'. John Hazle stated that Lord Eglinton had smiled when he saw the exciseman take a tumble and that, before the gun went off, Mungo had sat up, leaned on his right elbow and taken deliberate aim. Andrew Bartleymore painted a similar picture. John Brown, Mungo's companion, was of no help to him, too far off by now to have any clear idea of what had or had not happened. Mungo's own version of events, as documented in a voluntary statement made to William Duff, sheriff-depute of Ayrshire, was that, after seeing him fall, 'Lord Eglinton came up to him, and grasped at his gun, and the gun went off.'

It didn't seem to matter in court that Mungo had the landowners' permission to hunt on the nearby estates of Ardeer, Boydston, Grange, Seabank and Montfode. Nor were questions raised as to why a man who was able to produce a licence, endorsed by the Earl of Loudoun, authorising him 'to hunt upon his lordship's muir of Muirkirk, with dog and gun', would risk poaching on another laird's estate. Neither did it appear to cut any ice when evidence of Lord Eglinton's history of high-handed behaviour came to light. David Stirrat of Gourock testified to the effect that the Earl had once demanded his gun, allegedly striking him with his whip during their encounter near Saltcoats. Similarly, Thomas Brown claimed to have been assaulted near his home at Blacklaw on an occasion when Lord Eglinton had confiscated his gun. Court proceedings turned a little grubby when social snobbery reared its head. In response to the idea that surrendering his firearm might have offended an army veteran's sense of honour, the prosecution attempted to belittle Mungo by describing him as a 'common soldier' and 'an inferior officer of excise.' Evidently a working-class man had no right to a sense of his own dignity. Only Lord Eglinton and his set were entitled to that.

The verdict was guilty. Mungo was to be returned to the Edinburgh Tolbooth (where he had already spent some four months), fed exclusively on bread and water until, six weeks later on 11 April 1770, 'in the common place of execution in the Grassmarket of Edinburgh [he would be] hanged by the neck.' His corpse was then to be handed over to Dr Alexander Monro, professor of anatomy, 'to be by him publickly [sic] dissected and anatomized.' The condemned man's property would be forfeited to the crown.

As it happened, however, things fell out rather differently. Back in prison, Mungo was visited by well-wishers to whom he appeared calm and resigned to his fate. But when they returned the following morning, it was to discover that their friend had cheated the hangman and committed suicide overnight. There are those who have suggested that the silk handkerchief that Mungo made use of in hanging himself was one that those same visitors had provided the day before. Following his suicide,

Mungo's story appears to slip into the realm of myth when it tells of a paper, found in the dead man's cell, on which was inscribed a short, poignant poem:

> Farewell, vain world, I've had enough of thee,
> And now am careless what thou say'st of me.
> Thy smiles I court not, nor thy frowns I fear,
> My cares are past, my heart lies easy here.
> What faults they find in me, take care to shun,
> And look at home, enough it to be done.

Sadly matters didn't rest there, and a brief, unedifying postscript requires to be attached to Mungo's story. Incensed at being deprived of the spectacle of a public hanging, the Edinburgh mob exhumed his corpse and made sport by dragging it through the city streets. Eventually recovered by his supporters, in the end Mungo's poor battered body received a quiet burial at sea.

Demonised by the establishment and disparaged in court, might the real Mungo Campbell have been rather a decent, principled man, who was unfortunate in finding himself caught up in circumstances that spiralled beyond his control? Or simply a man with backbone who finally snapped under provocation and pressure? There is no way of knowing. One thing, however, that does emerge from the tragic tangle of events is the inescapable sense that Mungo's strength was also his nemesis. An eighteenth century man who rejected the peasant's role, Mungo Campbell declined to doff the cap, tug at the forelock and kowtow in the face of aristocratic privilege.

Lord Auchinleck's Guest

When a notably carnaptious Scottish laird goes head to head with one of the most highly-developed egos in eighteenth century England, you might reasonably expect a few sparks to fly. Small wonder, then, if James Boswell viewed with trepidation the prospect of introducing his learned friend and mentor, Samuel Johnson, to his rather formidable father, Alexander, Lord Auchinleck - a famously plain-spoken Scottish supreme court judge. When they met in the autumn of 1773, both Dr Johnson and Lord Auchinleck were in their sixties.

Johnson's fame was based on literary output spanning four decades – in particular perhaps on his ground-breaking nine-year opus, A *Dictionary of the English Language* - but he was known equally for an acerbic wit which he directed not infrequently against the Scots. In his 1755 *Dictionary* he famously quipped that oats were 'a grain, which in England is generally given to horses, but in Scotland supports the people.' His assertion that 'the noblest prospect that a Scotchman ever sees is the high road that leads him to England' was one that his acolyte, James Boswell, some thirty years Johnson's junior, was poorly equipped to refute, spending a substantial proportion of his time away from his family back in Edinburgh and enjoying whatever delights London offered. 'I do indeed come from Scotland,' Boswell had informed Johnson during the course of their first ever conversation, 'but I cannot help it.'

All the more surprising then when Johnson agreed to Boswell's proposal of a three-month Scottish tour to take place during late summer and autumn 1773 during which the pair would visit some of the furthest-flung reaches of the Highlands and islands. With Johnson's bulky frame and his hitherto sedentary disposition – never mind his legendary Scotophobia - the prospect of such a journey must surely have been a daunting one. Johnson was no longer a young man and, by his own admission, had 'passed [his] time almost wholly in cities.'

In the 1770s Highland wounds remained raw from savage recriminations in the aftermath of the 'Forty-five Jacobite Rising, and the tragedy of Culloden fell easily within living memory. Despite the best efforts of road-builders such as General George Wade, most roads in the Highlands were either poor or non-existent. As if to cap it all, Johnson and Boswell set out surprisingly late in the season when bad weather might easily be lurking just around the corner. For a portly man of letters such as Johnson, the three-month Scottish tour was unquestionably a tall order.

However, despite the inevitable hardships (not least the weather) things for the most part went well. Leaving Edinburgh by horse-drawn coach, the two men headed up the east coast, visiting St Andrews and Aberdeen along the way, and dropping in on Court of Session judge, Lord Monboddo, on his country estate in Kincardineshire. Routinely misrepresented as believing that humans were born with tails, James Burnett was a somewhat eccentric scholar whose thinking nonetheless is reckoned by some to be a precursor to evolution theory. Johnson and Boswell found his lordship relaxing in homely peasant garb. Johnson did not approve.

Moving west of Inverness, the men were obliged to switch to horseback travel, riding through dramatic Highland landscapes that left Johnson curiously unmoved. Boswell noted that 'at no time has (Johnson) had much taste for rural beauties,' but went on to admit, 'I myself have very little.' At Glenelg they dipped to the sea and spent the night in a particularly squalid inn before crossing the narrows of Kyle Rhea to land on the Isle of Skye.

During the course of a month on the island, Johnson and Boswell made the acquaintance of a variety of notables, not least Flora Macdonald, the Jacobite heroine who famously saved Bonnie Prince Charlie from capture in June 1746 when she disguised him as her Irish maidservant, Betty Burke. Johnson treated Flora, now in her early fifties, with utmost respect. At the harbour of Portree they saw a ship 'waiting to dispeople Sky [sic], by carrying the natives away to America.' Sadly, of course, they were witnessing the shape of things to come.

En route to Mull, Johnson and Boswell found themselves storm-driven instead to the small island of Coll where the two men were marooned by the weather for a fortnight or so. During this time, Johnson and Boswell were much taken with the kind attentiveness shown them by Donald MacLean, the absent laird's son and heir. Sad to say, Young Coll drowned less than a year later while crossing the Sound of Ulva.

When the weather eased up, Johnson and Boswell were able to continue south, skirting as they went the rugged west coast of Mull and sailing close to Staffa and Fingal's Cave – not made famous by Mendelssohn for another half-century or so – before finally they anchored at Iona. The tiny island's ancient buildings prompted what became arguably Johnson's best-known utterance inspired by his Scottish journey: 'That man is little to be envied,' he wrote, 'whose patriotism would not gain force upon the plain of Marathon, or whose piety would not grow warmer among the ruins of Iona.'

After returning to the mainland, the travellers spent two nights at Inveraray as guests of the Duke of Argyll who provided them with fresh mounts for a notably soggy crossing of the hill-pass known as the Rest-and-be-Thankful. Descending to Rossdhu, they spent time cruising around the islands of Loch Lomond in heavy rain but Johnson remained unimpressed, showing signs perhaps of having reached saturation point. Later that day, the two men crossed back into the Lowlands at Loch Lomond's southern shore and soon after they trundled into Glasgow by horse-drawn carriage - breathing a sigh of relief, as Boswell recorded, at having put the rigours of Highland travel safely behind them.

Even so, a significant hurdle of which Boswell was acutely conscious remained to be negotiated. In his journal, Boswell candidly admits that by preference he would not have 'ventured' to introduce Johnson to his father,

Auchinleck House

had not Lord Auchinleck 'out of kindness' extended an invitation to his home. A nervous Boswell anticipated three possible flashpoints. Unsurprisingly religion and politics featured in his list, Lord Auchinleck being a staunch Presbyterian Whig, his illustrious guest by contrast an Anglican Tory. The third potential hot potato was less predictable. It seems that discussion of Sir John Pringle, 'the father of military medicine', would be best avoided. Much admired by Lord Auchinleck, for whatever reasons Johnson thoroughly disapproved of this eminent Scots physician.

Initially all went smoothly. Confined to the house for two days by wet weather, Johnson and his host found a common interest in Lord Auchinleck's collection of rare Latin and Greek volumes in which Johnson readily became absorbed. 'Fatal topicks [sic] of difference,' Boswell observed with some relief, were thus avoided. The third morning dawned fine and dry, allowing Johnson and Boswell to step outside to tour the estate where Johnson particularly admired the present-day mansion's medieval predecessor whose timeworn remains stood on a rocky eminence overlooking the River Lugar. Ever varied in his interests, a local breed of cattle caught his eye which he was surprised to learn were naturally hornless.

It was at some point in the next couple of days that relations in Auchinleck House soured somewhat – a traumatised Boswell would later declare himself uncertain as to exactly when. With hindsight, a number of storm clouds could possibly have been seen, gathering on the horizon. Johnson had shown himself prickly in conversation with one of Lord Auchinleck's guests, and an unguarded remark made by an unnamed Church of Scotland minister concerning 'fat bishops and drowsy deans' (in the Church of England) provoked a scornful outburst. But when the time came, all that was required to ignite the touchpaper was a simple medal, part of a collection belonging to Lord Auchinleck, dating from the time of Oliver Cromwell whose effigy prompted discussion of King Charles I which led inexorably to the hot topic of politics.

Boswell, of course, had seen it all coming. In his account of the row that followed, he declines to go into detail, finding it too painful, but he does concede that Johnson and his father grew 'exceedingly warm, and violent,' and that 'in the course of their altercation, Whiggism and Presbyterianism, Toryism and Episcopacy, were terribly buffeted.' Lord Auchinleck held his own, it seems, though by his own (later) admission, at least partly through bluff and bluster. However distressing Boswell found the squabble between 'two men whom [he] reverenced', his sense of humour did not entirely fail him. 'Sir John Pringle,' he observed, 'never having been mentioned, happily escaped without a bruise.'

To his credit, Lord Auchinleck appeared to put the rumpus quickly behind him, taking an apparently cordial farewell of his son and Dr Johnson on the morning of their departure for Edinburgh – even if the old laird simultaneously breathed an inward sigh of relief at seeing the back of a man he would henceforth refer to as *Ursa Major*, or the Great Bear. For his part, Johnson makes no reference to the matter at all in his account of his visit to Auchinleck, paying tribute instead to his host's qualities as a landlord and complimenting him on his zeal in tree-planting. Is it possible, I wonder, that the crusty man of letters felt a tad embarrassed when he recollected an unseemly wrangle that he helped inflame in the home of his host? It is tempting to suspect so.

Johnson spent the final days of his trip in Edinburgh before boarding a coach back to England. Leopards are reputed not to change their spots but there can be little doubt that his Scottish journey had made a considerable impression on him. The year after his friend's death, Boswell quoted Johnson's oft-repeated conviction that 'this Tour was the pleasantest part of his life.' To Johnson – rain-lashed, saddle-weary and frequently exhausted - the Highlands had been less a series of picture postcard images than a setting for people he encountered who lived life very differently from what he was used to but whose hospitality and humanity at times had touched him deeply. At Auchinleck House, when asked an apparently innocuous question about whether he had liked the Highlands, Johnson's reply was characteristically waspish. 'Who *can* like the Highlands?' he had snapped, before adding immediately – 'I like the inhabitants very well.'

Lord Eglinton's Folly

Born in 1812 at Palermo in Sicily, Archibald William Montgomerie, the future 13th Earl of Eglinton, lived through a time of dizzying change. He was in his mid-teens when George Stephenson unveiled his famous Rocket, a prototype steam locomotive that helped launch the dramatic expansion of Britain's railway network during the decade that followed. On the high seas, sail was inexorably giving way to steam as new vessels crossed the Atlantic in a fraction of the time taken by their predecessors. Political reform too was in the air. The repeal in 1824 of the Combination Acts gave employees the right to band together to form trades unions, while the Reform Act of 1832 took a tentative first step towards universal suffrage. Predictably, of course, there were those among the established, conservative classes who viewed such developments with more than a little suspicion.

For them, the trimmed-down ritual of Queen Victoria's coronation in June 1838 typified what they saw as an abandonment of the nation's rich heritage. To their disgust, much of the ceremonial attached to the crowning of a British monarch had been ditched in favour of a much simplified procedure which the Whig government considered more in tune with the times. Out went the state banquet during which the Royal Champion, a knight in full armour, was expected to interrupt proceedings at Westminster Hall by entering on horseback and picking his way through the groups of assembled diners before theatrically tossing down his gauntlet as a challenge to anyone who might dispute the legitimacy of the newly-crowned queen. Robbed of a spectacle which he firmly believed to be his feudal right, it is reasonable to assume that the 13th Earl of Eglinton was one of those who bewailed the passing of such colourful pageantry.

While still a baby, Archibald had become heir to the Eglinton estates following the death of his father, aged 41, on his return from Sicily by boat. During infancy Archibald was comprehensively indulged by a doting maiden aunt and, on his grandfather's death in 1819, the seven-year-old could hardly have had any inkling of the colossal family debt, incurred through the 12th Earl's ill-starred involvement in ventures such as the overambitious Glasgow/Ardrossan canal scheme, which had now devolved to him, courtesy of his new-found title. Remarried and living in Sussex, neither his mother nor her spendthrift new husband, Sir Charles Lamb, was likely to be useful in promoting a habit of economy. Throughout his years at Eton and up until maturity, the 13th Earl made use of a generous allowance, administered by a small group of trustees, to dress like a dandy, become adept at billiards, conduct a variety of liaisons, involve himself in the world of horseracing and consume vast quantities of claret. It was as though the family debt didn't exist.

On reaching his 21st birthday, the young Earl gained financial independence, free at last of the trustees' grip. Turning a blind eye to the family debt, he had some time previously established a racing stable and stud and he went on, in the years that followed, to achieve a measure of success as a steeplechaser, winning both the Northumberland Plate and the Liverpool Cup in 1838, the same year that he became a member of the exclusive Jockey Club. His winnings, however, were insufficient to cover the costs of running the business and he resorted to selling off bits and pieces of his estates in order to maintain his lifestyle. In addition he was obliged to borrow.

During his frequent spells in London, Archibald had become part of an upper-crust set who subscribed to the fairly impractical view that a return to chivalric ideals would act as a welcome antidote to the ugliness and ills attendant on Britain's growing industrialisation. Their beliefs were surprisingly widespread. Interest in Gothic architecture was resurgent at the time, and it would be hard to exaggerate the popularity of Sir Walter Scott's historical fiction, most notably the medieval pageantry of *Ivanhoe*. Change was likewise afoot in the world of art that would lead in a few years' time to the emergence of the Pre-Raphaelite school with its focus on medieval and Arthurian subjects. When Lord Eglinton's equestrian interests are taken alongside the contemporary medieval craze, the Gothic extravaganza that he dreamed up for his family's ancient seat is perhaps a little easier to understand.

Some say that the whole madcap scheme was triggered by nothing more than a rumour. Whatever its origin, the proposed medieval-styled tournament to be held at Eglinton Castle seems to have become a *fait accompli* by the autumn of 1838 when the 13th Earl called a meeting in London to thrash out preliminary details. The project appears to have been put on the back burner over the winter months which he spent in his usual manner, following foxhounds across the English countryside, but when spring 1839 came round the newspapers started to pick up on the story and its leading light, Lord Eglinton, acquired a degree of press celebrity. A series of trial runs were held in London over the summer, the final dress rehearsal attracting a large crowd of spectators who had flocked to St John's Wood to watch nineteen competitors put through their chivalric paces in fine July weather. It all seemed to bode well for the tournament proper which had been scheduled for the last few days of the following month.

Eglinton Trophy

No-one anticipated just how popular the tournament would prove to be. Granted free entry, spectators converged on the castle *en masse*, travelling on foot, on horseback, by coach and even arriving by sea at the ports of Ayr, Ardrossan and Irvine. An entire boatload of Americans turned up aboard *The British Queen* for the specific purpose of attending the great event. On the day itself extra services, known as 'Tournament Specials', were put on - at grossly inflated prices - on the newly-completed railway line from Ayr. The roads were blocked by an estimated 80,000 or more spectators as they made their way to Eglinton Castle. For a great many of the out-of-town visitors accommodation, in short supply locally even at the best of times, proved impossible to come by, with all beds reputedly taken even as far away as Ayr and Kilmarnock.

Around one o'clock in the afternoon a lively spectacle looked in prospect as a colourful procession set out from Eglinton Castle, crossing the newly-completed Tournament Bridge to reach the 'Lists', a flat area within a loop of the Lugton Water where the jousting was due to take place.

Resplendent in his suit of brass armour and wearing a magnificently-plumed helmet, Lord Eglinton must surely have experienced a twinge of unease if he happened to look skywards as the cavalcade got underway. An ominous bank of cloud was gathering but clearly it was far too late for any second thoughts. Mounted on richly-caparisoned steeds and dazzling in their new armour, the thirteen combatants (not including their host) were already processing to the Lists, accompanied by their banner-bearers and by men-at-arms, both mounted and on foot. Music supplied by two military bands filled the air, though Lord Glenlyon - the self-styled Knight of the Gael - had arrived from Perthshire with seventy kilted Highlanders in tow who marched to the skirling music of their bagpipes. Members of Irvine Toxophilite Society - in plain English, archers - took their place in the parade and, not to be outdone, a band of Lady Archeresses were also present, uniformly clad in Lincoln green. A jester mounted on a decorated mule was charged with responsibility for entertaining the crowd. In view of the fact that the first droplets of rain had begun to fall, Lord Eglinton - the Lord of the Tournament - took the decision that, rather than ride, the Queen of Beauty and Love - the raven-haired Georgiana Seymour, Duchess of Somerset - and her handmaids should travel by coach in order to keep their rich costumes from spoiling. As she passed the crowds of spectators by, sadly the Queen of Beauty's opulent get-up and lavish display of jewels went largely unnoticed.

Of the knights preparing to do battle, the youngest were the Earl of Cassillis, Knight of the Dolphin, and Lord Eglinton's step-brother, Charles Lamb, Knight of the White Rose, both 23 years old, while at the other extreme the eldest competitor was 40 year-old Richard Lechmere, the Knight of the Red Rose. A Highlander, Alexander Fraser, Lord Saltoun, had been designated King of the Tournament, and the official guest of honour was no less a personage than the future Emperor of France, Prince Louis Napoleon Bonaparte. But not even this grand assemblage of the great and the good could do a thing about the weather. As the rain started to fall in earnest, much of the planned ceremonial had to be abandoned, but not before the participating knights had received favours of scarves and gloves from their lady admirers. Soon, however, matters took a turn for the worse when the tented pavilion of the Queen of Beauty became entirely swamped and, as the audience huddled miserably under their dripping umbrellas, it is not hard to imagine poor Lord Eglinton's bitter disappointment.

Delays, of course, followed and the jousting finally got underway several hours behind schedule. As the combatants hurtled towards each other, spray flying from beneath their chargers' hooves, the audience complained that they found it impossible to identify who each knight was, and in many of the contests the soggy participants failed to make contact at all, careering past one another in a dismal anti-climax. What was judged one of the better performances of the day took place between Lord Eglinton and the Marquis of Waterford, when Lord Eglinton's lance struck his adversary's shield squarely as planned. By now, however, the rain was descending in torrents and the decision had to be taken to abort the rest of the day's planned activities. For all that his cherished project had come close to being a total wash-out, it is to Lord Eglinton's great credit that he succeeded in maintaining an appearance of good spirits throughout, addressing the crowd at the close of proceedings and offering his apologies for having had to curtail the day's events. He was accorded a sympathetic round of applause.

His problems, however, were not yet at an end. A banquet for invited guests, scheduled for later that evening, had to be abandoned as the canvas pavilion where the meal was due to be served had become utterly deluged. Unable to return home along flooded roads, many of the humbler spectators were obliged to pass an uncomfortable night wherever they could find shelter - in farm outbuildings or huddled under dripping haystacks or, in some cases, taking cover beneath the tournament grandstand itself. One unfortunate soul was said to have spent the night shivering within a hollow tree-trunk in the castle grounds.

The following morning dawned dull and wet, and the competitors and their attendants resigned themselves to spending the day in mending damaged armour and equipment and attempting to dry out their sodden clothing. Thankfully the sun reappeared on Friday, 30 August, and Lord Eglinton's relief must have been palpable. Once again a large crowd turned out to view a variety of knightly sports, culminating in a *mêlée*, or mock-battle, between a Celtic alliance of Scottish and Irish knights and their English opponents. Two of the combatants added a degree of realism to proceedings when they appeared to lose their temper with one another, presumably to the audience's great delight. At the close of play, Captain James Fairlie, the Knight of the Golden Lion, was adjudged overall victor though, in a sporting gesture, the honours of the day were awarded to the host, Lord Eglinton himself. For invited guests scheduled events continued with the delayed fancy-dress banquet, during the course of which some rather dubious medieval-styled dishes such as boar's head and swan were served from gold and silver platters, and the day's events finally concluded with a candlelit dance. The following morning the combatants and guests set out for their homes under grey and rainy skies.

Undoubtedly the vagaries of the Scottish climate put a fairly major dampener on Lord Eglinton's great occasion - one, incidentally, that was estimated to have plunged his family finances £40,000 further into debt. In gratitude for his expenditure and efforts, 239 of the Earl's friends and associates commissioned for him what became known as the Eglinton Trophy, a five-foot Gothic confection in solid silver, crafted over four years by a London silversmith, depicting a scene in which the Lord of the Tournament - Lord Eglinton himself - was presented with a laurel wreath by the Queen of Beauty. In spite of its hefty price-tag - nearly £1,800 at the time - there are those who view the Trophy as a similar piece of Victorian frippery to the very event it was designed to commemorate. Lord Eglinton's attempt to recreate the medieval world was undeniably a gesture on a grand scale, but ultimately also a futile one. And quite possibly he knew it. Writing his memoirs in later life, he made a single bald reference to his medieval pageant: 'I gave a tournament at Eglinton.' No more.

It isn't easy now to picture Eglinton Castle in its glory days. Abandoned by the Montgomerie family during the 1920s, the building lost its roof some years later, then went on to suffer the indignity of being used for army target practice during the Second World War. Most of what was left was levelled during the 1970s, around the same time as the Irvine New Town authorities were pushing through a multi-lane by-pass that extended to within a stone's throw of the castle. With its single, solitary tower left standing, today's ruins are a far cry from the palatial Gothic mansion that hosted in its day one of the most bizarre and opulent spectacles ever seen in the annals of Scottish history.

The Free Hills of Old Scotland

America's first ever black president, Barack Obama, readily acknowledged the debt owed by the United States to Frederick Douglass, a one-time plantation slave from Maryland who escaped servitude and devoted much of the rest of his life to the struggle for racial equality. When the USA became too hot for comfort, Douglass crossed the Atlantic and spent the next two years touring Great Britain and Ireland where he lectured tirelessly on the horrors of slavery. In spring of 1846 he visited Ayrshire where he addressed a number of meetings.

Frederick Augustus Washington Bailey - as he started out in life - was born on the banks of Tuckahoe Creek, Talbot County, Maryland, the child of a plantation slave, Harriet Bailey. Removed from his mother during infancy, he was brought up by his grandmother, Betsy Bailey, a common enough occurrence at a time when it was deliberate policy to separate slave-children from their mothers. So intense was Harriet's pain at the loss of her baby that she was in the habit of walking through the night simply to spend an hour or two by his side before retracing her steps in time to start work at sunrise, a round trip on foot of almost 25 miles. As he grew up, Frederick was never certain of the identity of his father, though whispered rumours pointed at his master, Captain Anthony. Around the age of seven the young Frederick was sent to Baltimore to act as a servant in the household of Hugh Auld, where, recognising the boy's intelligence, Hugh's kind-hearted wife, Sophia, defied state law by teaching him to read. Lessons came to an abrupt halt when her husband caught on to what was happening, insisting to Sophia that teaching the boy to read was incompatible with the path laid out for him as a slave. But Frederick's appetite for learning had been whetted. He would later recall that he continued his education by gleaning what scraps of learning he could from white schoolboys in the street and by poring over sheets of discarded newsprint.

In his mid-teens Frederick was moved once again, this time finding himself put to work as a field hand under a white farmer with an unpleasant reputation for knocking unruly slaves into shape. On the aptly-named farm of 'Mount Misery', Frederick was regularly beaten and whipped until, presumably at the end of his tether, he finally faced up to Edward Covey, at which point, he recalled, the beatings ceased. Sometime later he was hired out as a shipyard worker in Baltimore where he spent his working days picking oakum, boiling pitch and assisting carpenters with their duties. In collaboration with three other workers, he planned an escape from the yard but their scheme was rumbled before it could be put into effect. Around this same time Frederick met and fell in love with a free black woman, Anna Murray, who assisted him in escaping by boat and train to New York City where she joined him soon after. The couple were married by a black clergyman before moving on to New Bedford, Massachusetts, where they set up home and Frederick undertook various forms of employment, from rolling casks on the quayside to working as a chimney-sweep. In an effort to evade the slave-hunters who were active in the area he changed his surname to Douglass, the name picked out for him by a friend who had recently read Sir Walter Scott's poem, *The Lady of the Lake*, whose heroine is Ellen Douglas. It was by this new surname that Frederick would be known for the rest of his life.

It was during his time at New Bedford that Frederick Douglass' life took a dramatic and unexpected turn, the result of a chance event. While attending a meeting devoted to the abolition of slavery, Douglass was invited to speak and, so moved was his white audience by his eloquence and sincerity, that he was immediately enlisted as an agent for the Massachusetts Anti-Slavery Society. From that point on, despite regular harassment and even serious physical assault, his dedication to the abolitionist cause never wavered.

In rebuttal of those who refused to believe that a man of such powerful eloquence could ever have been a slave, in 1845 Douglass published his autobiography, *The Life and Times of Frederick Douglass*. Ironically the book's instant success had the effect of further jeopardising his personal security. As a consequence of naming his former owner, Douglass could now be more readily identified, so in an effort to avoid detection and recapture he departed American shores on 16 August 1845 aboard the *Cambria* - on which, incidentally, he was denied a first-class cabin on account of his colour. In mid-Atlantic his life was threatened by fellow-Americans hailing from the deep south, and it was only thanks to Captain Judkins' timely intervention, threatening to clap those responsible in irons, that Douglass escaped being cast overboard. Crisis duly averted, later that month he disembarked at Liverpool from where he set out upon his demanding two-year lecture tour of Great Britain and Ireland.

It was January the following year by the time Douglass made it to Scotland, arriving in Glasgow by ferry from Belfast and stepping as he did so into a fairly major hullabaloo. A storm of controversy was raging over the Free Church of Scotland's acceptance of funds donated by churches in the southern USA that condoned the practice of slavery - 'blood-stained money' in Douglass's words and likewise in the view of a great many others. A vigorous campaign was being waged up and down the country based on the simple and direct slogan - *Send Back the Money!* - a phrase virtually ubiquitous in newspaper headlines of the time as well as splashed across town and city billboards. Astonishingly, in a packed-out meeting of the Free Church General Assembly held in Canonmills, Edinburgh (which Douglass attended), one of the church's co-founders and leading lights, Doctor William Cunningham, made efforts to justify its position by contending that nowhere in the scriptures did Christ condemn the institution of slavery. Reflecting later on what developed into a fairly tumultuous meeting, Douglass confessed to having been impressed by Cunningham's erudition and intellect, but not by his argument. The irony of the Free Church's position was not lost on him: 'That Church had taken the price of blood into its treasury,' Douglass wrote later, 'with which to build free churches, and to pay free church ministers.' In the event, the Free Church never did return its controversial funds, thus granting the pro-slavery lobby in the USA an unfortunate propaganda triumph.

Free Church controversy apart, it is clear that Douglass felt inspired by his travels through Scotland whose landscape and turbulent history he showed a tendency to view through the lens of his own people's predicament. 'Almost every hill, river, mountain and lake,' he wrote from Dundee, 'has been made classic by the heroic deeds of [Scotland's] sons. Scarcely a stream but has been poured into song, or a hill that is not associated with some fierce and bloody conflict between liberty and slavery.' Responding to an antagonistic white American with whom he had been acquainted during his dismal spell at Mount Misery, Douglass's reply was perhaps a little feistier than might have been expected: 'If I should meet you now, amid the free hills of old Scotland, where the ancient 'black Douglass' [sic] once met his foes, I presume I might summon sufficient fortitude to look you full in the face. You would see a great change in me!' In a land free of the scourge of slavery, it is as though Douglass breathed liberty in the very air itself.

Quite possibly, like many white people in the 'Old South' of the USA, Douglass had been influenced in his view of Scotland and the Scots by the works of Sir Walter Scott - the author, of course, who had supplied the surname chosen on his behalf. It is a little surprising that Douglass does not appear to have visited Scott's residence at Abbotsford, a popular literary destination then as now, while lecturing in nearby Galashiels, but no record of such a visit exists. What we can be certain of, however, is that during his time in Ayrshire, Douglass paid a visit to the Burns Memorial at Alloway, erected some 23 years earlier, where he declared himself charmed by the monument's scenic surroundings, revealing at the same time an appreciative familiarity with the poet's works. Honoured to be introduced to the youngest and last-surviving of Burns' three sisters, Douglass described Isabella Begg, in her seventies at the time, as 'a spirited-looking woman who bids fair to live many days yet.' It was a hunch that proved entirely accurate, as it turned out, when Isabella lived on for another twelve years until she reached the grand old age of 87.

From his remarks, both written and spoken, it seems beyond doubt that Douglass was conscious of a keen affinity between his own position and that of Robert Burns in eighteenth century Scotland, viewing the poet as a fellow-victim of injustice and oppression. 'The aristocracy,' he wrote, 'looked upon the plowman [sic], such as the noble Burns, as being little better than a brute.' Perhaps unconsciously, Douglass resorted to the language of enslavement when he recounted admiringly how Burns 'broke loose' from the stifling strictures that society had imposed upon him. Parallels with his own position are self-evident.

Of course, the time he spent in the land of Burns was a good deal more than simply a sightseeing trip. On two successive evenings in March 1846 Douglass delivered lectures in the Relief Church, Ayr, on each occasion in front of a full house. During his first speech he spelled out for his audience the cruel realities of slavery: how, for example, a slave-owner was free to dictate when and whom a slave should marry; how he had it within his power to separate a husband from his wife, or a mother from her children. He was even free to exert torture at will - 'by the burning brand, the thumbscrew, the chain, the whipping-post and the dungeon' - and no-one was in a position to intervene. Douglass went on to spotlight the hypocrisy of sections of the American clergy who promoted Christian virtues from the pulpit while habitually mistreating their slaves at home. At the close of his lecture, Rev. Renwick wound up proceedings from the chair by pointing out what would be superfluous today - namely, that, based on the force of Frederick Douglass' argument and the power of his rhetoric, no-one could now hold the opinion that the black man was a being of an inferior race. The chairman's concluding remarks were greeted with cheers of approval from the floor.

The following evening the Relief Church was full to capacity with the audience reportedly spilling from the pews to occupy the adjacent passageways. For his second lecture Douglass opted for a different tack, at one stage levelling both barrels squarely at the Free Church of Scotland for its entering into unholy fellowship with 'the props of slavery'. Before coming to this, he engaged his audience's sympathy by broaching the intimate subject of his own background and personal experiences. Douglass stated that he had been born a slave, the property of his master, as was his brother and each of his four sisters. As a baby, he was among a total of twelve infants who had been handed over to be brought up by his grandmother, all of whom had been snatched away when the time was ripe for them to be sold in the slave-market. His grandmother's mission complete, Douglass told his audience, the old lady was left 'desolate and forlorn.'

He moved on to portray for the audience some of the horrors he had witnessed during his 21 years of enslavement, describing in lurid terms the slave-owner's common practice of using a red-hot iron to brand his name on to the skin of his slaves. He referred to the use of bloodhounds to pursue fleeing slaves and, in one of his most shocking revelations, he recounted how, for all that his master was an office-bearer in a Methodist church, Douglass had observed him return from a Sunday service, tie up a female slave (Douglass's cousin, as it happened) and 'with his own hands apply the whip to her bare back till the warm red blood was dripping to her heels.' Towards the end of the meeting, items such as whips, collars, handcuffs, and fetters were put on display, the majority of these said to have been recovered from fugitive slaves. Lowering the tempo in conclusion, Douglass finished up by paying generous tribute to the 'brilliant genius' of Robert Burns and the poet's conspicuous love of liberty. For the last time Rev.

Renwick wrapped up proceedings, and all that remained was for the audience to rise and disperse through the streets of Ayr, sadder and wiser we may be sure for the heartfelt words that they had heard.

It was not yet time, however, for Frederick Douglass to depart from Ayrshire. He followed up his efforts in Ayr by delivering several more well-attended lectures in Kilmarnock, including one in the Laigh Kirk during which a resolution was adopted which condemned utterly the institution of slavery. Before leaving the town, a service was held in his honour in the Clerk's Lane Chapel. Perhaps surprisingly, Douglass delivered his final Ayrshire lecture to an audience in Fenwick, thus bestowing on the village the honour of being the smallest community to which he had addressed his remarks during the nine months of his Scottish tour. At a well-attended meeting in the United Secession Church, the inhabitants of Fenwick roundly condemned any church which maintained relations with slave-holding organisations across the Atlantic. Their message was clear and unambiguous.

By the time Douglass left Scotland at the end of October 1846, he had addressed no fewer than 50 meetings - each of his lectures, by his own account, delivered extempore. Audiences from Ayr to Aberdeen, Kilmarnock to Kirkcaldy, had been held spellbound by the dignity and intelligence of a man who a mere seven years previously had been classed by the society he had been born into as of no greater worth than a mere slave-owner's chattel. When Frederick Douglass departed from these islands, on the *Cambria* once again, and returned to the land of his birth, he made use of funds raised by the British and Irish public to purchase his freedom, and to acquire a printing-press in the city of Rochester on which he proceeded to publish his anti-slavery newspaper, *The North Star*. Following the victory of the North in the American Civil War of 1861-65, during which Douglass acted as consultant to President Lincoln, the evils of American slavery were finally brought to an end when the Thirteenth Amendment to the Constitution which banned slavery outright was ratified, state by state.

'I have never seen a people more deeply moved than were the people of Scotland.' So wrote Frederick Douglass in *My Bondage and My Freedom*, an autobiographical work which he published a decade or so after completing his tour of the British Isles. When invited to speak at a Burns Supper in Rochester, New York, on 25 January 1849, Douglass freely acknowledged the debt he owed to Scotland's national bard. 'Though I am not a Scotchman,' he told the company, 'and have a colored skin, I am proud to be among you this evening. And if any think me out of my place on this occasion' - at this he gestured towards a portrait of Robert Burns - 'I beg that the blame may be laid at the door of him who taught me that *a man's a man for a' that*". It is to their great credit that, by turning out for Frederick Douglass in numbers, the people of Ayr, Kilmarnock and Fenwick affirmed their unequivocal concurrence with the poet's noble sentiment.

Kirkdandie Fair

Whatever the early origins of the fair at Kirkdandie, they are long forgotten, lost in the distant past. More certain is the fact that for many years the annual spree became an Ayrshire institution, despite its secluded setting in the upper Stinchar valley. Every May the better-off farmers of the district would saddle up and set out for the fair on horseback, while their shepherds and farm-servants piled into horse-drawn wagons or simply made their way across the hills on foot.

Positioned on a bluff overlooking the river, the fair took place alongside an ancient chapel which is thought to have fallen into disuse at the time of the Reformation. When a new kirk was established at Barr during the 1650s, Kirkdandie's roof was transported the mile or so upstream to be recycled. The old chapel never recovered. Today its remaining stones languish, forlorn and half-forgotten, in a field of skinny saplings – oak, ash, rowan, and birch – that have been planted all around.

The western gable of the chapel is best preserved, rising steeply to a point with a window-space high-up, but the other walls are in varying states of disrepair, tumbling down or sundered by ash trees that have found a footing among the stones. A few yards to the north-east are the remains of a smaller building - accommodation perhaps for a solitary priest - where a gnarled plum-tree still produces tiny fruits in season. With no sound but the breeze in the long grass and the music of wild birds, Kirkdandie is steeped in the calm that descends on ancient places. It seems that the old chapel's fate is to be swallowed up in trees.

Things weren't always so peaceful. In the past, every last Saturday in May saw a mushrooming of tents and stalls on the old burial ground in preparation for Kirkdandie Fair, a yearly forum for business where close-fisted hill farmers would haggle over prices with wily wool merchants. Meanwhile disgruntled farm-workers would be working on improving their lot, attempting to negotiate more favourable positions for the term to come. But as well as work there was play. According to a ballad of the time, young men in holiday mood drank heartily while tucking into bread and cheese and haggis and ham and trying their luck with the girls. Proceedings grew increasingly riotous as competing strains of fiddle and bagpipe music rose into the air. The shenanigans that followed were perhaps inevitable.

The anonymous ballad tells of 'a country chap [who] had got a drap' and 'lent a chiel a clout.' Predictably his companions waded in … and the rest is folk history. Old scores were routinely settled at the fair, and ancient feuds rekindled. An enthusiastic combatant was the Laird of Changue: a man reputedly tough enough to have 'nail'd the Deil' in spectacular style over Changue's refusal to honour the terms of their agreement. Easier to verify are the mêlées that flared during the nineteenth century between cudgel-wielding locals and bands of Irish migrant-workers, widely employed throughout the district as farm labour. But with the passage of time the fair's significance dwindled: roads had nosed their way into the Ayrshire backwoods, and mobility and transport had widened local horizons. When a new fair became established at Girvan, seven or eight miles away, it proved the last straw and signalled the end for Kirkdandie. The world came to bypass the old chapel, and a century and more of silence settled down among the stones.

Kirkdandie

66

On a hillside overlooking the ruin are the remains of a second ancient site. Fragments of stonework are all that are left of an old archway, giving access to what was once a holy well. At the base of the rock-face ahead, half-hidden by the leaves of a spreading ash tree, a bubbling spring feeds a tiny pool, fringed with ferns and no wider than a few feet across, where pond-skaters skim and glide. Emerging from deep underground, the water of the Struil Well tastes cool and sweet, just as it did when it quenched the thirst of drouthy revellers in the far-off heyday of Kirkdandie Fair.

Early Ayrshires

Every year when the first early Ayrshires arrived, my father, a determinedly south Ayrshire man, would claim that he could taste the difference between his preferred Girvan tatties and their north Ayrshire counterparts, grown in the West Kilbride area. He would go further, maintaining that during his boyhood there had been shore farmers in the Girvan district who had had the ability to tell by taste which of their fields any given potato had been harvested from. As a non-partisan Galston girl, if my mother had doubts she chose not to voice them.

Less contentious possibly is the fact that the humble tattie had amassed a considerable history long before it settled down in Ayrshire's sandy coastal soil. The statistics are fairly striking: originating some 6,000 miles away, 12,000 feet above sea-level, *Solanum tuberosum* was first domesticated in South America an estimated 7,000 years ago, its starchy tubers playing a major role in sustaining the population of the Andes Mountains including the subjects of the powerful Inca empire. But even the Incas found themselves unable to withstand the ruthlessness and modern weaponry of Spanish adventurers who overran their mountainous homeland during the sixteenth century, plundering in the process unimaginable quantities of gold and silver. In addition to their looted treasure, the *conquistadores* took home with them to Spain specimens of what in Europe at the time was an unknown root vegetable but which quickly became an object of considerable curiosity.

Brought to England - reputedly by Sir Walter Raleigh - the potato took a little time to become established as a vegetable with anything more than mere curiosity value. Its arrival in Scotland was greeted with some uncertainty and for a time its tubers were widely suspected of being poisonous. Gradually, however, fears subsided and in time the new crop came to overtake oatmeal as the principal ingredient in the staple diet of ordinary Scots. By the late eighteenth century a potato patch was to be found in most kitchen gardens and, in an inexplicable turnaround, a belief had grown up that the tubers possessed useful medicinal properties.

The birth of commercial cultivation in Scotland can be credited largely to the enterprise of one man. As early as 1739, Robert Graham of Kilsyth planted half an acre of potatoes on his small Stirlingshire farm and his success as a commercial grower in the decades that followed encouraged others to follow his lead. It proved a timely development at a period when large numbers of rural Scots were migrating to towns in order to find employment in the mushrooming mills and factories of the Industrial Revolution. Unlike their forefathers, the new town-dwellers found themselves unable to grow food for themselves and their families, providing potato farmers with the opportunity to step in and plug the gap. The infamous potato famines of the 1840s - in Scotland as well as Ireland - served as a shocking reminder of the danger of relying too heavily on a single food crop, but curiously it was these very traumatic events that served in the years that followed to fuel advances in potato cultivation.

As farmers experimented with new and blight-resistant varieties, efforts were made at the same time to extend the duration of the potato season. At that time the maincrop harvest took place during October and November with supplies remaining fairly plentiful through the subsequent autumn and winter months, but by the time spring came round, stocks had become largely depleted, leaving an uncomfortable gap of several months before they could be replenished. Looking for a solution, two Ayrshire farmers, John Hannah of Girvan Mains and Quintin Dunlop of Morriston paid a visit to Jersey during 1875 where the island's mild, maritime climate enabled potatoes to be harvested a good deal earlier than elsewhere. The men were hopeful that growing conditions on the Channel Islands could be replicated on their own coastal farms.

As it turned out, their ambitions proved well-founded. Warmed by the influence of the Gulf Stream, the two men's farms benefited from free-draining, sandy loam which was quick to warm up in spring and troubled relatively rarely by late frosts. Returning home, they embarked on a series of small-scale experimental plantings, setting seed-potatoes in February and March and harvesting the resulting crop as early as June, some months earlier than the traditional Scottish maincrop. So positive were the results that a mere two years later farmers Hannah and Dunlop were growing the first 'early Ayrshires' on a commercial basis.

There was, of course, a problem. Potatoes make for a hungry crop, demanding rich feeding in order to thrive and, though a farm will always generate its own fertiliser, for potato growers it was never enough. For a time seabird guano was much in demand, shipped - like the potato itself - all the way from Peru. As more and more land was turned over to potatoes at Girvan Mains - in excess of 250 acres in the years leading up to the First World War, enough to keep as many as six ploughmen in employment - a team of Clydesdales was kept busy, hauling seaweed up from the shore, carting in farm and domestic waste from the surrounding district, and even piling offal from slaughtered animals on to what must have quickly become a highly disagreeable concoction. Girvan Mains' prodigious supply network was further extended when the railway stretched south to reach Girvan and provided the farm with not only a speedy means of dispatching its produce to city markets but also of acquiring in return what was known as 'Glasgow dung' - the accumulated manure from the city's horse population as well as the contents of the people's dry closets.

A few miles up the coast at Morriston, Quintin Dunlop didn't miss a trick when he secured an arrangement to relieve Irish cattle-boats, passing regularly up the Firth of Clyde to Glasgow, of dung that had accumulated during their time at sea. This he ferried by flat-bottomed boat to the harbour at Maidens before carting it to his farm, a little over a mile inland. At Girvan Mains, a malodorous mountain - clearly visible from the main road and as tall, it was said, as the adjacent farm buildings - gained notoriety to the extent that, on the death in 1942 of John M. Hannah OBE, son of the original John, his Glasgow Herald obituary saw fit to make reference alongside his various accomplishments to 'the imposing scale of the dung midden at Girvan Mains.'

It had not escaped anybody's notice that the earlier the crop, the higher its market value. In June 1917 the dubious morality of harvesting immature Ayrshire potatoes was raised in the House of Commons - a time, of course, when the nation was at war and domestic food production critical. A less wasteful method of ensuring an early crop had, however, been known since the previous century. The process known as *chitting* - encouraging potatoes to sprout before planting - had been found to be effective in giving the crop a head-start, the seed-potatoes normally being laid out for a number of weeks in a light, frost-free place. Some say that James Lyburn of Balchriston, near Maybole, was the first of the shore farmers to make use of special wooden trays for sprouting the seed after he had acquired a sample tray from the potato fields of Cheshire. In Maybole itself, agricultural merchant,

Thomas Hunter, similarly made use of an English model in the manufacture of his own sprouting-boxes whose use soon became standard in the local area.

In the early days a large number of varieties were grown with no particular one dominating, but a new early potato appeared in 1897 which very quickly became king. Bred in Hampshire by horticulturalist James Clark, Epicure was a vigorous hybrid with an ability to shrug off turbulent weather in addition to being comparatively impervious to both dry conditions and late frosts alike. Not everyone, admittedly, relished its taste: a dry, floury potato, during the 1930s it was considered unsuitable for the London market. Nonetheless Epicure settled down happily in Ayrshire and became for many Scots the archetypal 'early Ayrshire'. More than a century on, despite the development of new varieties, it is still favoured by some growers.

Though equable for the most part, it was not entirely unknown for the Ayrshire climate to throw up an occasional nasty surprise. At the beginning of July 1921 the coastal potato crop had been exposed to a prolonged spell of drought, and in some fields the yield was expected to be little more than a quarter of what was usual. Predictably, the prices paid by merchants for farmers' standing crops dropped accordingly. During the vital growing month of May 1938 many fields alongside the shore were ravaged by late frosts on no fewer than three separate occasions.

But for every lean year there were others that were bountiful. Harvesting in the early days was highly labour-intensive and was traditionally monopolised by Irish *tattie-howkers* who arrived in Scotland *en masse* each June and proceeded to spend the summer months following the harvest north and east across the country, starting with the early Ayrshires and finishing up during October or November with the maincrop in Perthshire and Angus. Families frequently became regulars at the same farm each year where men, women and children would labour side by side in a tradition that continued unbroken until very recent times. Finally during the 1970s it was increased mechanisation on Scottish farms and higher levels of affluence in rural Ireland that spelled the end of the annual influx of Irish tattie-nomads.

It is true that the number of shore farms still growing Ayrshire potatoes has shrunk somewhat in recent times, with the overall acreage under cultivation similarly down. On top of that, the Channel Islands might be suspected of engaging in something of a rearguard action, with drifts of Jersey Royals on ubiquitous display on Scottish supermarket shelves. But, for all that, there is little doubt that tucking into a plate of new Ayrshire potatoes, served whole and glazed with melted butter, remains for many Scots an unmissable rite of early summer.

The Last Pigeon Post

An old legend attributes to Ailsa Craig a rather curious origin. A notorious witch, it says, was flying across the dark skies of south-west Scotland, aiming to attend a coven on the northern Irish coast. For whatever purpose, she scooped up as she flew a great quantity of rock and soil, an action supposedly responsible for the formation of Penwhapple Glen in the parish of Dailly. Whether too heavily burdened or simply over-excited at the prospect of revels to come, it appears that the butter-fingered crone jettisoned her cargo some ten miles off-shore, making an almighty splash and creating in the process the giant rock we know as Ailsa Craig. Perhaps, then, it is fitting that the island remains part of the otherwise landlocked parish of Dailly, though - most would argue - for reasons more historical than supernatural.

Whatever the geological ancestry of Ailsa Craig (and experts are not entirely in agreement) there can be little doubt that a sheer-sided, thousand-foot granite pyramid, planted in mid-Firth of Clyde, would be likely to present something of a hazard to shipping. Following various shipwrecks, the island's lighthouse was finally established in 1886, whose winking eye could be seen, in clear conditions, from a considerable distance. As well as its light, the island was given its voice when twin fog-horns were positioned at both north and south ends, fuelled – like the light itself – by oil-based gas which could be manufactured on the spot. Contact with the mainland was to be maintained via a 'ball-signalling' system, monitored each day from Girvan using a telescope. But the system's effectiveness was frequently hampered by bad weather and poor visibility, and the Northern Lighthouse Board was forced into a rapid rethink in case an emergency should arise on the island.

The method finally adopted was one that harked back to earlier days. In prehistoric times, hill-top beacon fires were routinely lit in the event of disasters, such as war or imminent invasion. But beyond a simple call to arms, the beacon signaller's repertoire was severely limited. On Ailsa Craig, depending on where a bonfire was situated, it might indicate that medical attention was required, either for a lighthouse keeper or for one of the handful of workers in the island's granite quarry. Alternatively a fire in another location would signify that food supplies were running dangerously low. Any more elaborate message had no option but to wait for the arrival of the weekly supply boat - if sea conditions permitted.

Once again the Lighthouse Board looked to the past for a solution. As far back as the days of the Egyptian pharaohs, the domestic pigeon's legendary homing instinct had been made use of. During the twelfth century, the Sultan of Baghdad established an early pigeon post system, soon to be followed by the Mongolian warlord, Genghis Khan, whose messenger pigeons spread news of his conquests across the breadth of Asia – a feat that puts a ten-mile hop across the Firth of Clyde into some kind of perspective. A loft was duly erected on Girvan Green whose feathered occupants were to be responsible for communications with Ailsa Craig.

The Ailsa Craig Pigeon Post

In the mid-1890s, Richard Kearton, an eminent naturalist, and his younger brother, Cherry, one of the pioneers of early nature photography, paid a visit to Ailsa Craig. As they tucked in to an island breakfast of fried guillemot eggs, the two brothers listened to a remarkable tale. A child had fallen dangerously ill on Ailsa Craig, so a bird had been released, according to normal practice, carrying a request for medical assistance. The Girvan doctor braved choppy seas to reach the island, where he immediately set about examining his small patient. A certain powder, he decided, was urgently required, but the lateness of the hour and the worsening weather conditions made another crossing too hazardous to attempt. The problem seemed intractable, as the child's life hung in the balance, until finally matters were resolved when a second pigeon, this time bearing a request for medicine, was dispatched to the mainland. After what must have been a tense wait, a tiny speck finally appeared on the horizon: a carrier pigeon, aiming for Ailsa Craig and trailing what turned out to be a small phial of powder attached to its tail. Happily, the Kearton brothers were informed that the bird had arrived on time, and that the child's life was duly saved.

The pigeon post quickly became an institution. By the early 1930s, the Ailsa Craig lighthouse boatman - the aptly named Captain Archie S. Girvan - was being paid an annual sum of £4 on top of his regular salary for tending the Girvan loft. During his years in the job, Captain Girvan responded many times to the summons of the pigeon post. On one memorable occasion, he was called upon to convey police officers to the island, after George Rosie, a lighthouse keeper, had stumbled across a handless corpse stretched out on the shingle, washed up by the waves. Thankfully such grisly episodes were rare. Most call-outs were considerably less macabre.

In 1924, George Taylor, an Aberdonian by birth, was employed as a labourer in the Ailsa granite quarry. When the jib of a thirty-ton crane Taylor was operating broke loose and tumbled into the sea, the unfortunate workman found himself carried along with it despite his best efforts. Although he had taken a grievous blow, he managed to struggle ashore where the foreman, named Duffus, administered emergency first aid. A ragged wound in the quarryman's upper lip had to be stitched on the spot, but so severe was his body bruising that a beacon fire was lit to alert the Girvan doctor.

When it appeared that the bonfire had gone unnoticed, a carrier pigeon was released which failed to make it through the stormy conditions to the mainland. Tension mounted as a second bird was dispatched, this time with more success. When Dr MacDougall arrived, he patched up the injured man, declaring, to everyone's relief, that his condition was no longer critical. No doubt George Taylor was grateful to the plucky pigeon that had braved the blast on his behalf. But for many, the quarryman's unfortunate accident only served to underscore the need for a modern wireless link between Ailsa Craig and the mainland.

Not everyone, however, was put off by the island's isolation. There were those who found its sea-girt solitude exactly to their taste. When Alexander Thomson reached the end of his long career as keeper, he had spent a total of thirty-eight years on Ailsa Craig. Born the son of a lighthouse keeper on the Isle of Man, Thomson had married his boss's daughter in the first ever ceremony of its kind on Ailsa Craig. Tragically, one of the couple's sons died by drowning during the years of the First World War. But despite the tribulations of island life, Thomson announced at the time of his retiral his intention of passing his final years on Sanda – an island not much bigger than Ailsa Craig, and almost as remote.

But with advances in communications the Ailsa Craig pigeons were living increasingly on borrowed time. In December 1935, Captain Girvan shipped out wireless apparatus to the island which had been supplied by the Northern Lighthouse Board to enable the keepers for the first time to communicate directly with the mainland via equipment stationed at Turnberry lighthouse. The Captain's birds, of course, became redundant and the loft on Girvan Green was dismantled to make way for a public car-park. And so the era of Ailsa Craig's carrier pigeons passed into history, and with it forty years of gallant service.

It was only a matter of months before the first radio SOS reached Turnberry, requesting urgent medical attention for John Thomson, one of the lighthouse keepers. By the time the message was relayed by telephone from Turnberry to Girvan, the lighthouse boatman had already made his way to the harbour and was making his final preparations for departure. It transpired that he had intercepted the call at home, using his own recently-installed radio receiver. Captain Girvan, it would appear, had moved with the times.

Men & Myth

The Coilus Enigma

Loch Fergus is a quiet stretch of water set among rolling farmlands, its surface ruffled only by the passage of waterfowl. An off-shore island, the site of an early monastery, is tangled with wild wood, the memory of an older Scotland. The loch is said to have taken its name from a Dark Age warlord who led his troops to victory in the surrounding countryside. Yet, despite his success in battle, Fergus' name has slipped largely from local memory; while, strange to say, his routed enemy is still widely remembered. For some say that the chieftain who tasted defeat by the shores of Loch Fergus was none other than Old King Cole.

Legend has it that a warlike coalition of Picts and Scots led by King Fergus had wreaked havoc on the lands of their southern neighbours, the Britons, though a gallant British king named Coilus had put up a spirited resistance. But the pendulum swung emphatically in Fergus' favour when he surprised Coilus under cover of darkness, and such was the massacre that followed that only a tiny number of Britons were able to escape, including the king himself. Coilus led his men eastwards via Knockmurran, crossing the flooded Water of Coyle by means of a series of stepping-stones, known as the 'King's Steps', before fleeing into the densely wooded countryside that lay to the north. The fugitive Britons reached the banks of the River Ayr close to its confluence with the Water of Fail, and it was somewhere in this vicinity that the tattered remnants of Coilus' army made their last futile stand.

Folklore surely, rather than historical fact? Well, perhaps. But Robert Burns was one firm believer that his native Kyle had been named for an ancient king, steeped as the poet was in Ayrshire wisdom. Not every historian agrees, of course, but the map does display an intriguing cluster of place names in the locality: Coilswood Cottage, situated by the edge of Coilsholm Wood; the winding Water of Coyle which meets the River Ayr close to the village of Coylton.

Starting at Failford, where a sandstone monument commemorates Burns' final parting from his Highland Mary, a dairy-maid at Coilsfield House, it is possible to follow the Water of Fail upstream in the footsteps of the king. Passing beneath a tall railway viaduct, you will arrive at a narrow, wooded glen where the modern world quickly evaporates and time appears to stand still. Tucked between steep-sided bankings, a crescent of meadowland lies alongside a bow-shaped bend in the burn - an idyllic spot, looped in birdsong and spring blossom, which makes its name seem more strange. For the little half-moon meadow by the Water of Fail has been known for centuries as the Dead Men's Holm.

Loch Fergus

It would appear that things weren't always so peaceful on the banks of the Fail. Over the years the Dead Men's Holm has offered up an irregular harvest of relics from the past. As far back as the seventeenth century, a thing of wonder emerged from its rich riverside loam. An elegant bronze hunting horn, two feet in length and exquisitely crafted, came to light, whose ownership was attributed - perhaps inevitably - to King Coilus himself. The servants at Coilsfield House had cause to regret the horn's discovery when its shrill note was subsequently put to use in chivvying them along the mansion's rambling corridors.

Some of the Holm's other offerings proved distinctly more grisly. Fragments of bone and rusty armour were turned up by the plough, bearing out the belief that in olden times a battle had been played out on the banks of the Fail.

So, did Coilus and his remaining men resolve to face their pursuers for the last time here on the smooth green turf of the Dead Men's Holm? Or could it be rather that the Britons' grieving families bore their relatives for burial to this secluded place? Accounts vary. But a nearby tributary of the Fail is known as the Bloody Burn - its waters, according to legend, having run red with the blood of the fallen.

You can continue upstream, aiming for the farm of Coilsfield Mains, where it is possible to identify another piece in the jigsaw. For beside the steading of Coilsfield Mains, there is a prehistoric burial site which has long been known as King Coil's Grave.

Within a few yards of the byres a row of three whinstone boulders occupies the centre of a grassy mound, while an irregular semi-circle of smaller stones forms its western rim. An account of the cairn's excavation in the 1830s (carried out unaccountably by candlelight in the midst of a spring deluge) was kept by the Tarbolton minister, Rev. David Ritchie. Several feet down a number of cinerary urns were unearthed from beneath a flat, circular stone, as well as ashes and various bone fragments, all surrounded by unusual yellow clay. Ritchie reasonably concluded that the evidence that these discoveries provided went a long way to substantiating the local Coilus myth. Clearly, he argued, such a laboriously constructed tomb represented a burial fit for a warrior king.

But not, sadly, King Coilus. The theory began to unravel when modern dating techniques placed the Coilsfield cairn squarely in the Bronze Age, at least a thousand years adrift of our fugitive British king. And dates are not the only sticky issue. The question of Coilus' very identity remains unresolved, with a bewildering assortment of kings lining up in contention from pre-Roman times right through till the age of the Vikings. The plain fact is that, other than traditional tales and the folk memories of country people, hard evidence is thin on the ground.

But hope inevitably lingers. Perhaps one day a key will surface to the Coilus enigma, and matters can at last be settled. If the mysterious Holm lets slip a few more of its secrets, King Coilus yet may step from the shadows into the light of verifiable history. Till that day comes, he must remain the misty Dark Age hero who fought and lost by Loch Fergus, or the amiable old gentleman with a fondness for music from the pages of a book of children's verse.

Flitting the Sow

Time has not dealt kindly with the hills south of Kerse. For many years the countryside around it has been obliterated by an opencast site - a wilderness of mud and watery craters. The fields are marred by a procession of pylons, striding off towards the horizon. But of the old castle of Kerse, where once a redoubtable patriarch impatiently awaited the outcome of a most unusual conflict, there is not a trace.

Things were different five centuries ago, when Craufurd of Kerse held sway from his stronghold at Kerse Loch over vast acreages of Kyle, the feudal division of Ayrshire lying north of the River Doon. The only thorn in the veteran warrior's side was the running feud with his powerful neighbours to the south, the Kennedys, whose word was law all the way down through the Carrick hills and deep into Galloway. On many a moonless night bands of reivers had been known to ford the Doon and round up a few fat cattle before turning for home, pausing along the way to fire the thatch of a few Kyle farmsteads.

Family fortunes seesawed over time, with the Craufurds gaining the upper hand at one time, only to give ground in turn when providence smiled once more upon the Carrick men. So when Kennedy of Bargany threw down the gauntlet, we may never know whether he acted through arrogance and overconfidence, or rather in an effort to restore flagging fortunes. Either way, Bargany dispatched an envoy to Kerse Castle bearing word that, on Lammas Day next, he would tether a sow on Craufurd lands, despite what the Craufurds might do to prevent him.

The fierce old Laird of Kerse was said to have bristled with indignation at his neighbour's act of provocation, but the etiquette of the day demanded restraint and safe conduct for Bargany's messenger out of Kyle and into Carrick. The challenge for Kerse and his sons was to 'flit', or move, the sow back across the Doon before a summer's day elapsed – if they could.

The old laird knew for sure that the flower of Carrick's fighting men would rally to Bargany's standard, eager for a pop at the old enemy across the Doon. An octogenarian, Kerse's own fighting days were over, but he wasted no time in calling in favours from his kinsmen, allies and retainers; and the lairds of Drongan, Leifnoreis and Loudoun are said to have speedily answered the summons. All across Kyle soldier-farmers got belted and buckled and set about greasing pistols and muskets, while their shepherds, tenants and ploughmen left off hay-making and harvesting and set out for the fray by the Doon. The walls of Kerse Castle must fairly have echoed to the din of sharpening blades in preparation to flit the infamous sow.

Some say that she arrived at Skeldon Haughs in style, conveyed by horse-drawn float, while others maintain that her journey was more ignominious, carried in a sack. In any case, once tethered on the riverside meadow, a small boy was charged with the responsibility of frequently goading the unfortunate creature, so that her squeals of irritation could not fail to reach the ears of Esplin Craufurd, Kerse's eldest son, in command of the Craufurds' troops. Doubtless things got underway with a ritual exchange of insults, in all probability accompanied by a wild spattering of musket fire. Finally the Kyle horsemen advanced towards enemy lines but quickly became clogged in mire, so well had Bargany chosen his spot. The honours of the day, it seemed, were to be settled by hand-to-hand fighting.

A stretch of the riverbank near Dalrymple is where the trial of strength was said to have taken place, where the Kennedys' pig would have been shielded on three sides by the Doon, as accounts describe. Popular belief linked the farm of Boreland with the story – its name proving too strong a temptation - though a nearby pool does go by the name of 'Kennedy's Dub.'

How long that distant Lammas Day must have felt to the Craufurd chief, anxiously waiting for news in his castle beneath the Craigs of Kyle. Perhaps the old laird slumbered in the August sun, reliving in dreams his eighty years of love and combat acted out beside Kerse Loch. The day was well advanced by the time the first returning horseman appeared, a speck on the skyline, and began his weary descent towards the loch.

The eighteenth century poet, Alexander Boswell (related to the Craufurds by marriage) names this rider as Will o' Ashyntree. To the laird's annoyance, Will approached in gloomy silence, triggering the old man's impatient wrath: 'Is the sow flitted? Tell me, loon! Is auld Kyle up and Carrick doon?' With utmost reluctance, the exhausted soldier broke the news that Kerse's son, John, was numbered among the dead. Refusing to be diverted, the old man persisted: 'Gie me my answer, short and plain, is the sow flitted?' At that Will finally gasped out the news that the Kennedys were routed, their pig seen off across the Doon. The laird's reputed response reflected an age when reputation and the saving of face mattered more than the loss of a son. His old lined face lit up with terrible unholy joy. 'My thumb for Jock,' retorted the old man, snapping his fingers dismissively. 'The sow is flitted!'

Times change, and attitudes with them. Kerse Castle met its end in the eighteenth century, its stonework barrowed off as building materials for the new Skeldon House. The last remaining wall came down during a storm in 1797, and year by year local farmers carted away what was left of the rubble, whenever they found a need. Probably many of the dry stane dykes that criss-cross these windy uplands may have originated in the castle walls.

The Laird's Leavings

You'd be hard pressed to locate the ancient castle of Auchinleck at the height of summer. A quick beat about the bushes will reveal its seventeenth century successor, the so-called Place of Auchinleck, more extensive than its elder relative though almost as ruinous. But the ancient castle slumbers through the summer months unseen, shrouded entirely in greenery, and dreaming, you might imagine, of its more illustrious past.

It would be hard to quibble about the wisdom of the old keep's strategic location. Perched high on an outcrop of red sandstone, its walls teeter on the brink of a dizzying drop, overlooking the point where the Water of Lugar and the Dippol Burn converge, a hundred feet below. Ready access would only ever have been possible from the east, though even on this side a trench, traces of which are still visible, would have slowed the advance of any potential aggressor. In 1773 Dr Samuel Johnson investigated the ruin in the company of James Boswell - the son of his host, Lord Auchinleck - and deduced from the castle's immediate surroundings that it would have been likely to be equipped in past times with a moat and drawbridge, something not easy to visualise today.

When James Boswell's ancestor, Thomas, arrived from Fife in 1504, having acquired the lands of Auchinleck by royal charter, the crag-top fortress he gained possession of was already of considerable age. As far back as the thirteenth century the name *Nicol de Achethlec* (Auchinleck) appears on the infamous Ragman Roll whose signatories swore allegiance to Edward I of England. It didn't take Nicol long to renege, however, when he played a leading role in 'The Battle of the Bell o' the Brae' - the occasion when William Wallace launched a devastating attack on the English garrison at Glasgow, during which the enemy commander, Earl Percy, was killed and his forces put to rout. The medieval poet and chronicler, Blind Harry, records his belief that Wallace and Nicol of Auchinleck were kinsmen.

Thanks to the local topography, Auchinleck's nearest neighbour was strangely inaccessible. Effectively within hailing distance, Ochiltree Castle faced out from the opposite side of the Lugar gorge, its cliff-edge position presumably also dictated by strategic considerations. Since the mid-thirteenth century, the castle had been in the hands of the Colvilles, a powerful family of Norman descent, who held tracts of land across half a dozen Scottish counties from Inverness and Banff in the north down as far as Ayrshire and the border-country. Legend has it that for a goodly number of years the Colville lairds and their opposite numbers at Auchinleck Castle were successful in maintaining friendly relations, going so far as to put a pulley-system in place whereby a rope spanning the Lugar formed a link between their two houses and allowed greetings and other items to be passed readily back and forth. Almost inevitably, the good times didn't last. For reasons now unknown, cordial relations crumbled and were replaced by a feud between the two neighbouring families whose concluding events are recounted in a rather strange old legend.

It is tempting to imagine the laird of Auchinleck as a replete and contented man, pleasantly recuperating after a particularly hearty dinner, when he was suddenly struck by what seemed like a bright idea. Leaping to his feet, he immediately set about putting his plan into effect, gleefully arranging for the detritus of his recent meal - the picked-clean bones of a sheep's head - to be bundled up, placed in a basket, and conveyed to Ochiltree Castle via the rope-pulley which, for whatever reason, had remained in place following the breakdown in relations. It is not hard to picture Colville's outrage a few moments later when he took delivery of the parcel and proceeded to unwrap the leftovers of his neighbour's dinner.

Such an affront could not be overlooked. Once he had calmed down sufficiently, the Laird of Ochiltree applied himself to considering what form his revenge might take. Strong-arm tactics, he realised, were out of the question, his enemy's castle being well-nigh impregnable, therefore whatever plan he adopted would necessarily have to rely on stealth. According to one version of the story, Colville and his supporters slip quietly across the Lugar, secreting themselves under cover of darkness among trees and undergrowth near to Auchinleck Castle. Here they settled down to wait.

Colville's men remained silent and motionless until sometime later they saw their enemy's castle door thrown open, possibly either to admit a guest or alternatively to allow an inmate to depart. Seizing their opportunity, Ochiltree and his men burst from their hiding-place and, before the door could be secured against them, forcd their way inside, overcoming whatever resistance was offered. As they combed the castle's small number of apartments, sword in hand, it did not take the men long to locate the target of their mission and repay in full the insult of Auchinleck's leavings.

An alternative version of the story, however, saw Colville select a lonely spot in the woods where he laid a successful ambush for his discourteous neighbour. No matter what form it took, Ochiltree's act of revenge had consequences that quickly rebounded on his own head, as well as those of his family members and retainers.

When word reached the Earl of Douglas concerning the laird of Auchinleck's death, his response was both rapid and brutal. Declining to eat or drink until such time as his friend was avenged, the powerful nobleman amassed a band of followers and proceeded to ride into Ayrshire where he ravaged the lands of Ochiltree before surrounding the castle and calling for surrender. Colville, however, decided to stay put, hoping that he might be able to sit out the siege. Thus, Douglas's hand was forced. He ordered his men to storm the fortress and, during the course of the operation, they succeeded in capturing its laird alive but massacred nonetheless all other adult males in his household. Douglas' forces concluded their destructive orgy by burning Ochiltree Castle to the ground. In the five centuries and more that have passed since then, no attempt has ever been made to rebuild it.

Led away captive, legend has it that the laird of Ochiltree met his end in fairly peculiar circumstances. Somewhere in the vicinity of New Cumnock, Douglas and his men happened to cross an apparently unexceptional burn which prompted their prisoner, for inexplicable reasons, to make what turned out to be a most ill-advised admission. Sometime previously, Colville confided in his captors, it had been prophesied by a local 'spae-wife' that he would breathe his last at this particular place. On hearing the wise woman's words, the Earl of Douglas, it seems, wasted no time in ensuring their fulfilment. Some have even suggested that the laird of Ochiltree's summary execution was carried out by Douglas in person.

How long would it have taken for old wounds to heal, or for warring parties to become reconciled? We may well ask. One thing we know for sure is that in September 1513, a couple of generations after their feud's bloody culmination, the chiefs of the two rival houses, Thomas Boswell of Auchinleck and his neighbour, Robert Colville of Ochiltree, died alongside their king, fighting shoulder to shoulder on the star-crossed field of Flodden.

When the woods alongside the Lugar Water start to tint each autumn, the old castle of Auchinleck awakes once again and rouses itself from summer's leafy seclusion. Sunlight, slanting through newly-bare branches, falls upon a series of stone steps, half-buried under fallen leaves, that lead up to the sandstone outcrop that was selected long ago by the first Auchinlecks for their family stronghold. A few courses of the old walls remain in place, red like their parent rock beneath, but for how much longer? Swelling tree-limbs steadily prise the stonework apart while spreading mosses encroach more and more upon the ancient masonry, cloaking the dark events of the past in a dripping mantle of green.

The Minister's Curse

Craigie Castle reveals little of itself to passers-by. You might very well drive back and forth along the country road that passes within a few field-lengths of the ruins and still not be aware of the castle's existence. Yet the topmost of its crumbling battlements are visible from the roadside, rising above the sloping fields and hawthorn hedges like a pair of giant claws that give little indication of the building's former grandeur.

For Craigie Castle surely was a formidable sight in its day. Perched strategically on rising ground and several storeys in height, the castle undoubtedly dominated the surrounding countryside and in its time would been well-nigh impregnable. Unwelcome arrivals were slowed by tracts of marshy ground, now drained for pasture, and a series of deep ditches had been excavated to deter potential aggressors. In times of trouble, the laird's kinsmen and retainers would have flooded over the drawbridge, located beneath the watchful eye of a defensive tower, and during emergencies the castle precincts would have been capable of affording sanctuary to several hundred people.

But, despite its present ruinous state, it is clear that the old stronghold did more than simply meet the blunt requirements of self-defence. As well as being a fortress, Craigie Castle was also a family home. On an upper floor, remnants of the great hall's architectural splendour hint at gracious living. Stone arches can be seen, curving up from the base of decorative window openings, to converge in what would formerly have been a magnificent vaulted ceiling. Perhaps this was the very chamber in which a neighbouring landowner, John Wallace of Riccarton, was received as suitor to Margaret Lindsay, the young heiress of Craigie during the second half of the fourteenth century.

Hard facts about the castle's story are not easy to come by. But we do know that in 1371 it passed, through marriage, to John Wallace of Riccarton – a descendant of Scotland's hero – and a stone bearing the arms of both families, Lindsay and Wallace, is said to have been unearthed from the site and subsequently built into the steading at the nearby farm of Craigie

Mains. Wallaces lived on at Craigie for two hundred years until the late sixteenth century when the family departed for Newton Castle in Ayr, marking the end of the line for their old home. Craigie Castle became neglected and in time grew derelict.

Craigie Castle

But silence and slow time are not the stuff of folklore. Local legend would have it that there was a bit more to the castle's final chapter than that. In the devout days of the sixteenth century the Laird of Craigie had been seen to breach the sanctity of the Sabbath by receiving goods, delivered to his castle by a string of pack-horses. When the local minister got to hear, he took the first opportunity to launch a savage attack on the laird from the pulpit. So incensed was the laird at his public shaming, that in fury he hurled his sword at the clergyman who only just ducked in time to avoid the blade. Although the weapon clattered harmlessly to the floor, the damage had been done. Before his shocked and silent congregation, the irate minister invoked the wrath of God to punish the Laird of Craigie's wicked ways. Craigie Castle, fumed the clergyman, would be reduced to a pile of rubble and any attempt at repair would prove unavailing. In a final sting, he predicted that the laird's illustrious son would die a witless fool.

And things fell out much as the minister had foreseen. An army man, the laird's son suffered a fall from his horse, sustaining serious head injuries from which he never recovered. Shortly afterwards, a huge rock fall occurred during repairs to the castle walls, burying alive the masons who had been working below. And these were the tragic reasons why the Wallaces abandoned Craigie and left their ancestral home to crumble, a lonely roost for crows and jackdaws.

The Blackcraig Giant

Glen Afton of times past was undoubtedly a wilder place than it is today. Where conifer plantations now carpet the hills and only pockets of broadleaf woodland are left standing, at one time there was a tangle of native trees - oak, ash, birch, rowan and more – whose branches shaded a mossy under-storey of ferns, wild flowers and bracken. So thickly wooded was the glen that on one notable occasion a certain laird of Craigdarroch was reputed to have travelled a full five miles through the trees, clambering from branch to branch without once setting foot on the ground. Sadly no record survives of when exactly this remarkable feat took place; nor, for that matter, the reason why.

Not surprisingly the wild wood was said to contain some equally wild inhabitants. In the glen's upper reaches, the Afton Water passes along a narrow corridor between Yarngallows Knowe on one side and the slopes of Blackcraig Hill opposite, which rise steeply to a height of nearly 2,300 feet. The Spout Burn plunges down the hill's precipitous western flank, flowing between rocky outcrops known as the Black Clints to the south and their whimsically-named neighbours, the Merry Clints, further north. It was close to this spot, legend would have it, that an outlaw of unusually large stature once inhabited a hillside cave who, along with his similar-sized wife, lived by preying on the flocks and herds of his neighbours. But in the fullness of time this Blackcraig ogre was destined to get his comeuppance, in common with the majority of other storybook giants.

A mile or so down the glen, the farm of Dalhanna still has an obvious connection with giants. At any given time, a phalanx of steel colossi are to be seen, manning the distant skyline and revolving their arms in stately rotation as they front the prevailing westerlies. In former times, when giants seemed to conform more closely to storybook standards, the lairds of Dalhanna were Campbells, influential in the district since medieval times, and it was allegedly a Campbell who stepped up to the plate in tackling the Blackcraig rustler.

Confrontation eventually flared when Dalhanna's lawless neighbour ventured a step too far, stealing one of the laird's best beasts, a fine bull which he promptly dispatched before humping it across his shoulders to the cave by the Spout Burn – a considerable feat of strength, it cannot be denied. When Dalhanna discovered his missing bull, not one to take the loss lying down, he resolved to strike back without delay, surmising that he would find his foe resting in the aftermath of his earlier exertions. Arming himself with his broadsword, the laird mounted his grey mare and rode south through the Glen Afton woods, heading for the cave among the Blackcraig clints. Why he should have chosen to face his enemy alone we can only guess.

Blackcraig Hill, Glen Afton

A short distance from his destination, Dalhanna halted and concealed himself among trees and bushes where he settled down to wait. After some time he observed his enemy's wife leave the cave and descend to the Spout Burn where she set about washing offal that had been taken from the stolen animal. Confident now that the coast was clear, Dalhanna stepped out of the wood and approached the cave, sword in hand. Just as he had anticipated, the cave's tenant was sound asleep, snoring loudly with his massive mouth agape.

A large pot of water, bubbling on a fire nearby, presented the laird with an unforeseen opportunity. Setting his sword aside, he wrestled the heavy vessel from the fire and, creeping up on the sleeping giant, proceeded to tip its boiling contents into his gaping mouth. That the victim roared his displeasure goes without saying, but soon the boiling liquid did its work and his cries fell silent. When she heard the commotion, the giant's wife hurried back to the cave where she intercepted Dalhanna as he prepared to make his escape. Knowing at once what had taken place, she instantly gave chase as the laird mounted his horse and fled.

There followed a lengthy pursuit, Dalhanna's mare dodging tree-trunks and sailing over boulders and burns, until finally - in an action reminiscent of another celebrated chase - the giantess came close enough to stretch out her hand and grasp the laird's mount by the tail. When he became aware of what was happening behind him, Dalhanna swung round in the saddle and made use of his sword to sever with one blow his pursuer's hand from her body, and thus made good his escape.

Halted by her grievous wound, the giantess had little option but to turn and make for home where, lonely and forlorn, she died soon after of a broken heart. Legend has it that her body and that of her husband were laid to rest in a tranquil riverside meadow not far from the farm of Lochbrowan, more peaceful in death, perhaps, than ever they had been in life.

Maggie Osborne of Ayr

Legend claims that Maggie Osborne was born the illegitimate daughter of Walter Whiteford, the notorious 'Warlock Laird of Fail', from whom she acquired her famed dexterity in the black arts. Residing on the High Street of Ayr, Maggie's daylight hours were spent unexceptionally in managing the running of a public-house but as soon as night descended she reputedly took herself off, broomstick and all, on regular energetic jaunts over the Carrick Hills and down into Galloway where she took delight in harassing the natives and their unfortunate beasts, on one occasion cheekily taking communion at a local church. At the end of the service she was observed in the act of spitting out her communion wafer which was promptly swallowed by the devil himself who had apparently been waiting outside, disguised in the shape of a toad.

Maggie possessed all the routine skills of the witch's trade, in one case taking on the form of a cat and on another occasion disguising herself, more unconventionally, as a beetle crawling over the hill-pass known as the Nick of the Balloch, a hazardous situation from which she was fortunate to emerge unscathed. True to her spiteful reputation, Maggie undertook to revenge herself upon an unsuspecting shepherd, part of a funeral party, whose boot had inadvertently threatened to crush her and, in what most fair-minded observers might judge to be a fairly major over-reaction, she immediately set about conjuring up a mighty avalanche which duly descended on her victim's home, killing the man himself as well as his wife and many of his children forby. But that wasn't the end of it. On hearing that one of the shepherd's sons had happened to be absent from home at the time of her stage-managed avalanche, Maggie began plotting his demise in a manner that would undoubtedly have done credit to the weird sisters in Shakespeare's Macbeth.

On learning that the shepherd's surviving son was in the process of returning to Ayr by sea, Maggie ordered a servant-girl to fill the mash tun (a large vat used for fermenting malt) to the brim with water. That done, the girl was instructed to float an ale-cup on the surface and await further instructions. Meanwhile Maggie withdrew to a garret-room where, sure to be undisturbed, she invoked the devil to assist her in casting her spell. Sometime later she directed her servant-girl, waiting at the foot of the stairs, to check on the mash tun where the girl observed that the water was rippling gently with the ale-cup still afloat at the centre. Instructed to check once more, the girl - by now probably thoroughly frightened - reported back that the water was now swilling around, spilling over the rim, and that faint cries for help could be heard as the ale-cup rocked violently back and forth. When ordered to check for a third time, the girl advised her mistress that the water had once again returned to a state of calm and that the ale-cup now lay upended on the bottom of the vat, information that seemed to satisfy her mistress. Sometime later, of course, the news broke that a ship returning from the Hebrides had been wrecked on St Nicholas Rock, a treacherous reef situated close to the entrance to Ayr Harbour, and that none aboard had survived to reach dry land.

The time came around eventually when Maggie Osborne was obliged to pay for her crimes. After her supernatural activities were brought to the attention of William Adair, the local minister, she was quickly put on trial, the chief witness, some say, an elder of the Moor Kirk of Luce in Galloway whose church she had desecrated and throughout whose district she had wreaked persistent havoc. Convicted and sentenced to death by burning at the Malt Cross of Ayr, Maggie made a last ditch attempt to save her skin, calling upon the devil to provide her with means of escape, but the wings supplied by her diabolic master proved ineffectual and she was unable to gain sufficient height before a quick-thinking halberdier made use of his long-handled weapon to haul her by the petticoats back to earth. This time there was no avoiding her grisly fate.

Or so the story goes. But in reality not a shred of documentary evidence exists to the effect that anyone by the name of Maggie Osborne ever faced prosecution for witchcraft in Ayr. Yet who can be sure? Significant gaps in the seventeenth century town records leave a tantalising chink of possibility that the legends of Maggie Osborne may have at their core at least some small basis in fact.

Sir John's Leap

There is a dark tale associated with the sea-cliff known as Games Loup, situated a few hundred yards north of Sawney Bean's cave - no easier to verify, it has to be said, than the supposed cannibal's better-known crimes but possessing at least a degree of grim humour and with a happy ending of sorts. The villain of the piece is Sir John Cathcart, whose family's presence on the south Carrick coast dates back to the fifteenth century when, by royal charter, the Cathcarts were granted possession of the tall, grey tower of Carleton, glowering down from its hill-top perch above the fishing hamlet of Lendalfoot.

In the centuries that followed, the Cathcart family went on to produce a number of notable figures. Married to Margaret Cathcart of Carleton, Robert Cathcart of Killochan died in 1513, fighting for his country at Flodden. Later that same century, John Cathcart was a loyal backer of the Bargany faction during the great inter-Kennedy feuds but in later years

The Games Loup

became known as a 'wonderfully holy and heavenly' man whose wise counsel was widely sought. In 1702 the renown of the Cathcarts spread to the New World when Hew Cathcart of Carleton was created a baronet of Nova Scotia. But not every member of the family went on record as quite so illustrious or admirable.

In fact, if an old Ayrshire ballad is anything to go by, Sir John Cathcart was a thoroughly bad egg, using promises of marriage - backed up, some said, by the power of magic - to lure 'a maid of beauty rare', May Kennedy of Culzean, from her father's house - taking care first, of course, to remove the fastest horse from her father's stable and to deplete his coffers of gold. The pair rode south into Sir John's own territory, drawing rein when they reached the crest of a tall sea-cliff called Games Loup (on some older maps Gemmel's Loup), a couple of miles from Carleton Castle. This was the point where 'the fause Sir John' revealed at last his true colours.

'Loup off your steed,' he instructed May Culzean and, gesturing to where the waves surged over the rocks below, he told her with cruel irony, 'Your bridal bed you see.' He was unable to resist boasting that on this same spot he had already drowned seven wealthy women – or eight, depending on which version of the ballad you read – by plunging them to their deaths in the sea below, and it was now his intention to add May Kennedy to his list. But, being a greedy man through and through, 'the fause Sir John' could not stomach the thought of her jewellery and fine clothes being lost to the waves, so he ordered her to strip.

Sir John's greed threw May a lifeline. Appealing to his better nature, she begged him to look away while she undressed as, in her words, 'It ne'er became a gentleman/A naked lass to see.' Presumably believing he had nothing to lose, he duly obliged at which point May took him by surprise, gripping him tightly round the waist and, in a moment of palpable poetic justice, propelled him over the cliff and into the sea below. Predictably Sir John now changed his tune, pleading to be saved as he sank beneath the waves but May's resolve did not falter. 'Ye lie not in a caulder bed/ Than the ane ye meant for me,' she told him matter-of-factly, a point that was unanswerable.

The old ballad makes good reading, but its events are tricky to verify. Its nineteenth century collector noted that the people of Lendalfoot were firm in their belief that the castle above their village had been the abode of 'the fause Sir John'. The problem is that over the years more than half a dozen Lairds of Carleton went by the name of John Cathcart, and theoretically the ballad's anti-hero might have been any one of them.

Or none. Long before the Cathcarts rose to eminence, it has been suggested that the Games Loup cliffs may have been used by early hunters as a location for driving wild creatures such as deer to their deaths on the rocks below. For anyone keen to blacken the name of the local nobility, it would have been a simple task to adapt a distant folk-memory by substituting an innocent young woman for a cornered red deer hind.

The Devil and Lady Isle

According to the eighteenth century poet and folklorist, Joseph Train, there was once a widely-held belief that the Ayrshire coastline had been spared the depredations of foreign invaders by the timely intervention of a local sorceress, Elcine de Aggart, whose story he relates in his largely unread poem of the same name.

The events recounted by Train followed in the wake of England's defeat of the great Spanish Armada in 1588 - the occasion when Sir Francis Drake famously was in no hurry to lay aside his bowls - when a section of the routed fleet fled north, only to be driven by westerly storms towards the Scottish and Irish coasts. A number of the Spanish ships were reputedly wrecked on craggy Hebridean shorelines, the bloodlines of their survivors still allegedly discernible today, while others were believed to have slipped east of the Mull of Kintyre, progressing through the Firth of Clyde where they were viewed by the local population as potential aggressors.

Armed with nothing more sinister than a simple ball of blue yarn, Elcine de Aggart planted herself on a vantage point close to Turnberry Castle and proceeded to spool out wool in such a way as to control the destinies of the unsuspecting Spanish seamen - her method perhaps similar to that employed by the Fates of classical legend. And it worked. The sky duly darkened, the wind gathered strength and before long mountainous seas swamped the ill-fated Spanish ships, causing them without exception to founder with the loss of all hands. Their resting-place, Train informs us, lay alongside 'our good Lady's Isle' - a tiny, low-lying islet, a few miles south-west of Troon, where a chapel dedicated to the Virgin Mary once stood. What Elcine de Aggart's motivation might have been for such community-spirited intervention can only be guessed at, particularly in an age when witch-hunting had grown into a popular sport among the Scottish population.

Whatever the Turnberry witch's reasoning, there is a supernatural sequel to her story in which she plays no part. During his studies of Ayrshire folklore Joseph Train unearthed the tradition that one of the

Spanish ships which had sunk near Lady Isle had been carrying Vice-Admiral Alcarede himself, plus a cargo of valuables besides, most notably a golden throne intended for the use of King Philip of Spain's viceroy in England, had his great Armada been victorious.

Tormented by the thought of these untold riches on their doorstep which they had no possibility of accessing, the townsfolk of Troon enlisted the services of two expert divers from Holland in a bid to recover the sunken treasure. During their early dives the two men successfully undertook the macabre task of stripping the dead of their jewellery, and things continued well enough until one of the divers drew near to the ship's cabin when suddenly he was terrified by a loud, eerie cry, emanating from somewhere within. Such was his fright that he fled instantly to the surface and could not under any circumstances be prevailed upon to return. In spite of his grave misgivings, the second diver agreed to descend once more but not before he had secured a firm guarantee that his bravery would be rewarded with a grant of valuable crown-lands in Carrick.

Thus assured, the Dutchman plunged once again beneath the waves and, holding his breath all the while, entered the ship's apartments via a hatchway which he had located in the focsle. As he moved towards the cabin, he suddenly found himself mobbed by a host of malevolent spirits but continued nonetheless, and soon to his surprise came face to face with an amiable-looking elderly man, seated on King Phillip's golden throne, who reached out his right hand in an apparent gesture of friendship. Just as he was about to reciprocate, the diver noticed to his horror that the old man was extending not a human hand, but rather a cloven hoof. Backtracking rapidly, he almost drowned in his haste to resurface. Whether the promise of crown-lands was ever honoured, Joseph Train fails to mention.

Whether further attempts at salvage have been made I cannot say, but it may be the case that, four centuries on, Alcarede's ship still languishes today beneath the chilly waters of the Firth, its priceless cargo sinking year by year a little deeper into the mud and sand of the seabed. And, for all we know, it is possible too that King Philip's golden throne may yet from time to time be occupied by a genial old gentleman who is not quite all that he appears.

The Two Lairds of Changue

From the village of Barr, with its cosy cottages and tidy gardens, you can walk eastwards through the woods, for the first half mile or so following the chattering Water of Gregg, until the tar comes to an end, and where the track divides. If you take the left-hand fork, climbing steadily uphill with an irregular line of beech trees as your wayside companions, you may glimpse through a screen of trees the whitewashed walls and chimneypots of Changue House, with the conspicuous spire of a monkey-puzzle alongside and perhaps a bloom of rhododendrons in season. And if you are willing to climb a little higher, scramble up the slopes of Craigenrery to your left and you will shortly come across a very curious sight - on the spot, so it is said, where the Laird of Changue once stood alone and faced up to the forces of darkness.

To trace what led up to that legendary tussle, we must turn back the clock and the calendar - exactly how far no-one can say - to events first recounted by an anonymous balladeer whose tale has been retold - and embellished - many times over. From its various versions we learn that the Laird of Changue - our hero of sorts - was a man with something of a rumbustious reputation, based at least in part on his enthusiastic participation in the annual drink-fuelled fisticuffs that blew up each year during the Kirkdandie spring fair. Pleasure-seeking and profligate, the Laird supplemented the income he derived from his flocks and herds with what he could glean from smuggling wine and brandy and from the operation of the odd illicit still, tucked in a hollow among the hills. But still to his chagrin he found that his earnings remained incapable of supporting his lavish lifestyle.

One particular evening the Laird was making his way home, preoccupied as ever with his financial problems, when he was hailed at a lonely spot in the woods by a stranger who proceeded to engage him in conversation, revealing as he did so a surprising degree of familiarity with Changue's troublesome finances. This enigmatic stranger was, he claimed, in a position to ease at a stroke the Laird's difficulties, no recompense whatsoever being required until an unspecified date in the distant future when the Laird must agree to accompany the stranger to whatever destination he pleased. Changue, of course, was not fool enough to mistake the persuasive stranger's true identity or to fail to grasp that what was at stake was his own immortal soul, but so great were both his ambition and his need that he wasted no time in acceding to the stranger's terms, readily appending his signature to a copy of their agreement, whereupon the stranger turned quickly on his heel and melted into the darkening woods.

Time passed, and in the months and years that followed the Laird of Changue did indeed see his fortunes rise, with his harvest fields consistently bountiful and his livestock thriving on the hills with never a sickly beast to trouble him. His smuggling ventures prospered, and to the government excisemen who periodically scoured the surrounding countryside his lonely stills seemed miraculously invisible. But even as he revelled in his new-found affluence, the memory of his shadowy wayside encounter consigned to a dim recess at the back of his memory, the Laird was, of course, unable to halt the march of time, and after a long spell of security and prosperity the Prince of Darkness made his inevitable second appearance, on this occasion making no attempt to disguise his true identity.

This is the point where the Laird's story deviates from others of its type. How long he had been granted to repent of his youthful rashness is not on record, but when the day of reckoning dawned, presumably much to the Devil's surprise, Changue reneged on the deal, drawing his sword from its scabbard and refusing to come quietly. Confrontation was, of course, inevitable which flared in the appropriately dramatic setting of the hilltop of Craigenrery where Changue used the tip of his sword to etch a circle on the turf around him before proceeding to challenge his infernal adversary to eject him if he dared.

Presumably the skills of combat that Changue had perfected at innumerable Kirkdandie Fairs now stood him in good stead as he parried with unfailing accuracy the Devil's repeated sorties, during the course of which Auld Nick suffered grievous losses such as his wings, the sting on the end of his pointed tail and even his legendary horns. Notwithstanding his injuries, the Devil made one last, desperate attempt to eject his opponent from the ring but all to no avail - Changue proved too formidable a foe. Forced to concede that enough was enough, the Devil turned and fled the scene, leaving the Laird of Changue victorious. As the old ballad crows in its final line - 'Schang [sic] nail'd the deil!'

If the poem has a moral, it remains unstated and unclear with the greedy and arrogant Changue making at best an ambivalent hero. But there is a second ballad, anthologised during the nineteenth century (and credited to 'Mr Harrison, Edinburgh bookseller' though it is unclear whether as author or, perhaps more likely, as collector) which depicts the Laird of Changue in quite a different light as he faces up to adversaries more flesh and blood than supernatural. From the outset the author, whoever he might be, is at pains to establish his hero's credentials: Changue is 'a buirdly carl' - a sturdy fellow - though, in marked contrast to his alternative incarnation, this Laird is 'worthy', 'pious' and 'guidly' - 'a right rich man' who is 'kindly to a' the poor.'

His virtues, however, are not sufficient to impress 'auld father Grub, the parish monk' whose greed and envy are aroused by his neighbour's generosity and prosperity. Cynical that Changue's regular devotions must surely point to a guilty conscience, Father Grub accuses him of heresy and demands that he travel to Crossraguel Abbey and obtain from the abbot copies of 'the evangels four.' Thereafter, every evening without fail - just 'as the sun gaes down/O'er Arran's ocean isle' - Changue must repair to the Alti-kirk where Father Grub undertakes to correct his presumed shortcomings through instruction from the gospels. The location of the old chapel known as the Alti-kirk is no longer known. Its name appears on the title-deeds of the farm of Knockgerran, though the farmer of many years is unaware of the building's former location.

But there is a fairly major snag. For a time Changue is willing to comply but gradually becomes frustrated as Father Grub repeatedly lectures and berates him in French, the language in which these gospels happen to be written and of which he understands not a word. He finally protests that what knowledge he has gained during his lifetime has been acquired not through book-learning but rather by observation of 'nature's sacred lore': the movements of the stars and constellations, the calls and habits of wild creatures, and - a little more surprisingly - the activities of elves and fairies in the surrounding countryside.

This is too much for Father Grub who angrily dismisses him, demanding 'a hunner merks' for his pains, with 'three score o' ewes and lambs' to be forfeited in addition. Justifiably disenchanted, Changue declines to pay up, reproaching Father Grub for his greed, but the monk retaliates by accusing him of communing with the Devil and - almost as serious - of being present at a sermon preached by John Knox at the Barr Castle in Galston, an event that took place several times during the 1550s. Grub goes further, forbidding the local population to have any dealings whatsoever with Changue, and finishes by calling down a curse upon his head - 'By bell, book, and candle light.'

In addition to invoking the wrath of the Almighty, Father Grub takes the added precaution of enlisting the aid of Reiver Rab and his 'gipsy' gang who operate an extensive protection racket from their hideout beneath the Dhu Craig overlooking Penwhapple Glen. In accordance with Grub's instructions, Rab and his band of freebooters set about harassing the innocent Changue by day and haunting his house at night, wailing and caterwauling through the hours of darkness. The beleaguered Laird feels powerless to fight back, assuming that his enemies are 'deils, ghaists or witches', thus impervious to the effects of cold steel.

But finally he snaps. At the end of his tether, Changue rises one night, fortifies himself with a dash of Dutch courage and dons his old armour before stepping outside, weapons in hand, to confront his unseen foes. Immediately he is assailed by 'horrid yell(s)' and is pelted with missiles. But he refuses to be intimidated, challenging his invisible opponents to come out from where they are skulking behind dykes and in ditches and to face him in manly combat. Having thrown down the gauntlet, he sets off up the dark slopes of Craigenrery, presumably in the belief that possession of the high ground will give him an advantage over his foes.

On the hilltop turf, Changue scores 'twa rings' around him, an act traditionally reckoned to afford protection from evil spirits, and very soon finds himself encircled by a group of sinister figures - 'like ghaists wi' grave-claes o'er them.' Refusing to be daunted, Changue proceeds to spear and kill the first opponent bold enough to tackle him; then, wielding his great axe, he goes on to dispatch the others, one after another, until his last enemy left standing is felled by a single prodigious blow. Changue, it seems, emerges from the fray without a scratch.

While the Laird takes time to catch his breath, the breaking dawn gradually reveals the surrounding hillside littered not, to his surprise, with evidence of a supernatural tussle but with the bloodied corpses of Reiver Rab and his gang of toughs. The poem concludes by gleefully pointing out that lying amongst them is the villain of the piece, Father Grub himself, transfixed by the Laird of Changue's spear.

So, which of the two Lairds of Changue is the real Mackay: the oppressed hill-farmer who finally cracks in the face of Catholic church corruption and greed? Or Kirkdandie Fair's doughty fighter who lives a swashbuckling life at the Devil's expense, and finishes up by trouncing his benefactor? Well, very possibly neither. And yet the theory is routinely peddled that evidence of Changue's infamous encounter exists to this day in the shape of twin footprints, embedded side by side in the hilltop turf of Craigenrery, in which the grass refuses to grow. Some have claimed that the Devil himself was responsible, scorching the earth in fury as he prepared to flee in humiliation back to Hell. My own imagination is a little less lurid. To my mind the curious prints seem less the work of His Satanic Majesty's cloven feet, and more like those left behind by a pair of workaday boots, such as a shepherd might wear whilst doing his rounds on the hill. Their reputed longevity and the absence of vegetation I cannot explain.

Secret Stairs and Dungeons

When it comes to the location of their ancestral pile, the Earls of Cassillis may owe less to their illustrious forebears than they do to the power of magic. Their original plan was to position the castle on the summit of Dunree - a small, conical hill immediately south of the River Doon - presumably for reasons of defence.

But each morning, when the builders trooped uphill to resume work, they discovered to their dismay that their previous day's labours had been demolished overnight and the heavy stonework inexplicably transported to the banks of the Doon. A standoff thus ensued, ending only when the masons were forced to concede the point and relocate to the riverbank. And, if you look down from the breezy heights of Dunree to where the old house nestles among its couthy woods and meadows, you probably cannot help thinking that the fairy folk did the Earls of Cassillis a mighty favour.

Originally a Montgomerie stronghold, Cassillis by the fourteenth century was in the hands of the Kennedy family, following the marriage of Sir John Kennedy of Stair to Marjory Montgomerie. As time passed, the Kennedys grew in wealth and prestige as much of south Ayrshire and western Galloway came under their control, and the family came to wield considerable influence at state as well as local level. In 1509 James IV conferred the title of 1st Earl of Cassillis on Sir David Kennedy, a position he held until his death in battle at Flodden a mere four years later. Until recently the castle remained the residence of Kennedy chiefs, currently the 8th Marquis of Ailsa.

When viewed from afar, Cassillis House has parapets looming magnificently through gaps in the trees, as well as tall chimneys and crow-stepped gables. The ancient tower has a gracious nineteenth century mansion-house adjoining it. When viewed across sweeping lawns this is somewhat at odds, perhaps, with the old, grey keep, four-square and strong. Dating from times when high walls and stout defences mattered more than simple aesthetics, the old tower's outward strength was obvious, with walls said to be sixteen inches thick.

Cassillis House

In the early part of the twentieth century a secret panel came to light, reviving age-old legends of a tunnel linking the castle with the nearby riverbank. Behind this panel, a faded mural depicted a knight in armour, brandishing a vicious pike in one hand while pointing enigmatically downwards with the other to where a previously unknown staircase descended into the bowels of the building. No doubt the painted warrior had witnessed any number of clandestine comings and goings in his time. And who knows whether yet an ivy-covered trapdoor may one day be discovered, secreted somewhere along the banks of the Doon?

The hidden panel was not the castle's only puzzle. During the 1670s, a spiral staircase was added to the old keep which, as it wound upwards, enclosed within its centre a peculiar hollow cylinder - designed, some have suggested, as a possible escape route in the unlikely event of the castle's stout defences being breached. But the reason behind a grim chamber, hollowed out beneath the castle floor, is easier to see. An innocuous-seeming flagstone doubles as a trapdoor, giving access to a dismal, underground prison twelve feet beneath. In the course of a clean-up during more peaceful times, matters apparently took a distinctly grisly turn. Cartloads of skeletons were unearthed, in all probability the ill-fated victims of some long-forgotten conflict. The bones of the unfortunate souls were unceremoniously crushed to be spread as fertiliser on the surrounding fields.

Just outside the castle walls, a small, rounded hillock, still visible today, was the last stop for many on their path to oblivion. For the grassy mound served as an outdoor law-court, dating from times when local law enforcement was wholly at the laird's prerogative. A magnificent plane tree once shaded this spot whose colossal trunk and stout limbs suggested a great antiquity. Prior to many a fray, the Earl's warriors assembled at its side, returning thereafter to lay out their dead. Six hundred men are said to have gathered around the old tree in the aftermath of Flodden, anxiously waiting for news of their chief's sad fate on the far side of the border. Known as the 'dule tree' - or tree of sorrow – the woody veteran's sturdy limbs came in useful as a conveniently placed gallows-tree - hence the ballad of Johnny Faa, the 'gypsy laddie', who allegedly lured away the sixth Earl's wife, Lady Jean, and was strung up on the dule tree for his pains. According to one version of the poem, fourteen gypsies died alongside their leader.

And, despite the weight of contrary evidence, it is a story that has taken firm root. Behind a small, square window in the old tower is the chamber - known as 'the Countess's Room' - where Lady Jean was supposedly confined following her marital indiscretion. The Earl knew full well that the window would have afforded an unobstructed view of the dule tree where, in an act of summary justice, Johnny Faa paid the price for his presumption. For many years after, the country people of the district maintained that on certain nights Lady Jean's ghostly figure was still to be seen, gazing down to where Johnny and his hapless companions had swung from the dule tree's gnarled boughs.

It was another three hundred years before the dule tree met its end, blown down finally during the course of a violent storm. A replacement was planted but the new tree - still something short of a century old – looks a rather puny substitute for its aged, venerable predecessor.

Two Troglodytes

For many years a solitary, bearded figure was regularly to be seen tramping the roadsides between Lendalfoot and Ballantrae, dressed in a flapping, ill-fitting overcoat, a pair of wellington boots and a cloth cap. Snib Scott lived alone in a natural cave, a stone's throw from the shore, where he subsisted on the goodness of others and on what the sea washed in. But if folk tales and legends are anything to go by, Snib wasn't by any means the first to make his home in a cave near Bennane Head.

To the north of Snib's cave, the old coast road – now disused - curls around Bennane Head, hugging the shoreline all the way until finally it is forced inland by rocky crags near the tiny cove at Port Vad. The broader bay at Balcreuchan Port, a little further on, is concealed from the road by tall, grassy cliffs, and was once a popular dropping-off point for smuggled goods, arriving by sea. Almost certainly the publican of the nearby Craignaw Inn, a cliff-top hostelry with something of a boisterous reputation, found it to his advantage to turn a blind eye to the activities of the smugglers and their strings of pack-ponies, carrying French wine, brandy and tea inland for consumption in distant Edinburgh. By the turn of the twentieth century the old inn had closed its doors for the last time and it is difficult to pinpoint its location on the ground. Its last remaining stones may have been swept away some years ago during the re-routing of the A77.

The secluded cove at Balcreuchan Port seems an unlikely source for the raft of lurid tales that surfaced inexplicably in a variety of eighteenth century English broadsheets and chapbooks – the tabloid newspapers of their time – and which continue to be peddled even up to the present day. These news sheets alleged that during the sixteenth century – maybe earlier - a large sea-cave, accessible only at low tide, had provided a home for a criminal family who preyed for many years on travellers whom they waylaid on the hill road above their home.

The family patriarch was one Sawney Bean who as an impoverished young man had migrated from East Lothian to south-west Scotland. In

Ayrshire Sawney found a local wife, Black Agnes Douglas, and together they built up a considerable family who proceeded to multiply in turn – incestuously – forming as they did so a sizeable criminal gang. Over a period of 25 years the family members carried out a variety of nefarious activities: ambushing and murdering passers-by, appropriating their possessions and, most infamous of all, indulging their taste for human flesh. The eighteenth century news sheets claimed that as many as 1,000 travellers fell victim to Sawney and his cannibal kin during their years at Bennane Head.

Balcreuchan Port

It may be fanciful to suppose that these grisly events might be what gave rise to a saying favoured by many an old country gentleman, for whom 'traivelin' owre the Bennane' signifies leaving one's better days behind. Far-fetched perhaps, but undeniably apt. Even for Sawney himself, however, time eventually ran out when a troop of soldiers, commanded by the king in person, tracked his family to their coastal lair using bloodhounds. Captured and bound, the cannibals were taken to Edinburgh where they were executed according to the brutal fashion of the times.

But perhaps not all of them. A story tells how one of Sawney's daughters, perhaps constitutionally different from the rest of her family, fled from the cave below Bennane Head and settled in nearby Girvan where she embarked on a new life. Elspeth McCrudden, as the girl became known, took the precaution of planting a certain tree outside her new home as a time-honoured method of warding off the effects of witchcraft. Presumably well aware that her mother, Black Agnes, had been ejected from Ballantrae during her youth as a result of her occult activities, very possibly Elspeth feared recrimination.

In the end it was the downfall of the other members of her family that spelt Elspeth's own undoing. As the cannibals were escorted through Girvan at the start of their journey to Edinburgh, Elspeth was identified by one of her passing siblings and as a result was seized upon immediately by her outraged neighbours. Ironically the poor girl's fate was to be hanged from the very tree that she had planted for her own protection.

The tale of Sawney Bean has a claim to being one of Scotland's most frequently repeated legends despite the fact that not a shred of evidence for its ghastly events exists prior to the publication of the eighteenth century news sheets. Turning to East Lothian parish records will not help as their earliest entries date from the close of the sixteenth century, too late by a margin of several decades to pinpoint Sawney's entrance into the world. You might assume that a major military operation in Ayrshire, led by the king himself, would be preserved on record: apparently not so. Similarly there is no record of cannibals being put on trial, likewise no private or personal paper dating from the sixteenth century or earlier that makes reference to Sawney Bean or his activities.

If a kernel of truth does exist at the heart of the story – some gruesome murder case perhaps, or desperate measures forced upon local people during a distant time of famine – then surely with the passage of time it has been embellished out of all recognition. There were, of course, those who had a vested interest in deterring visits to Balcreuchan Port and its neighbouring coves and bays, especially on dark and moonless nights. It seems quite plausible that the brandy-smugglers and their associates would have made it their business to keep stories of horror and murder alive and in the minds of the local population.

In the years after the Second World War, Snib Scott left his home to settle in a cave just south of Bennane Head. In its time Snib's new home,

Bennane Cove (the Scots word for cave) had seen service as a blacksmith's forge, an overnight halt for travelling people, a place of refuge for local families in times of trouble, even as a short-term prison – though that Snib was aware of its chequered past may be unlikely. The peace and seclusion that the area offered appear to have been what convinced him to put down roots and during his years in residence Snib made no bones about his preference for self-reliance and solitude. Oddly enough he had reached his early thirties before his life started to diverge from the straight and narrow.

Born in 1912, Henry Ewing Torbet was the son of a Dundee insurance man. Bright and well-educated, after leaving school he held down a post in a local branch of the National Bank, during which time he became engaged to be married. What momentous event disrupted the equilibrium of Henry's life is unknown but, for whatever reason, he took the decision to sever connections with his past and take to a life on the road. After time spent travelling in the West Highlands, he eventually turned up in Ayrshire where he lived for a time in an unoccupied miner's cottage in the Doon valley before finally arriving at Bennane Cove, near Ballantrae. Here he settled down - as Snib Scott - to live out the rest of his days.

The name *Snib*, it has been suggested, resulted from meticulousness in securing field-gates but where the assumed surname Scott came from is harder to pin down. Living quietly, Snib claimed no state benefits, relying instead for his survival on nature's bounty and other people's cast-offs. Firewood was gathered daily from along the tideline, and food gleaned from the surrounding countryside. Initially resistant to what he perceived as charity, in time he came to accept 'unwanted' items, left for him by local people. Scrupulously honest, more than once Snib was known to hand in found property and to display acute embarrassment when presented with a reward. He left no litter behind him, and he drank no alcohol.

It can't be denied, however, that Snib did have one or two habits that might come across as a little irregular. Partial to a smoke, he made a point of recovering all discarded cigarette ends that he encountered during his wanderings. Road-kill rabbits invariably found themselves destined for his cooking-pot. Firm in the belief that campfire smoke counteracted the effect of germs, he was disinclined to wash, claiming that his body sweated out the dirt anyway. His sole companion was a stray ginger cat which adopted him, but remained nameless nonetheless. Snib fed the cat boiled potatoes on a plate, while he ate his own directly from the pot.

During his years at Bennane Cove there was a marked increase in traffic using the A77 trunk-road on his doorstep, and in the early 1970s Snib was involved in a road accident during which he was said to have stumbled into the path of an oncoming car. At Ayr County Hospital he was treated for a broken left leg but, despite such novelties as television and clean underwear, he signed himself out at the first opportunity and made his way home to Bennane Cove – a journey of some 30 or so miles - using crutches.

As the years passed, Snib was no longer able to cover long distances on foot and gradually his outings became restricted to walks to and from Ballantrae, two or so miles away. Providing himself with sufficient food became increasingly problematic and he came to rely more and more on the generosity of his neighbours. During the winter of 1983 a local farmer, Jim Melville, became aware that there was no smoke rising from Snib's fire and when he went to investigate he discovered that all was not well. Once again Snib was admitted to Ayr County Hospital where, despite receiving treatment for hypothermia, his condition worsened. On 19 December 1983, Snib Scott - the last of the Bennane Head troglodytes - passed away, aged 70.

Divided by four centuries or more, Sawney Bean and Snib Scott both left home in the east of Scotland to settle in apparently inhospitable caves on the south Ayrshire coast, but there all similarities end. Despite his unconventional lifestyle, Snib possessed qualities that were esteemed by his local community, and shortly after his death a simple shoreside monument, funded by public subscription, was erected in his memory outside the cave at Bennane Head. Snib Scott was 'respected and independent', as the legend on his memorial plaque affirmed.

LIVES CUT SHORT

The Loudoun Burning

The exact location of Auchruglen is a little tricky to pin down. Said to have crumbled to the ground many years ago, there has been ample time for the old tower to fade from local memory. However, it appears on a map of old Ayrshire – undated – where, tucked among the farms and fields to the south of the River Irvine, faded letters spell out the name. From this house, five centuries ago, a band of armed men set out, intent on carrying out what would go down in folk memory as one of the region's darkest atrocities.

The story begins some months earlier - in December 1527 - fifteen miles away, on the windswept links of Prestwick. Word had reached the old castle of Loudoun that Gilbert Kennedy, second Earl of Cassillis - and sworn enemy of Sir Hugh Campbell of Loudoun - was due to set out from Stirling to return home to Cassillis House, near Maybole, a journey of some sixty-odd miles. Sir Hugh was not at home to receive this news, but the opportunity was too good to let slip and his wife, Lady Loudoun, seized the initiative, promptly calling in her husband's most trusted friends – Campbell of Cessnock; and the Craufurds of Kerse, Leifnorris and Drongan. The men's first priority was to identify a lonely spot along the way that would be suitable for waylaying Earl Gilbert's party.

At that time a stretch of the Glasgow to Ayr highway hugged the Prestwick shoreline, and the conspirators reckoned that the maze of dunes and sandy hollows at the mouth of the Pow Burn would provide them with the cover necessary for a successful ambush. Backed by what amounted to a small army – 1,400 strong – Hugh Campbell's friends settled down among the sandhills to wait.

When he eventually appeared, Earl Gilbert was accompanied by only a small body of companions, feeling secure perhaps now that he was a mere stone's throw from his own lands beyond the River Doon. His confidence proved premature. Without warning, horsemen galloped out of the dunes and quickly engulfed the travellers. There could be no escape. We can only imagine the cries of shock and anger, and the clash of steel on steel that led finally to Earl Gilbert's death on the Prestwick sands.

The murderers melted quickly into the surrounding countryside, knowing full well that reprisals would be inevitable. But first there were forms to be adhered to. Earl Gilbert's body was carried in state to his ancestral seat at Cassillis House before subsequently being laid to rest at Maybole Collegiate Church. When some time later the law failed to give redress, a convocation of warriors duly gathered beneath the infamous Cassillis dule-tree - or hanging-tree – where, under the leadership of Alexander Kennedy of Bargany, the assembled men swore a collective oath to avenge their chief's death.

They had a trump card up their sleeve. A few short miles from Campbell headquarters, the house and lands of Auchruglen were held by their kinsman, John Kennedy, thus providing a convenient toe-hold in enemy territory and an ideal launching-pad for a revenge attack on Loudoun Castle. For details of what followed, we are obliged to fall back on folk tales and the oral tradition of the Ayrshire countryside.

There is a rough, old ballad that preserves an account of the Kennedys' revenge. An avenging war party, the anonymous poet tells us, descended upon Loudoun Castle at a time when the laird happened to be absent from home. (Implicated in Earl Gilbert's murder and outlawed as a consequence, Hugh Campbell had been obliged for some time to keep on the move.) Once again, however, the redoubtable Lady Loudoun, proved up to the occasion, refusing point blank to submit to demands for surrender and barricading the castle doors before retreating with her servants and children to an upper storey. Thus frustrated, the Kennedys proceeded to heap up brushwood against the castle walls with the clear intention of smoking out the occupants. But even then Lady Loudoun showed no sign of cracking, apparently willing to sacrifice her own life as well as those of her servants and nine children.

With the castle well ablaze, the Laird of Auchruglen was said to have made a last-ditch effort to avert total disaster, offering to break Lady Loudoun's fall were she to leap from an upper window. His proposal fell on deaf ears and, with this rebuff, Lady Loudoun sealed the gruesome fate of her children and entire household. And if her actions come across today as morally dubious, it is probably no more than a measure of her times. When it came to blood-feud, there were few perhaps who could claim to have hands that were spotlessly clean.

There is a final, curious twist in the tale. Alexander Kennedy of Bargany's son, Thomas - born in 1551, the year of his father's death - went on in due course to marry one Margaret Campbell, a daughter of the house of Loudoun. Given the half-century and more of bad blood between Campbell and Kennedy, it sounds very much like a determined effort at bridge-building.

The burning of Loudoun Castle is legend, not verifiable history. Conflicting accounts have surfaced over the years with one improbable - but much-repeated - version transposing the action back across the valley from Loudoun Castle to Auchruglen. As for the old Ayrshire ballad, it certainly cannot be taken as gospel with alternative versions in existence describing a similar atrocity as far afield as Aberdeenshire. Minstrels and storytellers, of course, were adept at modifying their repertoire for the audience at hand. But even so, the tradition that the old castle of Loudoun was burned to the ground in times past is one that proved remarkably persistent in the Irvine valley until very recent times.

Today the Auchruglen Burn burbles unnoticed through its steep-sided little glen before spilling into the River Irvine at Greenholm. Along its wooded banks, no trace remains of the old tower of the Kennedys. Meanwhile, on the other side of the valley, the old castle of Loudoun rose from its ashes only for its grand nineteenth century successor to suffer a similar fate to that of its predecessor when, in a curious echo of the past, it too was destroyed by fire in December 1941. On this latter occasion the first-floor library chimney, not blood-feud, was judged to have been responsible and, in marked contrast to four centuries earlier, there were no casualties reported.

Murder on Craigdow Moor

A few miles south of Maybole, a narrow, single-track road parts company with the main thoroughfare to wind unnoticed into the nearby hills. It skirts a few farmhouses and cottages along the way – not many – before finally reaching a point where the tar gives out and the road becomes a cart-track. The hills crowd in on a timeless world of dry stane dykes and ancient beech trees where the past feels as though it might be secreted round every corner. It was this same track that Andrew MacAlexander followed on a September afternoon four centuries ago, as he made his way home to the Girvan valley. As things turned out, however, he was destined never to arrive.

At that time the MacAlexander family had been established on their lands at Drummochreen for a little over a hundred years, ever since Andrew's forebear, John MacAlexander, settled by the Water of Girvan in the second half of the fifteenth century. He erected his new home within a picturesque bend of the river (since straightened out) - the respectable residence of a fairly prosperous small laird, constructed less for show than for sturdy practicality. In its time the house would probably have consisted of five or six apartments, placed over two storeys, and even today its sole upstanding gable suggests a building of considerable former solidity.

By the standards of their neighbours, the MacAlexanders' holdings were not extensive – in all about a thousand acres – but, despite its small extent, their Drummochreen estate had much to recommend it. From fertile, riverside haughs to ample woodland and hill grazings, it was capable of supporting a thriving small community of tradesmen, agricultural workers and labourers. Two mills worked on the Water of Girvan - one for handling grain and the second a 'waulk mill' for the processing of locally woven cloth – while, on the hillside above, generations of miners burrowed their way through a highly productive seam of coal. It is perhaps, then, no great wonder that Andrew MacAlexander was considered 'ane proud manne,' and pride undoubtedly contributed to his downfall.

The closing years of the sixteenth century were unsettled times in the south Ayrshire countryside as a long-standing blood-feud raged between the two main branches of the biggest local landowners, the all-powerful Kennedy family. A contemporary manuscript, *The Historie of the Kennedyis*, describes in pithy Scots prose the web of alliances and divisions, plots and counter-plots, that characterised the times, and it is to *The Historie's* anonymous author that we owe much of our knowledge of the fate that befell MacAlexander that autumn day of 1599.

Drummochreen

Money – predictably – played a part. In the aftermath of the Reformation, the teinds – annual religious bequests traditionally paid to the nearby Abbey of Crossraguel – of Drummochreen had inexplicably fallen into the more secular hands of the Earl of Cassillis, who proceeded in due course to sub-let them to his henchman, Hew Kennedy of Girvan Mains, on condition that he be supplied with fighting men and horses if required. Girvan Mains sub-let the teinds a second time: on this occasion to his near neighbour, Andrew MacAlexander, and on similar terms. But what he didn't allow for was the possibility that, by cutting out the middleman, the Laird of Drummochreen could effectively raise himself by one rung of the social ladder. MacAlexander jumped at the opportunity and Cassillis, it transpired, was willing to assent.

Girvan Mains, of course, lost out and T*he Historie of the Kennedyis* includes an account of a lively exchange that took place soon after, during which he sought redress for his perceived slight from the Earl of Cassillis. As it turned out, he was wasting his breath, Cassillis going so far as to warn him - 'ye dar nocht find falt with [MacAlexander]; for and ye do, we knaw quhair ye duell.' It is not hard to imagine Girvan Mains's furious resentment as he stomped out of Cassillis House, nursing thoughts of revenge. *The Historie* does not specify whether MacAlexander was witness to Hew Kennedy's humiliation, but in the light of subsequent events it seems almost certain that he was.

Girvan Mains departed under a black cloud, accompanied by his two servants ('Gilbert MacFedries and William MacFedries, ane boy'), following the track that today winds tranquilly among the ancient beech trees. By the time the three men climbed on to the open moor at Craigdow, his temper still had not cooled. His neighbour, MacAlexander, it struck him, would not be far behind, returning home by the same route, and he drew his plans accordingly. The author of *The Historie* tells us that Girvan Mains concealed himself 'behind ane knowe,' having posted his boy, William MacFedries, as look-out. And then he settled down for a wait.

Probably daylight was failing by the time MacAlexander (travelling with his brother, Thomas, and one Oliver Kennedy, presumably a friend) came into view. At the optimum moment, young MacFedries gave the signal and Girvan Mains launched his attack, pursuing his unsuspecting victim on horseback across the moor. So sudden was the onslaught, or perhaps so great the confusion that ensued, that MacAlexander's companions found themselves completely unable to protect their friend: it seems they did not strike a single blow in his defence. The Laird of Drummochreen died, the chronicle tells us, as a result of sword wounds to the head.

How word of the attack reached MacAlexander's family is not on record – domestic matters and personal heartache are not within the scope of the old Kennedy chronicle – but it seems natural that his brother, Thomas, and Oliver Kennedy would have galloped like the wind to break the tragic news. And if the events that the two men related sound like a virtual blueprint for the fate of Banquo in Shakespeare's *Macbeth*, penned only a few years later, it is no more than a sad reflection of the times. Violent death was no rare occurrence in sixteenth century Scotland - a fact that would have consoled but little the dead man's grieving widow and the 'fatherless bairns' that he left behind.

Fall-out from the murder quickly reached the capital and, in due course, the ears of the Privy Council. At the time James VI was endeavouring to stamp out the family feuds that plagued much of his kingdom - the Highlands in particular, as well as the wild lands along the border – and he would hardly have welcomed a further distraction, this time in the west. A proclamation was duly made on 21 September in which Hew Kennedy of Girvan Mains and Gilbert and William MacFedries were 'denounced rebels for the slaughter of Andrew MacAlexander of Drummochreen.' It was the first of several such actions but, a hundred miles distant from the south Ayrshire countryside, the Privy Council's impact was distinctly limited on the ground. A year later, John Kennedy of Blairquhan was still being cautioned 'not to harm Jonet (*sic*) Kennedy, relict of Andrew MacAlexander,' on penalty of a payment of 300 merks. And clearly Thomas MacAlexander was still intent on revenge for his brother's murder two and a half years after the event, being admonished 'not to harm Gilbert and William MacFedries.' All this time Hew Kennedy of Girvan Mains carried on with his life as normal, his activities apparently unaffected by his outlawed status.

By contrast, life at Drummochreen would never be the same again. In the aftermath of the murder, the dead man's friends and relatives gathered on Craigdow Moor where they set about retrieving rocks and boulders from the slopes that overlooked the scene of Girvan Mains's ambush. These they built into a memorial cairn among the whins and moorland grasses where their kinsman had breathed his last.

On Gallow Hill

High above the Irvine valley, a few miles outside the small burgh of Galston, there stands a unique Covenanting monument. Situated almost 1,000 feet above sea-level, the Gallow Hill cairn is made of red sandstone blocks, quarried locally and placed so as to form a stepped, circular plinth. From its centre rises an elegant, white cone into which mirrors have been set, facing the four points of the compass. For more than eighty years now the monument's winking eyes have been visible in clear conditions from as far afield as the Ayrshire coast, a distance of some fifteen miles.

The cairn dates back to tough times in the valley. Faced with the prospect of pay cuts and deteriorating working conditions, Britain's miners had downed tools in May 1926 and six months later many of the nation's collieries still lay idle. But a group of Galston miners - by their own request unnamed in later press reports - were determined that their spell of enforced leisure should not be wasted. When they discussed the possibilities, the idea cropped up of a memorial cairn on Gallow Hill.

It took stamina. The men sweated through the summer and autumn months, lugging gear and heavy loads of building materials up steep country roads before the skilled work of construction could even begin. Their task was not completed until late November and, shortly after, the grand unveiling took place. On the last Saturday in the month, strings of local people made their way to the cairn on foot while, for those able to afford a ticket, a convoy of six buses trundled up the narrow road from Galston, reportedly with all seats taken. An array of prominent citizens was on-hand: councillors, a local solicitor, teachers in valley schools, the factor of Lanfine Estate (on whose ground the cairn was located) and no fewer than three Galston ministers. Presumably the provosts of all three valley towns - Galston, Newmilns and Darvel – were gratified to note their respective burghs' civic mottos inscribed on the monument in quartz-chip lettering. Galston Burgh Band played to an estimated six or seven hundred who had braved the late autumn chill to honour a Covenanting hero, martyred for his faith during the dark days of the killing time.

Gallow Hill Cairn

The circumstances surrounding James Smith's death in 1684 are a little hazy. One account relates that he was shot on his own doorstep, a short distance across the fields from where his memorial now stands, for the crime of having provisioned a band of escaped Covenanting prisoners following their breakout from Newmilns Castle. An alternative version of the tale suggests that Smith perished at the point of a sword merely for having had his child baptised at an illegal conventicle. Encircled by a band of dragoons a cloak was flung over his head from behind, thus enabling him to be overpowered. Whatever the exact details, James Smith's death is commemorated in Galston kirkyard where a mossy memorial stone recounts that he was 'shot near Bank on Burn Ann 1684 and buried there.'

A headstone, once placed on the grave, is no longer in situ. According to William Wilson, a neighbouring farmer in the late nineteenth century, the stone was dislodged by a mischievous herdboy from the nearby farm of Middlethird and rolled into the small stream known locally as the Burnawn where it broke into several pieces. A fragment marked JS 1684 was subsequently salvaged and built into the nearby steading at Wee Threepwood - tricky to verify since the farm buildings have long been ruinous. The missing headstone was said to have been replaced with a rowan sapling which was nurtured by local people until it reached maturity.

A further puzzle concerning James Smith's martyrdom lies a few miles to the south. The churchyard at Mauchline contains a number of Covenanting relics including the tombstone of a martyr who fell prey to 'Captain Ingles, and his Dragoons, at the Burn of Ann in Kyle, and thereafter died of his wounds in Mauchline prison.' The date on the stone is 1684; the dead man's name: James Smith.

Perhaps we oughtn't to be too surprised. Frequently Covenanting memorials were not erected until a generation or more after the events they commemorated, thus allowing ample time for local memories to blur and accounting perhaps for the story's obvious discrepancies. It is quite credible that Smith would have been gravely wounded near his home before being transferred to Mauchline where he subsequently died as a result of his injuries.

But this version of events disregards an old tradition which maintains that, in the aftermath of the Newmilns jailbreak, Captain Ingles had not one but two innocent men shot. Could Ingles' dragoons, then, have been responsible for the deaths of two James Smiths, one buried where he fell at Burnawn, the other laid to rest in Mauchline kirkyard? Certainly cases where family members were martyred together were not unknown. Tragically, it is feasible that the Galston and Mauchline martyrs might well have been father and son.

Faced with a daily onslaught of wind and weather, in time the miners' monument started to crumble. Frost prised the stones apart and rainwater promptly washed out the mortar. In November 2006 the old cairn struggled past its eightieth birthday, but the prospect of a dignified centenary looked far from certain. A chapter of local history was in danger of being wiped out.

Thankfully action was taken. Refurbishment finally began during 2008 and, once complete, the cairn's rededication ceremony took place on a sunny August Sunday. Speakers paid tribute to the seventeenth century martyr, James Smith, and to those in the 1920s who gave their labour freely that he might be remembered. Though the turn-out was rather lower than eighty-two years previously, there was that day on Gallow Hill one remarkable link with the past. Well into her eighties, Annie Law of Hillhouse Farm had childhood memories of the original unveiling, having stood beside her mother as a five year-old among the milling crowds of 1926.

The Shepherd of Priesthill

He lies sprawled on his back with his hands thrust out from under a roughly-woven plaid, his face already grey in death. By his side, the murdered man's widow presses her right hand to her forehead, eyes closed in anguish, while his little daughter peers anxiously over her shoulder to where a party of mounted dragoons are in the process of leaving the scene, their work now complete. Under an ominous bank of cloud, one or two of the soldiers take a final backward glance towards lives they have left in ruins but the majority do not turn to look.

The dead man's Bible is dropped in the dust, its bookmark remaining in place. A black and white dog lies alongside his master and appears to have shared his cruel fate. But, more than to anything else on the canvas, our eyes are drawn ineluctably to the small child, right of centre, who clings to his mother's skirts while gazing at the prostrate form of his dead father. The look of horror on the little boy's face is nothing short of heartrending.

That at least was how the nineteenth century painter, Thomas Duncan, envisaged the day in 1685 when John Brown of Priesthill paid a heavy price for his principles. Among the myriad atrocities perpetrated during the years of the Covenanting era, events surrounding Brown's martyrdom are more than usually poignant, even by the dark standards of the Killing Time – the probable reason why Thomas Duncan seized upon the story as the subject for his painting.

Priesthill was, and remains, an isolated hill-farm close to Ayrshire's eastern rim: cross the skyline and the next four walls you encounter will be at the shepherd's house of Monkshead in Lanarkshire. If you park by the Greenock Water, you can pay a visit to Priesthill – a good half hour's tramp from the public road – the countryside you pass through appearing cared-for and prosperous. Sunny hill-slopes are tidily fenced and amply stocked with grazing flocks, and any potholes on the track are neatly filled with gravel. At various points, belts of young broadleaf trees have been established along the banks of the cleuchs, or steep-sided ravines, that cleave the hillsides, and from the variety of birdlife in evidence it looks very much as though nature approves. The old stone-dykes alone show signs of neglect, tumbling in places beneath the weight of the years, the skills required to maintain them now largely forgotten.

The seventeenth century farmstead that John Brown tenanted is located a mile or so beyond present-day Priesthill. You need stout boots or wellingtons to walk over the open moor. Three centuries ago John Brown herded sheep on these same moors, but in earning a living he had more than a single string to his bow. In a landscape where the wheel was of limited benefit, Brown acted as a haulier, ferrying goods across the hills by pack-horse and this, coupled with his legendary piety, led to his frequently being dubbed 'the Christian carrier.'

Brown would have been likely to enter the ministry but for the fact of an unfortunate speech impediment. Before settling at Priesthill, he conducted for a number of years weekly Bible studies at his previous home of Blackside which young men travelled considerable distances to attend, both summer and winter. A man of iron principle, he declined to attend services at Muirkirk, though compulsory by law, after Rev. Hugh Campbell had been supplanted by a government-appointed clergyman, and for a surprising amount of time he got away with it. In spite of his religious devotion, however, John Brown was not without human frailty, as parish records for 1666 demonstrate when they log his being rebuked for the sin of having transported goods by pack-horse on a Sunday. How he squared this with his religious convictions we can only speculate.

In 1682, at the age of 55, John Brown married for a second time. He had become acquainted with his bride, Isabel Weir, a woman from the neighbouring parish of Sorn, during his regular pack-horse travels throughout the area. In common with a number of other aspects of his life, the events of Brown's wedding appear through time to have become overlaid with myth. Living up to his reputation for making rather wild utterances, the presiding minister, Alexander 'Prophet' Peden, must surely have dampened spirits a little when he urged the new bride at all times to keep fresh linen to hand for use as her husband's winding sheet. At the time, Brown already had a small daughter from his previous marriage who was lovingly accepted by her new mother. Isabel Weir must have been a good deal younger than her husband as during the course of the next three years she bore him two more children.

In the years that followed Brown's marriage, the lonely farm at Priesthill remained a place of sanctuary for religious men on the run. The story survives of a youthful James Renwick appearing on the farm doorstep, unrecognised at first but subsequently incurring Isabel's gratitude when he lulled one of her fretful infants to sleep. On the last day of April 1685, Alexander Peden was once again an overnight visitor, leaving early the following morning and allegedly muttering ominously as he departed 'Poor woman, a fearful morning! A dark misty morning!'

John Brown's Grave, Priesthill

In the end it was Brown's continued refusal to attend church services that finally caught up with him, reported to the authorities, some believe, by the government-approved curate at Muirkirk. Early in the morning of 1 May, Colonel John Graham of Claverhouse led three troops of horse out of the garrison at Lesmahagow who, after a moorland ride of some ten miles, approached the vicinity of Priesthill. At the time of the troopers' arrival, Brown and his nephew, John Browning, were cutting peats on the moor and, prevented from detecting the soldiers' approach by a thick curtain of mist, both men were easily apprehended, neither one being armed. Surely Peden's wedding-day prophecy would not have been far from

Isabel's mind when she heard the news from John's daughter, Janet, that her husband was being escorted from the moor by a large group of horsemen. That spring of 1685, Isabel once again was expecting a baby.

The events that followed have been recounted many times. Invited by Claverhouse to pray for King James (VII and II), Brown declined, stating that he regarded Christ, not the king, as head of the church. Stubbornly he refused to attend services led by a curate who had been placed contrary to what he saw as God's law. These answers were more than enough to condemn him as a rebel, and Claverhouse duly extended to his prisoner the opportunity to pray prior to his execution. The story goes that Brown did so with such eloquence and at such great length that Claverhouse became impatient, interrupting on more than one occasion, but Brown remained unruffled. It would later be said that at this time his stammer had left him entirely.

As his devotions drew to a close, Brown committed his family to the care of God and pronounced himself ready to die. Varying accounts exist of what followed, but some versions of the tale assert that so moved were the government soldiers by Brown's piety that not one was willing to obey the order to shoot and that Claverhouse, in fear of mutiny, was forced to draw his pistol and fire the fatal shot himself. His report of the incident, contained in a letter written two days later at Galston, is equivocal. 'I caused shoot him dead,' wrote Colonel Graham, 'which he suffered very unconcernedly.' What Claverhouse failed to mention was the cruel taunt that many have alleged that he made following Brown's death, a taunt that reputedly rebounded on him. 'What think ye o' yer guidman noo?' he sneered at the murdered man's widow. 'I aye thocht meikle o' him, and I think mair o' him noo than ever,' was Isabel's spontaneous response.

Claverhouse had more work to complete. He turned his attention next to the dead man's nephew, John Browning, who was by now probably so thoroughly frightened by the scene that he had witnessed that he quickly confessed to his involvement in the violent release of Covenanting prisoners at Newmilns Tower some days previously. Browning had, he admitted, travelled directly from there to his uncle's secluded farm. As it turned out, Browning's candour did him no good. On Claverhouse's instruction, he was duly transferred to Mauchline where he subsequently faced the hangman's noose.

While Browning's interrogation was underway, Claverhouse's troopers conducted a thorough search of the premises, during which some have claimed that they located a large underground vault, capable of concealing a dozen men, in which firearms and swords were secreted. According to Claverhouse's own report to the Marquis of Queensberry, similar weapons were found within the farmhouse, as well as documents which he considered treasonable. As a professional soldier, Claverhouse was obliged to report the facts. But as to rumours of a secret bunker, up to the present day no such place has ever come to light.

Despite having been some ten miles away at the time of the shooting, Alexander Peden is said to have been the one who broke the news concerning John Brown's fate, the knowledge of which had come to him in a vision. However the tragic events were made known, Brown's newly-made widow was not left to handle matters alone with some accounts stating that first on the scene was a kindly neighbour, Jean Brown from Cumberhead, three or four miles across the hills, a woman who certainly understood loss, her own husband having lost his life some twenty years earlier during the abortive Pentland Rising, followed in turn by her two sons around the time of the Battle of Drumclog in 1679. It was Jean who observed that, while Isabel was normally so sensitive as to be unable to tolerate the sight of blood, somehow or other on this occasion she had been granted sufficient strength to endure the day's traumatic events. Probably, for the sake of her little ones, she simply had to.

The dead man's remains were laid to rest close to the spot where he had breathed his last. Sometime later – it is not known exactly when – a level, grey stone was placed on top of the grave on which a quaint acrostic inscription in verse paid tribute to his sacrifice. Two centuries on, a simple stone monument was raised on the site and the original gravestone enclosed within a low wall, the work funded by the proceeds of a memorial service held on the spot in April 1825.

The Dalgig Martyrs

Dalgig is a moorland farm whose loneliness has been lost. First came the foresters who blanketed the hillsides with alien conifers where blackface sheep once grazed. Bulldozers quickly followed, carving out a moonscape of opencast canyons in their insatiable quest for coal. As for the three murdered men who have lain three centuries and more on the heights above Dalgig, they would surely find their present-day surroundings quite unrecognisable.

The men died during the summer of 1685, at the very height of the Killing Time, when a simple refusal to swear an oath of loyalty to King James (VII and II) would lead almost invariably to summary execution. Despite the climate of intimidation, a large, illegal conventicle - or open-air religious service - had been conducted some days previously by the outlawed minister, James Renwick, in an isolated spot near Loch Doon on the Ayrshire/Galloway border. When proceedings drew to a close and the crowd started to disperse, a small band of men peeled away and turned their steps northwards, keeping to hill paths and lonely byways in order to avoid detection. Government forces were known to be active locally.

As darkness fell, the men stopped for the night in the shelter of the Tod Fauld, an isolated sheep-pen (of great antiquity) tucked beneath the soaring crags of Ben Beoch. But a local farmer – perhaps John Paterson of Pennyvenie, a known Covenanting sympathiser – arrived in haste to warn them of the near presence of government troops who were scouring the vicinity, probably in search of those dispersing from Renwick's conventicle.

The Covenanters were obliged to gather their possessions and move on, this time in darkness, stepping out across the vast morass now known as the Martyrs' Moss. At the north end of the moss they climbed on to the heights of Carsgailoch, at 1,200 feet above sea-level the highest point in the area. Here the exhausted men finally allowed themselves to rest among the peat-banks and coarse moorland grasses. Since leaving Ben Beoch, they had covered more than five miles of rough, boggy terrain under cover of darkness.

Sleep, it appears, proved their undoing. Colonel James Douglas - brother of the Duke of Queensberry - and his Highland troops had followed in the men's footsteps and, in the course of what must have been a rude awakening, only one Covenanter – Alexander Jamieson – succeeded in fleeing with his life. His three companions fell into the hands of Douglas's Highlanders who proceeded without ceremony to shoot them. Local tradition insists that the men were not even offered the option of 'taking the Test': swearing an oath of loyalty to the crown and renouncing the Scottish kirk. What is quite certain is that the bodies of Joseph Wilson, John Humphrey and John Jamieson (the escaped man's brother) were simply abandoned where they fell among the moss-hags and peaty pools of Carsgailoch.

Some accounts suggest that the lonely hilltop had been used for some time previously as a Covenanting hide-out, well-positioned as it was to act as a look-out over the surrounding countryside. Hugh Hutchison, the farmer of Dalgig on whose land the hill was situated, had proved a supportive neighbour, regularly ferrying provisions to the persecuted hill-men. On the day of the murders, Hugh happened to be closeby, presumably herding livestock, and when he witnessed the cold-blooded killings such was his shock that he let slip an involuntary cry of horror.

This, of course, alerted Colonel Douglas who ordered his soldiers to give chase. But, with the benefit of home-advantage, the local man was able to give his pursuers the slip, sprinting like a hare between the moss-hags before finally taking refuge in the depths of a nearby wood. Happily his luck held. Less fortunate, however, was Alexander Jamieson, the Covenanter who had fled at the soldiers' first approach. Arrested soon after, he was imprisoned in the tolbooth at Cumnock. His subsequent fate is unknown.

The Dalgig martyrs were not the only victims of the government crackdown: there were others who fell prey to royalist troops in the aftermath of James Renwick's conventicle including one woman. But eventually the heat died down, and Hugh Hutchison felt free to return home. As soon as he could, he climbed once again to the summit of Carsgailoch, accompanied this time by a number of others – friends from Galloway of the three dead men. So at last the bodies of John Humphrey, John Jamieson and Joseph Wilson were able to be decently laid to rest.

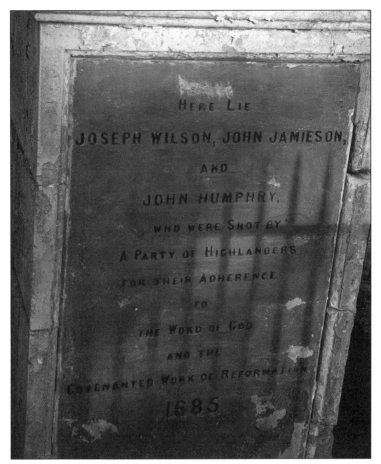

Carsgailoch Martyrs' Memorial

Despite a number of close calls, Hugh Hutchison survived the brutal years of the Killing Times, moving from Dalgig in due course to farm at nearby Fardenreoch where he lived out his life and raised his family in peace. At some point during the eighteenth century, the Dumfriesshire stonemason, Robert Paterson, arrived at Dalgig with his trademark white pony and his tools to record the martyrs' sacrifice in meticulously-lettered stone. Dedicated to the task of commemorating south-west Scotland's executed Covenanters, it was Paterson who provided the inspiration for Walter Scott's character, 'Old Mortality', in his novel of the same name.

By the early years of the next century Robert Paterson's stonework was seen to be crumbling. Following a local collection, the Marquis of Bute, the most extensive landowner in the district, made up the balance required to erect a replacement monument. In 1827 David Reid's firm of local builders was awarded the contract and, during their preparations for laying the foundation stones, what the workmen saw caused them to gasp. To their astonishment, as they sliced through the hilltop turf, the bodies emerged of the three seventeenth century martyrs, to all appearances as fresh as the day they were buried but for the fact that their complexions appeared a little sallow.

On closer examination, the workmen remarked that the dead men's clothing was for the most part intact, the heather-dyed fabric apparently preserved by the peat. One of those present, Ivie Campbell (Hugh Hutchison's successor at Dalgig farm) bent down and removed as a keepsake a small lock of hair from one of the Covenanters as well as a fragment of material from the man's 'pawkie', or mitten: items which would become in due course treasured heirlooms to be passed down through Ivie's family for generations to come. Finally the turfs were replaced with due reverence and peace restored once again to the Dalgig martyrs.

But they weren't forgotten. Nearly 70 years on, during the grandly-titled 'First International Convention of Reformed Presbyterian Churches' in June 1896, Rev. Dr David MacAllister of Pittsburgh, Pennsylvania, preached to a congregation of over 1,000 who had made their way on foot to the summit of Carsgailoch to attend a Sunday afternoon conventicle. Steeped as he was in Covenanting history, the visiting clergyman confessed himself humbled by the large turn-out and, by the close of proceedings, the not inconsiderable sum of fourteen pounds, ten shillings and threepence had been donated for the repair and upkeep of the martyrs' monument.

Today Dalgig lies empty and half-forgotten, its green fields fallen victim to the hunger for coal. Remarkably, Ivie Campbell's fragile keepsakes have fared rather better and now take pride of place in Cumnock's Baird Institute Museum. Adjacent to a fragment of Old Mortality's original memorial stone, all that remains of the material taken from the dead man's 'pawkie' is a tiny, frayed scrap. At its side, preserved within a small, circular frame, a simple yellow curl tells its poignant tale, still glistening like golden thread even after all these years.

Knockburnie's Ride

When the Circuit Court of Justiciary sat in Ayr in May 1811, no fewer than three of the cases to be heard related to the theft of livestock. The first case involved a spectacularly ham-fisted attempt at horse-stealing to which an Irishman, William Gillespie, had sufficient sense to plead guilty. Having some time earlier purloined a quantity of blankets, Gillespie had found his haul too heavy to carry, so came up with the idea of stealing a horse to assist in his getaway. Caught in the act, he ended up neither with blankets nor horse.

Sentenced to a year's imprisonment, Gillespie may have been a little cheered by the prospect of release from the Ayr tolbooth after twelve months on condition that he guarantee his good behaviour for a further three years. With horse-theft still a capital offence in Scotland, there is no doubt that the Irishman got off lightly. The reporter on the *Ayr Advertiser* didn't mince his words: 'The appearance of the prisoner indicated extreme wretchedness,' he wrote. 'His meagre and squalid countenance, long beard and projecting teeth, excited in the spectators a degree of horror mixed with compassion.' Poor Gillespie, then, was not exactly fair of face, but when it came to the crunch it was probably his looks that saved his bacon.

The next case to be heard was disposed of fairly quickly. James Campbell and his son - also James - were due to be tried on a charge of sheep-stealing, but young James failed to put in an appearance and was promptly outlawed by the court. After hearing the case against Campbell, senior, the jury declared itself satisfied that, although he had been found assisting in the slaughter of a sheep - a little tricky to explain away, you might imagine - there was no proof of his having been privy to the animal's theft. Campbell walked out of court a free man, though his son's ordeal would have to be faced another day.

The third case also centred around a father and son combination, accused of having two months previously stolen a pair of horses from adjoining farms near New Cumnock. The circumstances under which the animals were eventually recovered, and the thieves apprehended, are - to say the least - a little unusual.

John Kerr of Knockburnie was widely known as a kindly man who would never refuse a passing tinker a dry corner about his farm steading to spend the night in relative comfort. In March 1811, however, when George Watson, a travelling seller of stoneware, and his son, also George, stopped off at Knockburnie for the night, Kerr's hospitality was rewarded with an act of stupefying ingratitude. When the farmer got up the next morning, he received a rather unpleasant surprise when he discovered that his guests had slipped away under cover of darkness, taking with them as they went one of his farm horses: a fine, grey Clydesdale mare.

It is likely that his fury was compounded when it became clear that the Watsons had taken a second horse from the neighbouring farm of Marshallmark which was tenanted by John's brother, William. Without wasting any time the two brothers saddled up and set off in pursuit, so confident of catching up with the thieves fairly quickly that they didn't bother to take any food or money along with them. Gradually it became clear, however, that perhaps they were facing a tougher task than they'd bargained for. By the time they had covered the twenty-odd miles to Kilmarnock, they had still seen neither hair nor hide of their quarry, so they took the decision that William should return home - someone, after all, had to take care of the men's farms. John continued alone.

Stopping at intervals to make inquiries, John followed the Watsons up and over the Fenwick Moor before heading down through Mearns and on into Glasgow. He tracked the thieves through the city, a good deal smaller, of course, then than today, and before long found himself heading up Loch Lomondside and into the Highland hills. His task was made easier by the fact that his stolen mare had recently cast a half-shoe, and her distinctive hoof-prints were clearly recognisable on the muddy ground.

As one day ran into the next, how did John cope without a penny in his pocket? Possibly he managed to cadge a short-term loan from some acquaintance along the way, or maybe he simply relied on the goodwill of local people who, hearing his story, might well have provided him with food and accommodation. On reaching Tarbet, John veered west to Loch Long, then set out on the long climb to the Rest And Be Thankful, a hill pass rising to just short of a thousand feet. Of course, in the month of March it is quite possible that by now he was tracking his Clydesdale's prints through the snow.

Now among Gaelic-speakers, John had entered the mountainous heart of the West Highlands though somehow I can't imagine the stolid New Cumnock farmer being remotely daunted by the scale of the landscape. After all, wasn't he well used to the sight of the rocks of the Blackcraig Gairy, frowning darkly over the meadows of Glen Afton, all within a few short miles of Knockburnie? Nothing if not tenacious, he continued round the head of Loch Fyne and pressed on to the town of Inveraray where he obtained a warrant from the sheriff there who, when he heard John's story, provided him with two local policemen for the remainder of his journey. Now a posse of three, the men rode north to Dalmally and on through the pinewoods of Glen Orchy until they were faced with the prospect of crossing the wild rampart of Rannoch Moor. Having come this far, John was not about to give up now and the three men and their horses plunged ahead. Eventually, with the bleakness of the moor safely behind them, they dipped into Glencoe, riding in the shadow of some of Scotland's most magnificent peaks, though whether John showed any appetite for Highland scenery is not recorded. At last, eight days and 150 gruelling miles after leaving his home, the Ayrshire farmer finally came face to face with the thieving Watsons in an isolated glen in the hills north of Oban.

For brevity and understatement, the exchange that followed was one to rival Livingstone and Stanley's legendary encounter in the heart of Africa, and if George Watson got a bit of a shock he made a good job of hiding it. 'I didna expeck to see you, Knockburnie,' is supposed to have been his bland opening remark, and John Kerr's rejoinder, when it came, was equally terse and to the point - 'An' I didna expeck ye wad hae stown [stolen] my grey mare.' At this, Watson went on the attack, launching himself at John, but he was soon dragged back and restrained by the accompanying police officers. The captured men were then escorted back to Inveraray, the county town of Argyll, where they spent several weeks in custody before being sent on to face trial in Ayr. As for John Kerr, the chances are that he simply turned on his heel and headed for home, leading his newly recovered horses behind him.

No doubt, there are whimsical aspects to Knockburnie's long ride when viewed from our modern standpoint, two centuries on, but in 1811 the affair was seen very differently. Well aware of the gravity of his crime, Watson, senior, pled guilty nonetheless and threw himself upon the mercy of the court and, despite the best efforts of the defence, the jury found young

George similarly guilty. Both father and son were obliged to wait a further 24 hours before being informed of their fate.

There was to be no mercy. On Friday, 9 May, the presiding judge, Lord Meadowbank, took George, senior, to task for his shortcomings as a father, accusing him of being 'the most fatal enemy of one whom he was bound by every tie of nature and obligation of duty to guide in the paths of rectitude' - in other words, of being a bad role model. Watson displayed no emotion when he was sentenced to be hanged at Ayr in one month's time. George, junior, received less harsh treatment, sentenced to be transported to a distant land for a period of seven years where, the judge suggested, it might be within his power to recover his good name and return ultimately to Scotland. In sharp contrast to his father's impassivity, young George was unable to conceal his distress, at his father's fate as much as his own.

The executioner who presided on 7 June was one John High of Edinburgh, a man known familiarly by the name of 'Jock Heich' who, in a cruel irony, was rumoured to have taken up his trade in order to escape punishment for having stolen livestock himself, in his case poultry. While George Watson was said to have shown remorse during his spell in prison, when the time came to ascend the scaffold he was composed and apparently indifferent to his fate. Poor George Watson - the law relating to horse-theft was to relax some twenty years later and he had the dubious honour of being the last man in Scotland to steal a horse and pay for it with his life. Young George, in contrast, is thought to have fared rather better. Instead of suffering banishment, he is believed to have travelled no further than the rotting hulks that served as transport ships on the River Thames in London where for whatever reason he remained confined for a number of years. When he eventually regained his freedom, it is not by any means impossible that young George Watson turned his face to the north and found his way once again home to Scotland.

The Finisher of the Law

When the Wallace Tower bell failed to toll on Sunday, 10 August 1823, the townsfolk of Ayr were in no doubt that something was amiss. It was noted throughout the day that James Aird, whose responsibility it was to ring the bell, was not to be seen in his accustomed haunts and, when officials finally forced the door of the tower that evening, they found the bell-ringer's lifeless body, sprawled across the stairway that connected his apartments with the belfry.

Prior to his taking up employment in Ayr little appears to be known about James Aird's existence other than the fact that he was said to have been an old soldier who had come originally from Tarbolton. Though provided with accommodation within the crumbling Wallace Tower, ringing the hours wasn't his only civic duty and periodically his services were called upon elsewhere in the town. Certainly he must have cut a fairly conspicuous figure as he left his rooms and travelled down the High Street before turning left into the Sandgate where the Ayr tolbooth would have faced him, directly ahead. A grim, high-steepled building, the residents of its dismal apartments would hardly have welcomed Aird's arrival since, from 1815 until his death in 1823, he occupied the position of the town's municipal hangman.

Paid a basic annual salary of £30, Ayr's 'finisher of the law' was granted in addition a sum of £3 6s 8d (£3.33) for each execution that he carried out. During his years in the job, his hangman's bonus paid out on a total of eight occasions, the first of these occurring when the Duke of Portland's overseer, William Evans, was brought to the gallows, convicted of forgery, in May 1816. Evans never grew reconciled to his fate, declaring himself 'a murdered man' even as he took his place on the scaffold. The following October, Aird was called upon once more, this time to orchestrate a triple-execution. Two men from Wigtownshire, William Robertson and Joseph Cairns were to be hanged following their conviction for a series of robberies, while his third victim that day, coincidentally also from Wigtownshire, happened in this instance to be a woman. Under threat of eviction, Margaret Crossan had set fire to her landlord's byre at Carsegowan farm in May 1817 with the result that more than a dozen beasts had perished in the ensuing blaze. The fact that the condemned woman was leaving behind an infant child gave rise perhaps to a degree of public sympathy, and some of those who witnessed Margaret Crossan's execution insisted that the sky grew dark overhead and a dove was to be seen, fluttering strangely in the air above her head.

No such apparition was seen two years later, in May 1819, when Aird oversaw the execution of a 22 year-old housebreaker, John McNeil. In March of the following year he was called upon to usher William McGheer and Charles Brittan into the next world following the two men's conviction for violent housebreaking at Boreland farm, Dalrymple - a crime known as 'stouthrief' at the time. Those present were startled when McGheer dropped the signal handkerchief without a second's hesitation, indicating to the hangman his readiness to die and providing supporting clergy with barely sufficient time to step clear of the scaffold. In December 1822 James Aird's eighth and final victim was James Burtnay, a collier from Ayr who had been condemned for the rape of a minor, Janet Anderson, while harvesting potatoes in a field near Prestwick Toll. Burtnay claimed his dubious place in Ayrshire history by becoming the first man to be hanged 'facing Arran' on the west wall of the new prison which had recently replaced the old Sandgate tolbooth.

As things turned out, within a year of Burtnay's execution the hangman, James Aird, was faced with the prospect of his own demise, the result of a freak accident. In the afternoon of Saturday, 9 August 1823 Aird had apparently made his way to Ayr harbour where he spent time, watching timber being unloaded from the *Hercules*. At some point, it appears that he stepped aboard in order to obtain a better view of proceedings. During the course of moving a heavy log, at a given signal the crew-members withdrew their handspikes from the ship's capstan, thus leaving the apparatus free to spin rapidly around. One handspike, however, had been overlooked and was ejected by the rotating capstan at great speed and the unfortunate soul who happened to be standing in its path was James Aird. The flying handspike struck a fearful blow to the side of his body and, though clearly in great pain, it was said that the hangman did not cry out but simply left the scene of the accident with his hand pressed to the spot where he had been injured. It turned out to be the last time that anyone would see him alive.

Perhaps it should be no surprise that the hangman's personal tragedy quickly became a subject for - quite literally - gallows humour, prompting an anonymous local rhymester to pen an irreverent epitaph:

> The burglars now may loudly crow
> And doers of misdeed.
> No more the bad ones he'll off-throw,
> 'Tis true - the hangman's dead!

Within a very few decades, however, a rather darker mythology had grown up surrounding the late executioner. Ostracised by the local community, Aird was said to have been forced to fall back on pet mice, rats and birds for company. Weak of intellect and haunted by feelings of persecution, he never bought his bread from the same baker twice nor drew his drinking-water from the same well. A habitual night-wanderer, his solitary figure was to be seen, regularly tramping the town streets after dark and muttering all the while beneath his breath.

Yet the picture painted at the time of Aird's death by his obituary in the *Ayr Advertiser* is a rather less sinister one. While it appears that he did indeed keep a number of pets in his rooms, such as owls and rabbits, the newspaper makes clear that he was by no means shunned by his neighbours. On the contrary, he was known for carrying out small services, such as ridding their homes of vermin, invariably in such cases refusing payment. 'To his fellow-creatures in poverty he opened his hand liberally', the paper notes, and 'in the execution of his horrible duty he happily blended steadiness of purpose with great humanity.' All in all, the *Advertiser* concludes that Aird had conducted himself 'with a respect and modesty seldom or perhaps never combined with his office' and that he was viewed by the community as 'an object of respect rather than aversion.'

Whether James Aird's death was solely the result of his unfortunate accident, or whether perhaps the epilepsy from which he was believed to suffer had a hand in his final moments cannot be certain. Forty-seven years old at the time of his death, the hangman's remains were laid to rest in the Auld Kirkyard on the banks of the River Ayr. The town authorities paid his outstanding wages to his brother in Galston on the understanding that the money would be forwarded in turn to the dead man's widow and children in England. What the tragic circumstances might have been that led to

James Aird living alone in the ruinous Wallace Tower, isolated from his loved ones and occupying the reviled position of Ayr hangman, is unlikely ever to be known.

The Forty Acres Murder

By all accounts, Dudsday of May 1848 was a particularly busy one with both shopkeepers and public-houses in Kilmarnock reporting brisk trade as country people and their families converged on the town. Twice annually - first around Whitsun, then later in the year at Martinmas - Dudsday provided farm-workers disgruntled with their current lot with an opportunity to negotiate a better position for the forthcoming six-month term. Those content to stay put likewise benefited from the day's holiday, and many put it to good use by travelling to town and treating themselves to a new suit of clothes - hence *Duds*-day. It was for this very reason that James Young, a sixteen year-old local farm worker, made his way into Kilmarnock on Friday, 26 May 1848.

We know that, in common with many others, James made purchases of new clothing. Later in the day, in the company of his father, John Young, he visited his married sister's new home - she had flitted that very day - following which the two men made their way to John's home at Knowehead farm, Riccarton, stopping off briefly at a friend's house where John accepted the offer of a dram and James a glass of ginger beer. They continued to Knowehead where James intended to leave his new purchases. Because of the lateness of the hour, his mother suggested that her son stay over but, keen to get back to his workplace, James left around 11 p.m. to cover the couple of miles or so to Forty Acres farm (now more commonly spelt 'Fortacres'). Sadly, as events turned out, he would never arrive at his destination and, when he said goodbye to his parents at Knowehead, it would be the last time that they would ever see their son alive.

Some hours later - between 3 a.m. and 4 a.m. on Saturday, 27 May - John Gebbie, a Kilmarnock weaver, and his companion, John Scott, a calico printer, were walking near Forty Acres Toll when to their horror they stumbled across a lifeless body, sprawled in a pool of blood. Shocked, the men rushed to rouse Robert Hendry, the toll-keeper, and Joseph Smith, the farmer of Forty Acres, who instantly recognised the dead boy as his employee, James Young. Shortly before 7 a.m., James's father arrived on the scene and was faced with the unenviable task of identifying his son's body. Ironically, when fate caught up with poor James that night, he was probably within hailing distance of his destination.

Later in the morning, Police Superintendent Thomas Penny arrived at the crime scene, followed shortly afterwards by Sheriff-Substitute James Robison and the local Procurator-Fiscal, James Murdoch. The cause of the boy's death wasn't hard to see. An injury to the back of his head appeared to have been caused by a stone which was lying close by - the size of a large potato. A bloody chisel, retrieved from an adjacent field, appeared responsible for a savage gash on the side of his neck from which a large quantity of blood had spouted. The boy's pockets had been rifled and, presumably knocked from his head, his cap lay not far away. Closer inspection revealed that his pocket-watch, a gift from his older brother, was missing as well as fifteen shillings in silver. A post-mortem investigation, carried out later that day by Dr Haldane of Ayr and Dr Paxton of Kilmarnock, revealed no possible clue to the attacker's identity.

Remarkably, although no witness to the crime ever came forward, within a few short days a suspect had been apprehended, charged with murder and placed under lock and key at Ayr, largely through a series of fortunate events. On the morning of Sunday, 28 May, a toll house at Lochwinnoch - some fifteen miles north of the crime scene - was found to have been broken into overnight and £35 in cash removed, in addition to a watch. The previous day a stranger's odd behaviour had aroused the suspicions of a local farmer, William Orr, so he saddled up his horse and set off in pursuit, eventually catching up with his suspect some five or six miles away in the town of Johnstone where he succeeded in pinning the man down until a local police constable, Alexander Davidson, could arrive to effect his arrest. When searched, the man was found to have in his possession a sum of nearly £35 as well as the watch that was missing from the toll house. Charged with theft and housebreaking, by Sunday night he was securely locked up in Paisley jail.

The following morning, Monday, 29 May, a Dalry police officer successfully put the next piece of the jigsaw puzzle into place. Descriptions of James Young's stolen pocket-watch had been circulated fairly widely and, when Constable Hutchison examined a watch pawned two days previously at William Lowry's establishment in New Street, Beith, he was able to verify from its serial number - 908 - that it was indeed the one which had been removed from the murder victim. From his records Lowry was able to advise police that the watch had been deposited (through a third party, as it transpired) in the name of one James McWheelan, an Irishman who had previously been employed in the nearby Glengarnock Iron Works. When it emerged that McWheelan had caught a train for Johnstone but had failed to complete his journey, disembarking at Lochwinnoch instead, the penny must very definitely have dropped.

At Paisley jail police soon identified the individual charged with the Lochwinnoch burglary as one and the same as James McWheelan, the man in whose name the stolen watch had been pawned at Beith. Denying all knowledge of the watch, the Irishman was nonetheless unable to offer any credible explanation and quickly found himself sucked into far deeper trouble than a simple charge of housebreaking. The following day, Tuesday, 30 May, he was escorted by train to Ayr where he was charged with the murder of the farm-servant, James Young. The fact that less than four days had passed since James's death was a tribute both to meticulous policing and in particular to the plucky efforts of the Lochwinnoch farmer, William Orr.

It would be another four months before the McWheelan case came before the Circuit Court of Justiciary in Ayr - on Wednesday, 4 October - and, although the accused man showed no hesitation in pleading not guilty, it soon became clear that he had an uphill struggle on his hands. One of a total of 93 witnesses called by the Crown, a Kilmarnock labourer, Robert Thom, described how in the early hours of Saturday, 27 May he had been having a drink with a stranger in Andrew Anderson's public-house in Waterloo Street when he noticed bloodstains on the man's clothing. 'You have surely been murdering somebody, or killing somebody's swine,' Robert Thom had quipped. His drinking-companion, whom he identified as James McWheelan, replied that he had been involved in 'a skite' over a girl, then drained his glass abruptly and departed. The testimony of successive further witnesses allowed the accused's route towards Beith to be traced. One man, John Marshall, recounted how an agitated McWheelan had accused him of insulting him and had proceeded to assault him on the roadside near Stewarton. A barber in Beith, John Crawford, told the court how the Irishman had attempted to skip the queue in his urgency to have his beard shaved off in what looked suspiciously like an attempt to disguise his appearance. In a development that seems to owe more to detective fiction than to real life, it emerged that a distinctive, pink-patterned handkerchief, recovered from the vicinity of the murder scene, could be reliably linked with the prisoner who persisted nonetheless in maintaining that he had never at any time set foot in the parish of Dundonald, where Forty Acres farm was located. In an effort to explain away his blood-stained clothing, he claimed to have taken a lift sometime earlier in a farm cart transporting slaughtered calves, a story corroborated by the cart's driver, Hugh Allan of Dalry.

But it wasn't enough. After hearing a summing up by both Crown and defence lawyers and the concluding remarks of the presiding judge, Lord Mackenzie, the members of the jury took a mere fifteen minutes to reach a unanimous verdict of guilty on charges both of robbery and murder. Turning to the convicted man, Lord Mackenzie advised him that in a case of murder Scots law permitted no discretion, and that he should hold out no hope of reprieve. 'You must,' he told McWheelan bluntly, 'consider your life in this world at an end.' The judge concluded by informing the prisoner that he would be sustained by bread and water alone until he faced execution in three weeks' time, on Thursday, 26 October. McWheelan cried out at this, still denying the murder but admitting for the first time an association with James Young's pocket-watch. 'I got the watch, although I never said it before,' he confessed, 'from a man named Hall in Kilmarnock.' Of course, his outburst sounded exactly like what it most probably was - a last, lame attempt to stave off what was inevitable.

McWheelan was not a model prisoner. Hostile and suspicious, he was easily roused to anger if pressed to confess his crimes. In discussion with two local clergymen, he stated that, Protestant by birth, he had attended church during his childhood years but had long ago fallen by the wayside. To the ministers' horror, he claimed no knowledge of the existence of God and was happy to ridicule the notion of Hell. His lapse into crime, he insisted, was the result of his lowly position in society and he freely admitted to having served a number of spells of imprisonment. We might imagine that the two clergymen's eyebrows shot skywards when McWheelan inquired of them whether the punishment to be suffered by a triple-murderer in Hell would be subject to proportionate increase. Of course, it is quite possible that he was simply mischief-making. Then again, perhaps not.

For all his bluster, McWheelan was a deeply troubled man. While awaiting trial he had already attempted suicide - a small blade from a pair of weaver's scissors had been found, concealed in his cell - and he made a second attempt after being sentenced. When a bent nail, sharpened to a point, was discovered, secreted among his bedclothes, he was kept thereafter under close watch. He was made to wear hand-cuffs at night which were removed during daytime. Although barely able to read, the condemned man surprised his visitors by his ability to repeat virtually verbatim extended passages of any book which had been read to him. Perhaps surprisingly, the person to whom he appeared most responsive was Prison Governor McKissock and, in the weeks leading up to his execution, the two men spent many hours in private conversation. Bit by bit the prisoner began to relax, to sleep better, even - it was noted - to put on a little weight. We might wonder whether it could have been the first and only time in McWheelan's life that he was free to benefit from a spell of leisure. Gradually his trust grew and he started to open up concerning his own personal circumstances. Since he was unable to write, this information was noted down at his dictation.

McWheelan stated that he had been born in Dublin, maybe 30 years earlier - maybe 32. He was led to believe that his father had died before he was born. While he was still small, his mother removed from Dublin to Belfast, where she had friends and, in what must have been a fairly hand-to-mouth existence, she and her young son subsisted on what income she could glean from selling small items out of a basket. When McWheelan was around seven years old, his mother left Belfast on a return visit to Dublin and he never set eyes on her again. After what must surely have been a time of excruciating uncertainty, it was finally concluded that she had either died or been murdered. For a while he was cared for by his mother's Belfast friends but, when they died, he was sent to live in a household of three unmarried brothers and a sister who put him to work herding cattle. His new guardians, he recalled, treated him kindly enough, but from that time on he received no education whatsoever and very soon he forgot the rudiments of reading which he had learned from his mother.

In an effort to improve his prospects, McWheelan left Ireland in his early twenties and sailed to Glasgow where he took up a gardening job. His memory of his subsequent employment history was hazy, but sometime later he had started work with a contractor in Ardrossan whom he named as Mr King. Here he remained for a number of years and, during this settled spell, it looked for a time as though things might just turn around for James McWheelan when he became romantically involved with a servant in King's household to whom he promised marriage. But by this time excessive drinking had started to exert a grip on him and the girl, he recalled, warned him frequently against its dangers but, sadly, to no avail. In recent years alcohol-consumption had taken a devastating toll on him. There is no question that, when it suited him, McWheelan could be an inveterate and accomplished liar but, somehow or other, his sad tale has a ring of truth about it. As a child, he had no father's hand to steady him and, in the person of Governor McKissock, he may have belatedly discovered the father-figure that he had never previously known.

On Tuesday, 24 October - 48 hours before the scheduled time of his execution - McWheelan received a visit from a distressed young woman who arrived at the prison in the company of his former employer, Mr King. The condemned man made repeated efforts to distract the girl from her grief, declaring himself happy and resigned to the fate that awaited him, but without success. The old McWheelan resurfaced, however, when she tearfully urged him to confess to his crimes. 'Ay!' he is said to have snapped. 'Who learned you to come with that story? It's strange that everyone wants me to go to the scaffold with a lie in my mouth.' It seems likely that his words, spoken in anger, were ones that he would later regret.

The following day, Wednesday, 25 October, McWheelan finally appeared to crack, confessing his guilt for the first time, then immediately recanting, only to repeat his confession in the presence of Governor McKissock. He went on to give his startled listeners an account of events which he maintained had taken place on the night after James Young's murder, which he had spent alone in a rented room at Lochwinnoch. A single candle on the table before him, he told them, had suddenly blazed out with the light of a dozen candles and illuminated one of the room's two doors. Overcome by fear, he made a vow before God that he would desist from leaving by that particular door, yet immediately found himself passing through it nonetheless. The most likely explanation, of course, was that the overwrought McWheelan had mistaken dreams for daytime reality, but what a Freudian might make of it all, I couldn't say. He went on to ask that the girl who had visited him the previous day be sent for but it could not be done. She had returned with Mr King to Ardrossan and was unable to be contacted in time. McWheelan later confessed that his employer had provided him with a sum of money to allow him to marry the girl, but that he had failed to do so.

Whether the ministers' persistence finally paid off or, what is possibly more likely, imminent death exerted its influence, McWheelan's attitude to religion mellowed somewhat, or at least appeared to. He made what Rev. Graham believed to be a full and candid confession, during the course of which he admitted to his involvement in James Young's killing but for the first time implicated a partner-in-crime. He divulged the fact that on Dudsday evening his accomplice and he had sized up an earlier possible victim but in the event had taken pity on the man when he revealed that he had an elderly mother who depended on him. A little later they had overheard James Young and his father bid one another goodnight on the doorstep at Knowehead and had subsequently shadowed James as he made his way down the Forty Acres road and where they had launched the now infamous attack. McWheelan's own intention, he insisted, was robbery alone, never murder, and his accomplice had been the one who had struck the fatal blow. Though he confessed to having previously considered highway robbery as a means of obtaining money for alcohol, McWheelan maintained that, until allying himself with his accomplice, his nerve had always failed him. After listening to the condemned man's confession, Rev. Graham was convinced that he had at last come clean, almost at the eleventh hour. McWheelan's story, however, spectacularly unravelled when the first potential victim - the man with a dependent mother - was identified and revealed that he had been approached on Dudsday by one man alone whose description answered remarkably closely to that of James McWheelan. As for the shadowy accomplice, it is tempting to see him as some sort of alter-ego - a Gil-Martin-type figure as in James Hogg's *Justified Sinner*, published some 24 years earlier - though the chances of McWheelan's having been familiar with Hogg's disturbing novel are surely virtually nil.

On the morning of the execution, Thursday, 26 October, proceedings began when the magistrates and authorities met just after 7 a.m. The condemned man arrived shortly after, accompanied by the Revs. Knox and Graham whom he requested to pray for him. McWheelan's appearance made a strong impression on the large crowd of men, women and children who has assembled to witness his final moments. Roughly 5 feet 10 inches in height and of a muscular build, McWheelan was described as having jet-black hair and bushy whiskers, with the dark eyes and complexion of a man of foreign birth. He walked upright and with apparent total composure. When he addressed the crowd, those who heard described his voice as deep and resonant. 'I bear anger at no man,' McWheelan told them. 'I owe no man any ill will. Fare-ye-well.' At this, he turned to ascend the scaffold which was surrounded by a guard of Special Constables and local Yeomanry. McWheelan was heard all the while to be uttering prayers - 'Lord, take me to thyself. O Lord, do not let my guilty soul die in sin' - words that didn't quite perhaps qualify as remorse, but were at least an admission of wrongdoing. Once the prisoner was in place, the executioner - the octogenarian John Murdoch of Glasgow - drew a cap down over his face.

The crowd and assembled officials waited expectantly while McWheelan remained unmoving on the scaffold - a full thirty minutes during which the tension mounted unbearably, and still the condemned man did not release the handkerchief which would act as the signal that he was ready to die. Finally it was left to the magistrates to prompt the executioner who, on receiving his cue, drew back the bolt and sent the prisoner plummeting to his death. Several minutes passed while his dangling body convulsed repeatedly until finally all signs of life departed and it was able to be cut down for burial within the precincts of the prison. It was noted that throughout the entire procedure only one single, solitary groan was emitted by the crowd. Once the grisly proceedings were complete they filed out, quietly, and proceeded to disperse.

The tangle of truth and deceptions that James McWheelan built around him, his confessions and immediate retractions, untruths, half-truths and evasions all hinder our ability to take a balanced view of the man he was and the life he chose to lead. That he was an alcoholic and a murderer seems beyond doubt, but his claim that poverty and social exclusion were what determined his descent into crime was not, I suspect, a notion that the family of James Young might have felt disposed to accept. One thing seems certain. On 26 October 1848, when the trapdoor was released and McWheelan plunged out of this world and into the next, he surely carried many of his secrets along with him.

The Drowning of John Gallon

In July 1873 *The Newcastle Courant* ran the death notice of a local man, John Gallon, aged 60, of Street House, Ponteland. News of his death would have come as something of a shock to many, for he had been well regarded in the district and his pack of otterhounds was a familiar sight throughout the north-east countryside. The circumstances in which he perished were both tragic and unusual.

During Gallon's time as master of the Bishop Auckland otterhounds, his thirty-strong pack was generally acknowledged to be the best bred and most rigorously trained in the business. With some forty years' hunting experience, his knowledge of north-eastern waterways – the North Tyne, Coquet, Wansbeck, Reed and Till – was second to none. But local knowledge would prove no help on his final excursion which took place in less familiar territory, some 150 miles from home on the Scottish side of the border.

At 7.30 a.m. on Wednesday, July 16 1873 a substantial crowd assembled at Barskimming House, near Mauchline, to see Gallon and his otterhounds off. Accompanied by local followers, the hunt proceeded to the nearby banks of the River Ayr. Doubtless the prosperous, green farmland with its gently sloping woods and meadows held no terrors for John Gallon that summer morning. He could have had no idea of the fate that awaited him.

Once freed, the hounds plunged upstream, scarcely pausing in their stride until they reached the confluence of the Ayr and its major tributary, the Lugar Water. Here, scenting quarry, the pack set up a furious baying and diverted along the lesser stream, entering a narrow defile with their master hard on their heels. Bringing up the rear, the other hunters balked, it seems, at the prospect of entering the gloomy gorge, opting instead to detour across country to where a footbridge crossed the river a little upstream at Slatehole. Here they paused to wait.

At first Gallon's failure to appear brought little concern, the assumption being made that he must already have passed by - his hounds could be heard in full cry some distance upstream. Therefore the hunters resolved to proceed, but with still no sign a mile or so on, suspicion crept in that all was not well. Retracing their steps to Slatehole Bridge, the hunters contrived a makeshift raft to enter the steep-sided gorge and, fearing the worst, equipped themselves with a grappling iron which they had borrowed from a blacksmith's premises nearby. The first thing they sighted was Gallon's cap, eddying ominously on a gentle backwater, and an hour or so later his drowned body was dragged from the depths of a pool, some 150 yards below Slatehole. Ironically, the veteran hunter was known to be unable to swim a stroke.

'A thorough gentleman'; 'unassuming though accomplished'; 'good and kind to the last': following Gallon's death the tributes rolled in. Yet, seen through twenty-first century eyes, there are aspects of his lifelong passion that many would find hard to accept. In pursuit of a wild creature that often weighs little more than a stone, crowds numbering in the hundreds (in addition to hounds and terriers) were commonplace. Spears - frequently of the three-pronged variety - and lengths of convoluted netting formed a routine part of the hunters' tackle, equipment more suited to a gladiatorial contest, you might think, than to a day spent enjoying the countryside. The chase might last for many hours, and 'tailing the otter' – where a huntsman seized the beleaguered creature by the tail before flinging him to the hounds - was viewed as a fitting finale to a day's sport.

A contemporary memoir, *Recollections of an Otter-hunter*, helps lift the lid on nineteenth century attitudes. Its author, William Turnbull (in his seventies at the time his book was published in 1896), had been inn-keeper at the Fox and Hounds, Bellingham, where Gallon was a regular visitor, and over the years the two men had hunted together on numerous occasions. Perhaps the biggest surprise is that Turnbull's memoir frequently refers to his quarry in terms suggestive of a sincere and deep-seated admiration: 'king of the deeps' and 'king of the flood' are two favoured expressions. Conservation appears to have been practised, female otters being spared whenever possible, but nonetheless the *Recollections* betray a naive faith that the supply of wild creatures to be hunted will prove inexhaustible.

As well as a short tribute in verse, Turnbull devotes two whole chapters to John Gallon, highlighting his friend's sense of fairness and his humanity. And by all accounts Gallon was a thoroughly upright individual, a decent and devoted family man. In 1866 when his own daughter was a little girl of nine, he willingly assumed responsibility for his teenage nieces after their father, a master tailor in Rome, had died, leaving them without a guardian.

John Gallon's Gravestone, Elsdon

Margaret, Jane Eliza and Mary were still living under John Gallon's roof in the years leading up to his drowning.

Gallon's grave is still to be seen in Elsdon Churchyard. The red granite headstone brings to mind the events of a century before, when on Saturday, 19 July 1873, a sombre procession of relatives and friends travelled the twenty-odd miles from Ponteland to see John Gallon laid to rest. Present was his Scottish wife, Margaret, distraught at her unexpected loss, and the couple's daughter, Margaret Jane, not yet through her teens, and of the sad, orphaned girls who had arrived from overseas to find a home in Northumberland.

Times have moved on, and attitudes with them. No longer do Britain's otters face the prospect of a grisly end, while, in a curious reversal of fortune, it is their old adversary, the otterhound, whose future now looks less assured. What would John Gallon have made of it all? A countryman whose actions and beliefs were those of his time - would he have come round to a new way of thinking? We have no way of telling. Be that as it may, it is hard not to wish the old otter-hunter peaceful slumbers beneath his native Northumbrian turf.

Laurienne's Cross

In the centre of a small, hummocky field, a short distance east of Auchinleck, there stands a tall Celtic cross. Sculpted from red sandstone over a century ago, nowadays the monument's most frequent visitors are likely to be the blackface sheep that come and go, cropping the turf in its shadow. Things weren't always so tranquil. It was close to this quiet spot, on a late Victorian summer's day, that tragedy struck.

The highest ground in Auchinleck parish is found on its eastern rim, a handful of miles from the elegant, sandstone cross. An ancient hilltop cairn on Wardlaw Hill sits at over 1,600 feet while the summit of Stony Hill at 1,843 feet above sea-level is the highest point in the parish. Rising from the peaty slopes around, the Gass and Glenmuir Waters descend through windswept moorland, barren and treeless, since time immemorial the lonely preserve of the shepherd, the fugitive Covenanter and the burbling whaup. But change came to that quiet countryside, change that not only remoulded the landscape but also transformed utterly the fabric of local society.

The sullen moorlands waited until the turn of the nineteenth century before relinquishing their long-held riches. Concealed under an enveloping blanket of peat, commercially viable seams of coal and ironstone came to light, both commodities much in demand at the time for use in burgeoning industry. Rows of miners' cottages sprang up to accommodate an expanding workforce, a large number of whom consisted of Irishmen and their families fleeing poverty and hunger in their native land, as well as a smaller group of Spanish immigrants employed for their expertise in iron-working. New communities came into being at Birnieknowe, Cronberry, Darnconner and Lugar, and a railway station was established a few yards east of the miners' row at Commondyke. Steel rails snaked their way across the moor, ferrying goods to and from the new mines.

In the 1830s the sum total of Roman Catholics in Auchinleck parish had been estimated at two: a humble hawker and his sister. Barely ten years later, swelled by the influx of Irish and Spanish workers, Catholics were resident in sufficient numbers to justify being served by visiting clergy. Even after the district was assigned its own resident priest, Father William McCabe, around 1850, worshippers were still obliged to celebrate mass in a succession of various halls around Cumnock. McCabe's successor in 1855 was Rev. John O'Dwyer who, finding this situation intolerable, set about raising funds from his congregation for the purpose of erecting a custom-built church. A major local employer, the Eglinton Iron Company, added its support, contributing the sum of £50, and a plot of land beside the Lochnoran Well at Birnieknowe was donated by Lady Boswell of Auchinleck House and earmarked as a suitable site. Using volunteer labour, construction took place over a number of years, until in 1867 Our Lady of Lourdes and St Patrick Church opened its doors for the first time.

Sister Lauriene's Cross

Just over a decade later, O'Dwyer's successor, Father Patrick Wright, expanded operations with the establishment of St Patrick's School, adjacent to the existing church and presbytery. Lord Bute provided financial backing, and soon a schoolteacher, supported by two pupil teachers, was educating some 150 of the local children. In 1885 a convent was built adjoining the chapel to accommodate a number of the Sisters of St Joseph of Cluny who had arrived two years earlier to assist with the running of the school. For the best part of the next century the nuns of Birnieknowe would be closely involved with the life of the local community.

In the spring of 1888 Sister Columba became head of St Patrick's School. Her predecessor,

153

Sister Laurienne Cusack, had stepped down following an ear infection which had left her hearing impaired. On her return from convalescence at Girvan, Sister Laurienne had devoted a large part of her time to visiting the sick and needy of the district in their homes, a position for which her popularity locally admirably suited her.

But clearly her remit went rather wider. When Sister Laurienne went in pursuit of a truant schoolboy on the fateful afternoon of Tuesday, 7 August 1888, her timing proved critical. Crossing a branch-line line of the Glasgow and South Western Railway as she made for the High Row at Commondyke, the chances are that Sister Laurienne heard nothing of Engine No. 90, approaching from the east. What is beyond doubt is that her injuries were such that the unfortunate nun died soon after the tragic collision.

Within two hours a crowd assembled – not only Roman Catholics – many people anxious to assist, others simply to pray in the church. Over one hundred subsequently offered to maintain a vigil by Sister Laurienne's body throughout the night. When word of the tragedy reached Father Murphy (the current priest, who happened to be in Rothesay at the time) he immediately returned to conduct a memorial service, and on the day when the body was due to be taken by train for burial at Girvan, such was the crush on the platform that Commondyke station had no option but to close its gates to latecomers.

In the aftermath of the tragic collision, life of course went on. Probably entirely blameless, Johnnie Goodfellow, the driver of mineral train No. 90, had to live with his memory of the fatal day, as did the errant schoolboy but for whose actions the accident might never have happened. But in the months to come Sister Laurienne's loss seemed to sap the resolve of the Birnieknowe religious community. Sister Columba fell ill and, unable to continue with her duties, stepped aside. When the remaining sisters' health showed similar signs of failing, they had no option but to withdraw their services. Within a year of Laurienne's death, the nuns of St Joseph had gone from Birnieknowe.

They were replaced in due course, but though their successors – the Sisters of the Order of the Cross and Passion – were active for some 75 years, latterly the nuns appeared to be living on borrowed time. During the twentieth century social housing was established at Auchinleck (which by now had its own Roman Catholic church), leading to a steady depopulation of the surrounding mining communities. It was perhaps with a sense of inevitability that Birnieknowe school and convent closed their doors for the last time, their buildings left stranded in the depths of the countryside.

To Sister Laurienne's contemporaries, today's Birnieknowe would scarcely be recognisable. The name survives in a nearby farm, but the miners' rows have vanished entirely. Green walkways for sheep now follow the course of the old branch lines, and of Commondyke station itself only fragments remain. Where the convent once stood, a modern dwelling-house nestles among a band of sheltering trees. By contrast, the tall, sandstone cross has weathered the changing times, a lasting symbol of the esteem in which a reverend Sister was held by the local people she had served.

On Kilantringan Moor

December 1908 had ushered in a spell of unseasonably mild weather and a green end to the year seemed assured. But shortly after Christmas conditions took a turn for the worse, when the first blizzard of winter whistled in, causing the mercury to plummet. Ponds froze overnight and curlers took to the rinks for their first ends of the season while heavy snowfalls blanketed the country: sixteen inches of snow in Edinburgh, with a similar depth in the west at Dumbarton. Greenock and Pitlochry both recorded a foot, and even Millport on the balmy isle of Cumbrae registered a fall of nearly six inches.

The south-west of the country didn't escape unscathed, though some of its worst calamities were enacted not on land but at sea. On the south Ayrshire coast, the *Deloraine* ran aground on a rocky shore to the north of Ballantrae, though by sheer good luck the entire crew of nine was plucked to safety by a passing Clyde-bound steamer. Four other seamen were less fortunate, succumbing to the waves off Arran when the *Bessie Arnot*, carrying a cargo of iron ore from Dublin, foundered in mountainous seas.

Inland districts fared no better, with hill shepherds reconciled to the chore of digging out their snowbound flocks. Meanwhile the Glasgow to Stranraer train, with fifty luckless passengers aboard, became trapped among mammoth drifts on moorland to the south of Barrhill. A snow-plough was promptly dispatched from Ayr, only to become quickly snowed up itself. It was twenty-four hours before railway officials, assisted by squads of the unemployed, succeeded in relieving the beleaguered passengers. No doubt the rescue party received an enthusiastic welcome – the train's dining-car, it was reported, had already run short of provisions.

Robert Cunningham lived with his parents, brothers and sisters on Ballantrae's Main Street that fickle December of 1908. Twenty-six years old, he was a kenspeckle figure in the locality, having worked for eight years as the Glen App postman, prior to which he had delivered bread around the farms and cottages of the district by horse and wagon. By all accounts, Robert was a likeable young man, keen on sport, who was known for his cheery whistle and carefree nature. It was said that he had recently become engaged to be married.

It was a white world that he stepped into on the morning of 28 December. The mail's arrival had been delayed at Ballantrae, but it was perhaps typical of Robert that, despite the short hours of daylight available to him, he set off, determined to complete his deliveries. As he crossed the moorland ridge separating Ballantrae from the head of Glen App the wind must have buffeted him furiously, and what a relief it would have been to drop into the relative shelter of the woods at Carlock. Robert continued downhill, stopping off at the familiar farms and cottages, until finally he arrived at the foot of the glen where Finnarts, a large house no longer standing, signalled the terminus of his round. Before turning to retrace his steps, he tucked into a hearty meal at Finnarts. As things turned out, it would be his last.

On the return journey, it was dark by the time he paused at the schoolhouse and accepted a cup of tea from the teacher, Jane Leask. Meanwhile the snow fell ever more thickly. At the head of the glen the gamekeeper, James McLean, offered to put him up for the night but Robert declined, apparently eager to return to his fiancée. The route across the moor was probably so familiar to him that it held few fears, even in conditions that might have given a more cautious man second thoughts. James McLean would later recollect that Robert had departed Carlock in pitch darkness and wild weather at 6.20 p.m. The Glen App keeper was the last person to see him alive.

When he failed to return that evening, Robert's brother Matthew and two friends set out to search for him but high winds and the intense cold soon forced them back. In spite of this, no-one was yet unduly concerned: it seemed certain that Robert must have taken shelter with some kindly resident of the glen. But with no news the following day there could no longer be any doubt that something was amiss. Search parties were drawn up comprising virtually the village's entire complement of able-bodied men, plus an insistent few who were not. For a time their efforts were hindered by rough weather but finally, on the last day of the year - nearly 72 hours after Robert had left Carlock - they located his body, huddled beneath his empty mailbag on the snows of Kilantringan Moor. Some said that his brother was first on the spot.

In the days that followed it was suggested that perhaps he had struck his head during a fall and thus was rendered unconscious. But it seems more likely that, having become disorientated in whiteout conditions, Robert was simply overcome by cold and exhaustion. On a night like 28 December, hypothermia would not have been long in coming. Whatever his final moments, Robert's death was keenly felt throughout the small community of fishermen and farming folk. Ne'erday 1909 was a sombre occasion for many.

Robert Cunningham's Memorial, Kilantringan

Money was raised locally for a commemorative tablet to Robert to be placed on the wall of the parish church. When his sad story reached the ears of the Postmen's Federation, its members contributed generously for the erection of a stone cross on Kilantringan Moor to mark the tragic loss of a colleague. In time the monument became weathered, its lettering no longer legible, so in 1991 the Communication Workers' Union - successor to the Postmen's Federation - stepped in a second time with funds for its restoration by a local stonemason. And rightly so - Robert Cunningham was an unassuming postman, held in much affection, who displayed bravery and dedication to duty during his final hours. He deserves to be remembered.

The Northbank Mystery

Anchored on its rocky promontory, the old castle of Portencross has viewed for centuries the ebb and flow of human affairs. In the thirteenth century King Haakon's Norwegian longships were to be seen, melting away behind the Cumbraes, defeated as much by wild autumnal weather as by the Scots under Alexander III.

A hundred years later, King Robert II and his son, Robert III, both made use of Portencross as a convenient launching point for the ten-mile sail across the Firth of Clyde to their royal residence at Rothesay Castle. But castles and kings weren't the only ones over the years to be caught up in momentous events along this craggy coast. A simple whitewashed cottage, situated just north of the old castle, bore witness one stormy autumn evening to a grave domestic tragedy of its own.

By October 1913 the new tenants of Northbank Cottage had spent some six months settling in. They had arrived at Portencross from the West Highlands during May – Alexander MacLaren, a native of Highland Perthshire; his wife, Jessie; and Jessie's younger sister, Mary, who had lived with the couple for many years. Alexander had been employed as a storekeeper at the Glengarnock Iron and Steel Company in Dalry, when he met and married Jessie, the daughter of a well-known local contractor, George Gunn.

Soon after their marriage, the couple moved south to Port William to set up a bakery and general store, and a little later Jessie's mother and her younger sister, Mary, joined them in Wigtownshire to assist in the running of the business. Before leaving home, Mary had given up her job as telephone operator – the first such ever in the town of Beith where her good looks had earned her the nickname 'the beauty of Beith.' In spite of her striking appearance, Mary was destined to remain unmarried.

Alexander quickly became established at Port William where he played a prominent role in the local community, establishing the Ebenezer Hall where he conducted regular evangelical meetings as well as occupying a seat on the local school board. Despite his high public profile, Alexander moved on once again, this time north to Taynuilt, Argyll, where he took charge of the local post office and subsequently set himself up as a sheep farmer. Once again Mary accompanied her sister and brother-in-law.

But it appears that she didn't take to life on a Highland farm, possibly missing the social buzz of the shop and bakery. Following repeated invitations, Mary resolved to embark on a new life overseas by joining another married sister and her husband, Mr and Mrs John Craig, at their home in Canada. However, as matters turned out, things did not go to plan for Mary on the Saskatchewan prairies either, for in little over a year she was back at Taynuilt, fleeing, it seems, an abortive love affair. It was shortly after her return that Alexander took the decision to retire from sheep-farming and in May 1913 the MacLarens and Mary left Argyll to take up residence in an isolated cottage on the north Ayrshire coast. At the time of their move to Northbank Mary was not yet 50, a decade or so younger than her sister and brother-in-law.

Little more than a stone's throw from the waves, the cottage was situated on a raised beach at the base of a wooded cliff whose triple peaks were known locally as The Three Sisters. Northbank's nearest neighbours were at the tiny settlement of Portencross, half a mile to the south along an unfenced track, but obscured from view by the slopes of Auld Hill where they plunged towards the sea. To the north, the nearest neighbour was the farm of Fences, more than a mile away on the Hunterston estate. If undeniably isolated, the setting of Northbank was certainly picturesque and the cottage had sufficient land attached to keep a retired farmer occupied. Alexander had the space to keep a milk-cow.

Mary Gunn spent Saturday, 18 October 1913 shopping in the village of West Kilbride, some three miles south-east from Northbank along the coast road. During the afternoon her brother-in-law set out with the intention of meeting her and escorting her home – on the face of it innocuous enough, but an action which would provoke some comment in the days ahead. The pair met somewhere in the vicinity of Ardneil farm, roughly the halfway point, and together walked back to Northbank. By the time they arrived at the cottage darkness had set in and the weather had taken a turn for the worse.

After their evening meal, Jessie, Mary and Alexander settled down by the parlour fire, the two women busily knitting by lamplight while Alexander read aloud from a novel by Mary's favourite author - *At Sunwich*

Northbank

Port by W.W. Jacobs - on loan from West Kilbride Public Library. A strong wind was blowing and from time to time rainy squalls drummed against the window-panes. In the absence of neighbours the parlour blinds were not closed, though the window was screened by a lace curtain. For events that followed, the account later supplied by Alexander to the police is virtually all we have to go on.

Around 8.30 p.m., by Alexander's reckoning, the cottage was suddenly rocked by the report of gunfire, accompanied by the sound of glass shattering at the parlour window. Mary leapt to her feet, uttering the words 'Oh Alec, I'm shot!' before crumpling to the floor – words, as it turned out, that would be her last. After several more shots, fired in quick succession, Jessie collapsed into her husband's arms with a bullet lodged in her back. By comparison Alexander got off lightly, his left index finger injured by a bullet which subsequently passed through the book he was reading. Six shots in total were fired - then silence. Just as abruptly as the shooting had begun, it ceased.

Alexander faced a quandary. Should he remain close at hand for fear that the unknown gunman might return? Or alternatively run the risk of leaving the women unattended – one grievously wounded, the other already dead – in order to raise the alarm? In the event he chose the latter, but before leaving Northbank he released his collie and Scottish terrier pup from an outhouse and, accompanied by the two dogs, he scouted around the environs of the cottage. Why these creatures had failed to give notice of the approach of a stranger proved one of the case's unsolved puzzles. The dogs had not so much as given a bark.

Satisfied that the attacker had absconded, Alexander headed through darkness and driving rain towards his nearest neighbour at Portencross farm. 'They're all shot at my house!' he blurted out to Alexander Murray and his wife. 'My wife and Miss Gunn are lying shot on the floor!' The startled farmer accompanied him to Auchenames House where the laird, William Adams, heard Alexander's tale and promptly telephoned a friend at West Kilbride who in turn alerted the local police by word of mouth. The village police station was still not connected by phone.

Twenty minutes or so after Adams made his phone call, a car ferrying two police officers plus a local doctor arrived at Northbank where they found Jessie alert and fully conscious. She reported that all had remained quiet since Alexander's departure. Dr More dressed her wounds before putting her to bed, and then attended to Alexander's injured finger. Sadly, there was nothing to be done for Mary who was declared dead at the scene - struck, as it turned out, by a total of three bullets, one of which had passed through her heart. Meanwhile more police converged on the cottage from the nearby towns of Ardrossan, Dalry and Largs. Late as it was, Alexander was invited to accompany officers to West Kilbride police station for further questioning.

At first light - around 8 a.m. – the police inquiry at Northbank began in earnest. For fear that her injuries might prove fatal, Jessie was interviewed and the statement she gave was found to correspond closely with her husband's version of events. Officers searching outside the cottage identified a number of footprints below the parlour window, blurred as a result of the night's rainfall but sufficient to reveal that the gunman had worn tacketed boots - not much of a distinguishing feature in a country district at this time. A check was made and it was noted that the boots did not match any pair in the cottage. Though indistinct, these prints were carefully covered over in order that plaster casts might be taken. A spent bullet was retrieved from alongside the window, apparently the result of a stray shot which had ricocheted from surrounding stonework.

Meanwhile a constable searching indoors came across a shotgun - and his pulse may have quickened a little - but Alexander had a ready answer, explaining that he was routinely in the habit of shooting for the pot. A dead rabbit as evidence lay on the kitchen table. Ballistics experts would later confirm that the bullets recovered from Northbank had been fired from a handgun.

As the search widened, some twenty officers set about combing the surrounding countryside, scouring the precipitous slopes of The Three Sisters and picking their way along the shoreline in the hope of apprehending the murderer, of recovering a discarded weapon, or even of stumbling across the body of an unhinged criminal who might have committed suicide in the aftermath of his brutal attack. Not least they were looking for some compelling motive for what looked like a motiveless crime - no attempt had been made to enter the cottage, even during Alexander's absence, and no property appeared to have been stolen.

Seen through twenty-first century eyes, there are one or two aspects of the investigation that might come across as a little eccentric. The local press reported at the time that a well-meaning local joiner had provided police with a number of custom-built wooden boxes, each equipped with a glass bottom, enabling officers to study the seabed in hopes of recovering evidence such as a discarded weapon. Probably to no-one's surprise, the boxes proved less than effective, frustrated by rough seas and by a shoreline whose forests of swaying seaweed might have concealed an entire armoury. The newspapers also noted the necessity of securing accommodation at Northbank for the dozen-plus bicycles that investigating officers made use of in carrying out their inquiries.

At the end of the day, however, the police search revealed precisely nothing - and in the absence of hard facts the rumour-mill started to grind. A grey-bearded stranger, it was reported, had been seen on the day of the murder, turning up on the doorsteps of several local farms and in each case asking for directions to Portencross. A group of local schoolchildren were happy to testify to that but the man was never identified. A male passenger at West Kilbride railway station aroused suspicion by requesting permission to board the Largs train and pay for his ticket at his destination – he briefly became a suspect but was subsequently eliminated. A dubious character was spotted lurking in the Ardneil Woods, though when police investigated he turned out simply to be a local man setting snares for rabbits.

At one point West Kilbride was agog with rumours of an imminent arrest in Glasgow but this too came to nothing. When even the prospect of a police £100 reward failed to prompt any new information, the Ayrshire Constabulary went so far as to make contact with their counterparts in Saskatchewan to investigate the possibility of a spurned Canadian lover's involvement in the crime. Once again, however, they drew a blank when word came back that the man in question was innocently at home on the night of the murder, some 4,000 miles from Portencross. But if the police inquiry appeared to be stalling, there were others who were rather quicker off the mark. As the horror of the story became known further afield, an enterprising Glasgow printer rushed out a picture postcard of Northbank Cottage which was said to have sold in its thousands.

Inevitably suspicion fell on Alexander himself. Some suspected that the wound to his left hand might well have been self-inflicted, possibly the same people who chose to interpret Northbank's domestic arrangements in terms of an 'eternal triangle' and who viewed askance his close relationship with his sister-in-law. Shortly after the murder, a scene blew up on a local bus when Alexander felt that his good name had been called into question. In spite of his understandable sensitivity, he showed little reticence when voicing his suspicions of others. Elizabeth Gibson of Portencross guest-house took legal action following an alleged slander but puzzlingly the case against Alexander was dropped at the last minute leaving the landlady substantially out of pocket.

Following a setback, Jessie had been admitted to Kilmarnock Infirmary and there she remained an in-patient until January 1914, a stay of over two months. Once discharged, Alexander took her to a friend's house in Dalry where she spent time convalescing in the aftermath of her injury and traumatic experience. Jessie and Alexander wasted little time in moving out of Northbank but events of October 18 appeared not to have destabilised their marriage, and if Jessie harboured any dark knowledge of her husband it was something that she kept firmly to herself.

Three days after her death, Mary Gunn's funeral took place at the Southern Necropolis, Glasgow, with her brother-in-law, Alexander, in attendance. Today, the only remaining monument to a woman who was hailed in her time a beauty and for whom life must once have seemed rich with promise is a toppled headstone, indistinguishable from the scores of others that surround it. A century on, it is hardly likely now that the identity of whoever ended Mary's life so abruptly will ever be known for sure.

In the Howe of Laggan

The few hundred souls who inhabit the village of Barr are fortunate indeed, living as they do in one of the prettiest and most secluded parishes in south-west Scotland. A network of walking trails radiates from the village, tempting visitors to stretch their legs and blow away the cobwebs. If you follow a woodland path alongside the winding Water of Gregg, you will reach a point where the trees fade out and views open up of the higher hills. A lonely cairn, raised almost a century ago, commemorates the bravery of a local shepherd who left home during an epic snowstorm, sadly never to return. Christopher McTaggart was only nineteen years old.

The blizzard of New Year 1913 was as prodigious in the south Ayrshire hills as it was elsewhere in Scotland. For a week beforehand cold south-easterlies had been scouring the country until finally, in the early hours of Saturday, 11 January, the wind swung north-east and reached gale-force, accompanied by blinding snow flurries. Exposed to mountainous seas, east coast shipping was first to feel the force of the storm. The gravest loss of life occurred when a Danish steamer, the *G. Koch*, ran aground on the Aberdeenshire coast with the loss of seven crew members, while further to the south three more seamen drowned when a Dutch vessel foundered in Carnoustie Bay. A Norwegian steamer, *Ortra*, was wrecked near Peterhead.

Inland districts fared little better. All over the country telephone and telegraph wires came down. Derailments on the rail network were widespread and trains became marooned, unable to proceed or go back through sheer volume of snow. Perthshire was particularly badly hit, with 2 feet 8 inches of lying snow recorded at Blair Castle. Inevitably fatalities followed - a Lundie woman, Annie Armstrong, fell victim to the elements, dying of exposure beside the main Dundee to Coupar Angus road, while pit worker John Henderson perished in attempting a short-cut along the North British railway line in Midlothian.

The south-west didn't escape unscathed. During a function in Ballantrae village hall the dancers' merriment was abruptly curtailed when a savage gust blew in one of the windows. More seriously, for the best part of a week rough seas prevented the Ailsa Craig mailboat, the island's only link with the mainland, from delivering essential provisions. Seven-foot snowdrifts lay like frozen waves in the streets of New Cumnock, and food supplies for patients at the nearby Glenafton Sanatorium had to be transported by horse-drawn sleigh. Not surprisingly, exposed upland districts were worst affected, putting shepherds and their flocks in peril.

Christopher McTaggart prepared to set out from his home near Barr around 8 a.m. that snowy Saturday morning. At this point the story takes on the trappings of folklore, as it is said that the young shepherd took up the family fiddle and played a hymn tune before he left. Accompanied only by his sheepdog, Wag, his job was to bring hill sheep down to lower ground. His father left at the same time on a similar solitary errand. Despite the harshness of the weather, Christopher probably felt few fears, having herded the Changue hills for a number of years. He must have made this same journey on countless previous occasions - though probably not in conditions as severe as those that prevailed that particular January morning.

As the day wore on, the blizzard showed no sign of abating and concern started to mount regarding Christopher's safety. Around midday one of his brothers ventured out to search but, in a wall of driving snow, soon became disorientated and lost. Five hours later – long after dark – he stumbled home, frozen and exhausted but bringing no news. It was now nine hours since the young shepherd had been seen. A search party of local volunteers was quickly assembled – including Christopher's twin brother, David, and, with lanterns swaying through the darkness, they set off into the storm.

Great wreaths of snow hindered the searchers' progress, making for slow and arduous going. Finally they reached a broad hollow known as the Howe of Laggan that lay between the heights of Larg to the west and the Haggis Hill, lying further east. It seems likely that they had surmised that Christopher might be found in the vicinity of the buchts, or sheep-pens, that were located alongside the Laggan Burn.

It was surprising that the men were able to hear anything at all above the howl of the gale. Perhaps the wind lulled for an instant, allowing them to pick up the distant barking of Christopher's dog and thus locate the spot where the young herd lay, slumped against a fence, unconscious. His hands were bleeding from his efforts at rescuing sheep from a nearby drift and his body was dusted with no more than a thin covering of snowflakes, suggesting that he had collapsed only recently through cold and fatigue.

But sadly the search party's arrival was too late - despite their best efforts to revive him, Christopher McTaggart's life slipped away a quarter of an hour after they reached him.

Kirstie's Cairn

Carrying the young man home through the storm was well-nigh impossible, so he was placed for the night in a nearby shepherd's hut. The following day the weather had cleared sufficiently for a party of twenty men to be mustered in Barr who subsequently made their way to the Howe of Laggan where they recovered Christopher's body, bringing him back by stretcher to his parents' house. His faithful collie, whose barking had first alerted the searchers, had refused to leave the lonely shelter, insisting on keeping a lonely night-time vigil by his dead master's side.

Christopher wasn't the only local shepherd who ran into difficulties associated with the weather. On Glendrissaig Hill south of Girvan a shepherd lost his bearings completely but eventually managed to struggle home, chilled to the bone and weary but otherwise unharmed. At Pinclanty, in the Stinchar valley, another herd named Seaton collapsed in a snowdrift and found himself unable to rise. In an act of unsung heroism, his workmate, Murdoch, lifted his exhausted companion and carried him bodily to safety, a distance of over two miles.

Christopher's funeral and subsequent memorial service at Barr were well attended. The Free Kirk minister, Rev. John Angus, praised the young man's dedication to duty, highlighting parallels with the good shepherd of the scriptures. In words of high poignancy, the minister charged the young men of the area with the responsibility of raising a cairn in Christopher's memory. 'Let it be built of the patient weather-beaten stones that lie scattered around,' he intoned, 'stones that witnessed his struggle, that listened to his last sigh, silent stones that have brought no tale to us from dim days of the past. Let us make them our messengers to carry down to future ages the record of a noble death in the storms that swept these hills.' Rev. Angus noted that the last sermon that Christopher had heard preached had been based on the text 'Prepare to meet thy God.' The 'Death March' was played at the close.

Life gradually returned to normal in the aftermath of the great storm, and the name McTaggart became in time a byword for the good shepherd among the south Ayrshire hills, as Christopher's brothers followed in the family footsteps, despite their tragic loss. Sam McTaggart, co-founder in 1921 of the Carrick Sheep Dog Trials Society, herded sheep until his retiral in 1954, his last 39 years having been spent on the farm of Glendrissaig, near Girvan. Robert McTaggart of Glenauchie, near Straiton, was known in his later years for regaling listeners with tales of the days when he had driven sheep to market on foot - sometimes as far away as Lanark – sleeping by the roadside along the way. And back at Barr, Jimmy McTaggart herded the Changue hill until a sudden ill-turn, while gathering sheep for dipping, ended his life in July 1943. He was 55 years old. Jimmy's body was discovered by his neighbours no more than a short distance from the cairn marking the spot where thirty years previously his younger brother, Christopher, had perished in the snow.

PEOPLE & PLACES

The Deil's Back Door

Auchtitench was hard to reach. That was the point. If you were a Covenanter looking for a bolt-hole in seventeenth century Ayrshire with the King's dragoons hot on your tail, then you could hardly have chosen better.

Even today – more than three centuries on – it's still not an easy place to get to. The tarmac fizzles out some six miles away at Dalblair, a hamlet whose assortment of old and modern houses overlooks the meeting-point of two moorland streams, the Guelt and the Glenmuir. From there one needs to walk along a stony track that follows the winding Glenmuir Water.

There are no occupied houses beyond Dalblair. A couple of moorland miles will bring you to the old farm of High Dalblair, crumbling among a stand of tall trees, and two more to Glenmuirshaw, likewise abandoned. A settlement with a long history, in prehistoric times a stone-chipping factory operated nearby while in the late seventeenth century the renowned Covenanting minister, Rev. James Renwick, conducted open-air services on the farm's grassy holms. Looking over the riverside meadows, it is easy to imagine the happy haymakers of yesteryear and hear their busy cries. Now no sound breaks Glenmuirshaw's silence other than the baa-ing of blackface sheep and the cackle of grouse from the hill.

A mile or so further north-east is another ruined house, High Shaw, sitting on the banks of the Thorter Burn. But to find Auchtitench, you need to to stick with the Glenmuir Water, bypassing a complex of rees, or sheep-pens, before gingerly negotiating a rickety wooden bridge where dippers bob and chirrup from boulders mid-stream.

This is where the going starts to get tough. A series of telegraph poles (curiously without a cable or any obvious destination) leads across broken country into a steep-sided cleft, The Deil's Back Door, whose shaley cliffs plunge to where the Glenmuir Water takes a spectacular tumble over the Connor Linn. Apparently shunned by grazing sheep, the surrounding slopes can be rich with late summer colour: pink yarrow, growing in isolated clumps, lilac scabious, and the delicate white stars of parnassus grass. It was here, in the safety and seclusion of the ravine, that the Covenanting preacher and prophet, Alexander Peden, is said to have baptised many of the children born among the surrounding Threeshire Hills.

But Peden and his contemporaries would surely have recognised little of the landscape that now faces one at the head of the gorge. Beyond a sweep of brown moorland, a rampart of mature conifers stretches left and right as far as the eye can see, well into neighbouring Lanarkshire and Dumfriesshire, screening from view the headwaters of the Glenmuir. Somewhere behind that dark curtain lie the ruins of Auchtitench.

Stories about the old place abound, few – if any – verifiable. Among the more plausible is the belief that it might have acted as a safe-house for James Renwick and other Covenanters during the killing time of the 1680s. Close to the lonely farmstead, the government-appointed curate of Kirkconnel, Rev. Samuel Mowat, is said to have defected to the Covenanting cause following a chance wayside encounter with a charismatic stranger – one Alexander Peden, as it turned out. But thanks to activities of the foresters, longstanding rumours of a secret vault in the vicinity of Auchtitench – haunted, some have alleged, and tenanted periodically by brandy-smugglers and fugitive Covenanters alike - are unlikely ever to be verified.

Despite nature's takeover bid, it is still possible to identify the remnants of Auchtitench. Half-hidden by tall nettles and bracken, the corner of one gable remains upright, its stones squared, balanced and positioned by masons long ago. Most of the remaining walls have collapsed into heaps of mossy rubble. From its destitute state, it is hard to believe that the farm was tenanted as recently as the 1920s when James Hope shepherded the surrounding moors and hills.

In the past the Threeshire Hills were always remote, but not necessarily cut off. Remarkably, in the mid-nineteenth century a teacher was employed at Auchtitench, 1,200 feet above sea-level, who was paid an annual salary of £1 by Auchinleck School Board to instruct what must have been no more than a handful of pupils. In 1890 the Threeshire District Association was formed to set up joint-schooling for children in adjoining areas of Auchinleck parish, Ayrshire; Kirkconnel, Dumfriesshire; and Crawfordjohn, Lanarkshire; but the scheme quickly foundered over the thorny issue of funding. Latterly, however, isolated Ayrshire pupils had crossed into Dumfriesshire for schooling at Fingland, a fee being paid on their behalf by Auchinleck School Board.

In later years the Threeshire Hills suffered a steady loss of population, as one by one the old farms fell vacant - Clocklowie, Friarminnon, Penbreck and, of course, Auchtitench - too isolated to be deemed compatible with modern life. Rugged all-terrain vehicles made tending livestock possible from afar, while vast Sitka spruce plantations thrive with minimal attention. The jobs moved out, and the people, of course, went with them.

A Monumental Mystery

No-one can say for sure who built the Shaw Monument, or pinpoint with any degree of accuracy the date of its completion. Even the old tower's purpose remains something of a mystery. Its name doesn't provide much of a clue, deriving simply from the farm whose land it stands on. One thing seems certain. So changed are its surroundings that whoever was responsible for the monument's existence would face a tough task in recognising it today.

Situated on rising ground on the outskirts of Prestwick, the Shaw Monument is a cylindrical stone structure, 50 feet in height, with a three-arc crown piece placed across its airy summit. An internal staircase gives access to a rooftop gallery which in its day would have afforded broad views across peaceful farmland. Today, by contrast, it overlooks a busy stretch of the runway attached to Prestwick Airport. Sandwiched among the factory units of a modern industrial estate, the tower stands adjacent to a high-tech aero-engineering plant whose owners during the 1970s rescued their old neighbour from probable oblivion when they secured and repaired its crumbling masonry. Beyond a high barbed wire fence, the airport control tower isn't far away.

Some historians believe the tower to be of nineteenth century origin, while others are inclined to place it rather earlier. The august Ayrshire Archaeological and Natural History Society concede rather limply that 'records are lacking.' With evidence so thin on the ground, folk memory and guess-work have been used in order to plug the gaps. One theory contends that the monument was the work of a local hawking enthusiast, constructed for use as a look-out in connection with falconry. Others believe that some landowner raised the tower purely as a folly, designed for nothing more than visual effect. More banally, the suggestion has even been made that the monument might simply be the elaborate cover of a coalmine's ventilation shaft. Whatever the truth, the Shaw Monument and its early origins have been exercising minds now for some considerable time.

The Shaw Monument

During the late 1950s, when officials of the Ordnance Survey were revising maps in the vicinity, they invited the local community to supply details concerning the monument's past. Their request drew a blank, it seems, until two employees happened to attend a lecture entitled 'Auld Ayr' in the Sandgate Church Hall. The speaker that evening was Andrew Shearer, a local tradesman, fitness enthusiast and well-known public speaker, who proceeded to offer up a plausible account of the tower's beginnings.

Some time ago, Shearer told his audience, the proprietor of the nearby country estate of Auchincruive, Richard Oswald, was a gentleman much given to persecution of the local fox population. His wife was equally devoted to the chase, being in the habit of enthusiastically accompanying her husband on horseback. However with the passage of time Mrs. Oswald faced increasing difficulty in keeping up with the body of the hunt, until finally the day arrived when a day's riding was quite beyond her. So, rather than leave his wife brooding glumly at home, Oswald constructed a viewing-tower on a hillock on Shaw Farm, from the summit of which she could still enjoy the pleasures of the hunt without incurring the discomfort that attended a day in the saddle. And that, suggested the Sandgate speaker, was the origin of the Shaw Monument – though he was careful to add that his version of events was 'based purely on hearsay.'

Records show that the first Oswald of Auchincruive was indeed named Richard, a wealthy businessman in his late fifties at the time he acquired the estate in 1764. Born into a family of prosperous Glasgow merchants, he had amassed a sizeable personal fortune largely through trade with the American colonies. He lined his pockets still further when he married Mary Ramsay, a well-heeled heiress whose father owned extensive plantations in America and the West Indies. Richard moved in elevated circles, numbering among his acquaintances the economist Adam Smith, as well as Lord Shelburne, the British Prime Minister, and the foremost American of the day, Benjamin Franklin. Such indeed was the Prime Minister's faith in the well-connected Scot that he entrusted to him the peace negotiations that followed the American War of Independence, a treaty being duly signed in Paris in November 1782. Richard Oswald died two years later, leaving behind his widow, but no children. His gravestone is to be found in the country churchyard of St Quivox, a short distance from his home at Auchincruive.

However, it would be overly hasty to conclude that Richard Oswald was without question the builder of the tower. For, following Mary Ramsay's death four years after her husband, Auchincruive passed by a roundabout succession to the son of Richard's nephew, rather confusingly also named Richard. This second Richard Oswald married Lucy Johnston, a noted Edinburgh belle whose beauty and musical accomplishments prompted no less a personage than Robert Burns to praise her as 'that incomparable woman,' and who had her portrait painted by Sir Henry Raeburn. Lucy Johnston died tragically young, succumbing to tuberculosis in 1798 in Lisbon where she had gone in an effort to restore her health. Perhaps then it was Lucy, not Mary, who gazed down from the Shaw tower, too infirm to follow the hunt despite her tender years.

A glance at the Oswald family tree does nothing to clarify the situation, revealing a bewildering array of Richards, no fewer than four of whom were known to have lived at Auchincruive. To compound the problem, a local minister, Rev. Kirkwood Hewat, recorded in the 1890s that the estate factor at the time maintained that the Shaw Monument predated the arrival of the Oswalds at Auchincruive. But how far back to go? Four hundred years of Cathcarts reach back until they meet the Wallaces of the fourteenth century - related, some say, to William Wallace. And while few, if any, have suggested the tower goes back that far, it is clear nonetheless that it's had a good, long time to nurture its ability to baffle.

Not so long ago a story did the rounds about an American pilot who had just completed his first ever landing at Prestwick Airport. As he taxied towards the terminal building, the crumbling outline of the Shaw Monument caught his attention. 'Say, what's the old hulk on the hill?' he asked a local member of the crew. Evidently the pilot was unaware of a leg-pull being hatched. 'Why,' came the reply, 'that's the old air traffic control tower!' 'Well now,' the pilot was heard to murmur, 'ain't that just somethin'...'

The Stones of Knockbain

In the year 1821 Mexicans gained their independence from Spain after a long and violent struggle. The emperor of France, Napoleon Bonaparte, died that same year, in lonely exile on the far-flung isle of St Helena. Cloistered in his London studio, John Constable added his final brushstrokes to 'The Haywain', his vision in oils of a rural English idyll. And on the heathery slope of an unremarkable Scottish hillside ten drystane dykers straightened their backs and stepped back to survey their handiwork, noting – surely with some pride - that their names and their efforts had been preserved for posterity in stone.

When Paul and Julie Secord acquired the farm of Knockbain nearly 170 years later, they were all too aware that they had taken on a considerable task. The farm had been bought over by the Forestry Commission in 1960 and since then the house and steading had been entirely neglected. The Commission's tenant until 1990, an elderly gentleman whose preferred mode of transport was a horse and cart, had clearly not been one to instigate home improvements.

Born in Canada, Paul had spent his early years in Ontario where his Scottish antecedents, through intermarriage with the French-Canadian community, had acquired for him his fairly unusual surname. After moving to England, Paul spent a busy working life managing large-scale plumbing and heating projects in the London area, but he never forgot an elderly relative in Canada - probably in her eighties at the time - spinning tales of her native Scotland, a place which developed something approaching mythical status in the impressionable young boy's mind. Had she only known it, Great-Auntie Lizzie had sown a seed which would lie dormant a good many years before finally taking root in 1990 when he and his wife, Julie, had their offer accepted for the farm of Knockbain.

It came about purely by chance. Despite having no farming experience whatsoever, Paul and Julie had set their hearts on acquiring a bolt-hole in the Scottish countryside, a small farm where they might periodically escape the hurly-burly of their busy city lives. While holding out for the right property, they happened to attend a family wedding in Sheffield where Paul met Scottish relatives, farming folk from Bargrennan in Galloway, who spoke of a small Ayrshire farm which was currently on the market. From its description, it sounded to Paul as though Knockbain might just fit the bill.

He recalls his first speculative visit, turning off the twisting A714 at Pinmore and driving along the tiny, single-track road that rambles through open sheep-pastures before dipping after a few miles into the wooded glen of the Lendal Water. The approach to Knockbain was undeniably picturesque but only after Paul had nosed up the final slope and switched off his car engine did the full beauty of the farm's situation reveal itself. From its elevated position, the house commanded a clear view north over the Water of Lendal to the summit of the Grey Hill beyond, while round to the west a blue ribbon of sea was visible through a conveniently-placed gap in the hills. Although it was obvious that Knockbain required urgent upgrading, Paul was instantly hooked. The farm was exactly what he had been dreaming of.

Even on that very first visit, Paul quickly became aware that there was something unusual about Knockbain. Composing a photograph from high on the slope behind the house - the resulting print now framed and on display on his sitting-room wall - he was puzzled to notice three unshaped stones, spaced as the corners of an inverted triangle, which protruded from the gable end of the byre. At the bottom of the triangle, the largest stone had suffered considerable erosion but still bore a strange resemblance to a human skull, or perhaps the grotesque form of a gargoyle. Not acting as a water spout, however, the stone's purpose was unclear.

The three mysterious stones were no more than the first in a series of surprises that Knockbain had in store. As Paul and Julie spent time getting to know their new home, they unearthed a number of messages from the past. On the west wall of the byre, facing into the close, a square-ish stone located just below eye-level records the year - 1829 - before adding in neatly-carved lettering that the building was 'Erected by Anthony and Thomas.' Perhaps surprisingly no surname is given but an adjacent expanse of unmarked stone suggests the possibility that the inscription may for whatever reason have remained incomplete. A few paces away, a second stone is similarly dated - AD 1829 - with a mark alongside identifying the stonemason as well as a curious heart-shaped engraving, a few inches tall.

Stone in Knockbain Dyke

On the opposite side of the close, a longer inscription emerged recently from beneath multiple layers of whitewash, recording the fact that the stable had been 'Built by William Turner and Thomas Logan 1830' - a year later than the construction of the byre. A strange little poem follows:

> For this poor land brave Wallace fought
> Though his reward on earth was nought
> But now he's gane above the sky
> Where southron foes he does defy.

Any connection that Knockbain might have had with the activities of Scotland's hero is unclear. We can only conclude that its builders simply felt an urge to preserve their patriotism in stone.

Shortly after taking over the running of Knockbain, Paul was all set to embark on a drainage scheme when he received a communication from Scottish Natural Heritage. Part of his eighty acres, he was advised, was to be designated as a Site of Special Scientific Interest due principally to its remarkable richness in native flowers and their associated wildlife. Paul admits to having had initial reservations, suspecting at the time that SSSI restrictions might undermine the farm's ability to operate as a going concern.

But with the passage of time his attitude mellowed. Business boomed in London, allowing Paul and Julie to relocate full-time to Knockbain and to tend their farm with nature, rather than simply profit, in mind. Each year small numbers of cattle are released on to the hill during late summer where they graze and where Paul believes that the trampling of their cloven hooves plays an important role in anchoring wild flower seeds. Then, during the early months of the year, the beasts are removed before the onset of the new growing season and the hill is left to its own devices - with dramatic results.

Today the farm is brimming with birdsong, the hill-ground in season a carpet of colour. Orchids compete in shades of purple with mats of wild thyme and vivid cushions of bell heather. Yellow spears of bog asphodel grow in profusion, while the scabious flowers present myriad butterflies - including exquisite blues - with a sweet temptation. Everything on the moorland looks rosy though, as Paul admits, the SSSI isn't entirely without its problems, his greatest bugbear probably being the invasive bracken which can increase by some 5% a year, he estimates, if unhindered. Young hawthorns have sprung up, probably from seeds dispersed by wild birds, and these need to be cleared. But notwithstanding the difficulties, the land is clearly in good heart and nature is responding with gusto.

Of Knockbain's original 400-odd acres, just over three-quarters disappeared under conifers during the 1960s and, when partial felling took place recently, one of the farm's hidden wonders re-emerged into daylight. On the southern periphery of the conifer plantation, a march-dyke separates Knockbain from the neighbouring farm of Knockdaw, doubling up in the past as the boundary-line between the adjoining estates of Carleton and Bargany. Obscured for some 40 years by closely-planted Sitka spruce, a large, squared stone, built into the dyke, is inscribed as follows:

Erected by Sir Andrew Cathcart & Sir H. D. Hamilton. Undertakers & Builders: John Dick, James Campbell, Anthony & Robert Milroys, Gilbert Dick, John McWhirter; Carters William Milroy, Thomas Kennedy, David Galt, William McClure.

With sore fatigue we reached the head
& many a heavy stone we laid.
In unity we did agree
& on this stone our names shall be.

The year is added -*1821* - along with a mason's mark which appears similar to the one on the wall of the byre.

The existence of this memorial, with its simple dignity and understated pride, in a deserted spot among the hills might today seem a little surprising, but in times past its location would probably have felt a good deal less isolated. Nineteenth century maps show a cart-road stretching from the farm of Millenderdale (less than half a mile from Knockbain across the hill; more than three by road) over the shoulder of Knockdaw Hill and down to the farm of Garnaburn in the Stinchar valley and, though no trace of the old track now survives, an opening in the dyke a few short strides from the dykers' stone is likely to mark the route it followed. It was no coincidence that the men sited their memorial at the highest point of the dyke ('the head') but it must surely also have entered their calculations that a traveller between the Lendal and Stinchar Waters could hardly have passed without seeing it.

Knockbain is a special place whose landscape, flora and fauna have been preserved through the efforts of its dedicated twenty-first century guardians. But it is more than that. Through its uniquely-lettered stonework, it enables us to span the centuries and make contact with the past - not with those Cathcarts and Dalrymple-Hamiltons who simply owned the great estates; but rather with ordinary men, humble and frequently overlooked, who strained and sweated and shivered as they laboured a lifetime on the land but whose pride and humanity speak out loudly from the stones of Knockbain.

Tammie Raeburn of the Ark

A fairly obscure nineteenth century poem, John Ramsay's *Fasten's-E'en*, uses good broad Scots to paint a vivid tableau of the shenanigans that accompanied old Kilmarnock's Shrove Tuesday celebrations. These took place every year for five centuries or more until the Magistrates and Council finally put an end to them in 1831. Any connection with the festival's religious origins (as the day prior to the start of fasting associated with Lent) appeared to have been long forgotten. On the morning of Shrove Tuesday, proceedings got underway with rather a rumbustious ice-breaker. The town's horse-drawn fire-engines assembled at the Cross where large numbers of merry-makers were already gathered and, for a riotous hour or so, certain individuals were given the responsibility of hosing down with cold water anyone and everyone within reach.

Once the crowd was thoroughly wound up, not to say drenched, the day's events continued as town officials marched through the streets to the accompaniment of fife and drum, holding aloft as they did so a halberd from which were hung a cloth purse, a pair of leather breeches, a pair of shoes and a blue bonnet, items representative of Kilmarnock's principal trades. At the Town-house the marching crowds were joined by the town Bailies and Councillors who led the parade to an area in the vicinity of Kilmarnock House - possibly today's Howard Park - where Fasten's-E'en races were traditionally held. Cake and confectionery sellers hawked their wares among the crowd, and the town's 'light-fingered lads' weren't slow to seize the opportunity to mingle.

It wasn't unheard of, of course, for revellers to partake of a small refreshment or perhaps go so far as to hazard a modest wager on the outcome of one of the races. Men from the countryside, identifiable by 'plaid and dog', were often deemed the surest bet, brawnier of limb and fleeter of foot perhaps than their more sedentary cousins in town. A less savoury side to the festivities could be seen in the cock-fighting contests that sprang up in a variety of venues around the town, such barbaric tussles frequently umpired by - of all people - local schoolmasters who claimed by right any birds which fled the ring, known as 'fugies', plus the carcasses of those unfortunates killed during the fighting.   As the day wore on, drunkenness and disorder routinely broke out. To the vexation of the magistrates, the dykes used for drying laundry on the Town's Green were maliciously destroyed during the Fasten's-E'en revelry of 1775, an act for which four local glovers were subsequently prosecuted.

According to John Ramsay's poem, many out-of-towners were drawn to the annual extravaganza, hailing from such distant parts as Beansburn, Riccarton, Kilmaurs, Fenwick and even the far-flung towns of the Irvine valley. The Fasten's-E'en crowd must have made a motley brigade, but one figure consistently stood out from the rest. Dressed in clothes that consisted almost exclusively of patches and darns and with hair and beard uncut and uncared for, in John Ramsay's poem this 'craw-deil' - or walking scarecrow - attracts the attention of two gossiping townswomen. Who might this be, asks 'blear e'ed' Meg, 'sae tousy an' sae duddy'? It doesn't take her friend, fish-wife Jean, long to identify the kenspeckle figure. 'That's Tammie Raeburn o' the Ark,' she replies - far prouder of his rags, she goes on, than any smart young man in the latest fashions. And there is little doubt that Tammie Raeburn did indeed cut a distinctive figure in and around Kilmarnock during the early part of the nineteenth century.

For all his tatterdemalion appearance, Tammie was in fact a small-scale local landowner. Following the death of his father in the early years of the nineteenth century, he had fallen heir to the modest smallholding of Holmhead, flanking the River Irvine two miles or so to the east of Kilmarnock. The dwelling house, a low, thatched building divided between its human occupants and their livestock, was locally nicknamed 'the Ark' - a Scots term signifying a chest in which meal or grain might be stored - which possibly gives the impression that Tammie's apartments were rather less than commodious. Unseen from the public road, the Ark was shrouded in ivy and screened by trees and bushes.

For details of Tammie Raeburn's life we are obliged to fall back on minor local writers of the nineteenth century whose accounts shed little light on his early years beyond the fact that he had been born in 1769 - the same year as both Napoleon and the Duke of Wellington, and precisely a decade after Robert Burns. Tammie's education extended no further than the basic skills of reading and writing and in due course he found employment as a labourer on local farms and also as a gardener on the estate of Shawhill, situated just across the river from Holmhead - he was said to have used stilts for the purpose of commuting. By all accounts, Tammie Raeburn was a strapping young man, of good appearance, who stood over six feet tall. As far as can be told, his life at this time appears to have run along fairly conventional lines, though there is a story - quite possibly apocryphal - which demonstrates how a debilitating shyness effectively put paid to his attempted courtship of a neighbour's daughter. He never subsequently married.

It looks very much as though something in Tammie's life went badly awry. Some have claimed that his problems started when he became involved in a dispute with a neighbouring farmer who had insisted on closing off a footpath which Tammie was in the habit of using on his way to and from the Ark. Matters escalated to the extent that the affair ended up in court, probably around 1816, and when the judge's decision went against him, Tammie is said to have taken it very much to heart. It has been suggested that this was what prompted his resolution neither to cut his hair nor change his clothing until such time as the wrongs against him were righted. Whether or not there is any truth in the theory, it is at least possible that the sense of injustice that dogged Tammie for the rest of his life may be traced back to this time.

He did eventually achieve at least some degree of redress. Returning late from Kilmarnock one evening, this same neighbour chose to cut across Tammie's land, a curiously insensitive move that apparently was made under the influence of drink. Quite understandably, Tammie was outraged and did his utmost to force the man to retrace his steps. Hard blows were exchanged. Once again the matter came to court and on the day of the trial, presumably much to everyone's surprise, Tammie presented himself dressed in a respectable suit of clothes, though apparently he could not be prevailed upon under any circumstances to trim his hair or beard. In contrast to his previous experience in court, this time the decision was made in Tammie's favour when the offending neighbour was convicted of assault and Tammie himself awarded damages. Strangely, though, the justice of the verdict appears to have done nothing to restore his faith in the law.

Over the years Tammie was obliged to negotiate his way through a number of brushes with authority. On one occasion he found himself locked up for refusing point-blank to pay poor rates - statutory taxes which were earmarked for relief of the poor - and only when the sum outstanding was paid by a well-wisher on his behalf was he released from Irvine Jail. Further problems resulted - strangely enough - from his aversion to trimming which, it became clear, extended far beyond the sphere of personal grooming. During the course of a heated exchange, he threatened to shoot a farm-worker whom he had discovered in the act of cutting a hedge which Tammie regarded as entirely his own property, but which his neighbour believed to be a boundary marker. In this instance he got off with a fine, something that would have pained him grievously nonetheless as his love of money was legendary.

Through time Tammie became known by the name of 'The Ayrshire Hermit', though the circumstances of his life suggest otherwise. He did not, it seems, live in total isolation but shared his home with an elderly woman (of whom nothing appears to be known) whose responsibility it was to attend to his dairy and domestic matters. He was known to have a fondness for animals and kept a number of cats as pets. Most unexpected of all, his home was frequented by a regular stream of visitors, for whom he provided refreshments - at a price - landing himself in trouble on one occasion for supplying alcohol in contravention of the licensing laws. He appeared to enjoy performing for his guests, feeding tame birds in his garden with crumbs which they pecked from his beard and from between his lips. (He was, nevertheless, quite prepared to use his ancient firearm to do away with any of the feathered flock which had the temerity to be caught pilfering from the garden, and he prided himself on the skill of his marksmanship.) He was said to have taken pleasure in social banter, and fancied himself apparently as something of a wag. Though not by habit a church-goer, he enjoyed company, and the attention that his eccentric appearance stimulated he appeared to welcome. In 1839, at an age of nearly 70, he was successful in obtaining a ticket for the famous Eglinton tournament where he enjoyed himself immensely milling with the holiday crowds. The fetching good looks of Georgiana Seymour, the Queen of Love and Beauty, were said to have made a strong impression on him and, long after the medieval pageant was over, he treasured as a souvenir the ticket which had granted him admission. All in all, for a man deemed a hermit, Tammie was possessed of an improbably sociable streak.

Whether Tammie ever ran into William Stevenson, another Kilmarnock worthy in the early nineteenth century, does not appear to be on record. Originally from the parish of Dunlop, Stevenson lived in Glen Street, a mason by trade, who opted, for reasons unknown, to abandon his chosen profession in favour of begging. In 1887 he and his wife were said to have parted on rather unusual terms, a condition being set whereby the first of the two to propose reconciliation must pay the other a forfeit of £100. The prospect of such a penalty must have acted as a powerful deterrent as apparently they never came face to face again. During his final years, Stevenson became bedridden as a result of a painful condition known as 'the stone' (kidney-stones or gallstones perhaps) and only during his final days on this earth, aged 87, did the full extent of his eccentricity become apparent. Aware of imminent death, he gave instructions for the purchase of a large quantity of provisions and spirits for consumption at his forthcoming funeral. He then summoned a local joiner and ordered a coffin to be built to his specific requirements, emphasising in particular the need for the woodwork to be entirely watertight. Finally he instructed the Riccarton gravedigger to locate a plot which was spacious, comfortable and dry, and content presumably at last, he lay back and proceeded to expire within the next few hours.

When the dead man's effects were gone through, an enormous quantity of gold and silver coins came to light - crowns, guineas and dollars - as well as bonds and securities which, when combined with cash in hand, totalled some £900, a vast sum in 1817. Under the terms of Stevenson's will, the greater part of the money was to be divided amongst distant relatives, but £20 had been set aside for his elderly housekeeper and a sufficient sum earmarked to cover expenses associated with his funeral purvey. It wouldn't be cheap. He had left explicit instructions that an invitation was to be extended to Ayrshire's beggars - all of them - and any who turned up were to receive a gratuitous payment of either sixpence or threepence, dependent on age. When the word got out, an almighty convocation of 'gangrels' and 'gaun-bodies' gathered in Kilmarnock from far and wide who, following the funeral ceremony, embarked on a colossal spree during which they were treated to copious quantities of food and drink, served up in a local barn. Predictably the evening that ensued was a roistering one, enlivened by all manner of wild and drunken antics. As for William Stevenson - a man whose lifestyle was, to say the least, parsimonious - at the end of the day he was given a send-off that was both spectacular and in all probability unique. Be that as it may, it is likely that the townsfolk of Kilmarnock breathed a collective sigh of relief over the next few days as their dishevelled guests gradually sobered up and departed.

In years to come no less a flow of visitors descended on Tammie Raeburn's Ark, their motives only to be guessed at, though it seems likely that a certain number would have come simply to gawk and snigger. Inevitably Tammie's credulous nature led to him being exploited, and there were those, predictably, who derived pleasure from hoodwinking their host outrageously, or plying him with alcohol - which he did not normally drink - or making him the too-easy butt of their practical jokes. His miserly reputation was something else that led to trouble. A year before Tammie's death, an armed gang broke into the Ark and, in what must have been a deeply unpleasant experience, forced him at gunpoint to hand over his money and valuables. Their objective achieved, the gang members made off with a haul of some £30 in gold, silver and copper, firing their guns in the air as a scornful farewell. Sometime later, however, one of the ruffians, Thomas Duffy, was apprehended and sentenced to ten years' transportation for his crimes, while his wife was found guilty of reset and jailed for six months. A third member of the gang managed to evade capture and was outlawed by the court. Whether Tammie's beloved money was recovered is not on record.

Viewed through twenty-first century eyes, there seems little doubt that Tammie Raeburn suffered from significant mental health problems, and his ever-present feeling of persecution suggests possibly some kind of paranoid condition. Rather pathetically, he vested his hopes in Queen Victoria herself who, he was entirely confident, would obtain for him instant redress for the injustices he had suffered, if only he could alert her to his sad plight. In an effort to open channels of communication he posted to the monarch the gift of a silver coin, dating from the reign of Elizabeth I of England, and was disappointed to receive in return nothing more than a standard, impersonal acknowledgement.

Late in life Tammie suffered a broken left arm after slipping on ice and, having no faith in the medical profession, he declined the attentions of a doctor, losing, as a result, virtually all use of the arm. His fear and paranoia seemed to intensify with increasing age and appeared to contribute to an overall decline. His matted hair and beard grew snowy-white, and his once-brawny physique diminished markedly. Finally on 23 June 1843, at the age of 73, Tammie Raeburn passed away, leaving behind him as he did so all of his worldly cares and anxieties. Such money and property as he possessed were divided among his relations, and his land was sold and subsequently absorbed into the estate of Grougar. Somehow it made for a sad ending to the story of one of Ayrshire's most singular, not to say tragic, characters.

Wallace's Forgotten Tower

It was a late summer evening in the year 1297, and darkness was dropping. A group of horsemen reined in on a grassy hill-top, and turned to scan the coastline below them. The sky was bright from a blaze of mighty flames that leapt from the barns where enemy forces had been garrisoned in numbers: several thousand English soldiers had paid a hefty price for the treachery of their king, Edward I. One of the shadowy riders was the Guardian of Scotland, William Wallace himself. He gazed down at the conflagration and offered his terse assessment of a job well done: 'The barns o' Ayr burn weil!' And from that night onward the breezy summit they stood on became known as Barnweil Hill.

Well, maybe it wasn't quite like that. Although the story has long been embedded in Ayrshire folklore, the chances are that the name, Barnweil, was in use long before the famous firing of Ayr barracks. But that small detail wasn't enough to stop one local landowner from digging deep in his pocket. William Patrick of Roughwood commissioned Robert Snodgrass, mason and builder in Beith, to devise a tribute to William Wallace in stone, and the spiky Gothic tower that Snodgrass came up with in 1855 can still be seen on Barnweil Hill today.

The monument's scenic location may have helped to smooth over any minor historical quibbles. Its internal staircase spirals up to where a narrow trapdoor opens on to a roof-top gallery, some 60 feet above ground level. Four splendid stone thistles were originally the highest points of the tower until a red beacon light for Prestwick Airport was added – something mason Snodgrass could scarcely have predicted.

Engraved on the wall in small, neat lettering are Wallace's legendary words as he watched the barns go up in smoke. Nowadays the outlook is likely to be more peaceful with the hills of Arran and Kintyre rising from the Firth of Clyde and occasional matchstick planes dipping in slow motion towards Prestwick Airport. Inland, a patchwork of farms stretches out to hilly horizons, all the way round from the rolling Galloway skyline to the distant blue bowl of Ben Lomond and, in good visibility, jagged Highland

Wallace Memorial, Barnweil Hill

ridges beyond. The view from the top of the tower is undeniably fine, but it's one that no-one has enjoyed for some time.

Unfortunately, modern-day visitors to Barnweil will find a notice, posted by the local authority, which intimates that, 'In the interests of health and safety, Barnweil Monument has been closed until further notice.' There is no apparent urgency - the notice dates back several years – and the tower is starting to wear a distinctly uncared for appearance.

Things weren't always thus at Barnweil. In the past the monument could be a busy place with open-days and flag-flying ceremonies on the anniversaries of Wallace's most famous victories. In August 1955, the year of the tower's centenary, Tarbolton Literary Society held a meeting there to mark the 650th anniversary of Wallace's execution. Rousing speeches were delivered, votes of thanks given, and the proceedings rounded off by a moving open-air rendition of 'Scots Wha Hae.' No more.

William Wallace cast a long shadow over this corner of Scotland, and even in these post-Braveheart times his name still bubbles up from time to time. Controversy rages periodically over the claim that he was born at Ellerslie, Ayrshire, and not Elderslie, Renfrewshire, the traditional frontrunner. A commemorative stone stands outside Kilmarnock Fire-Station, marking the birthplace of Malcolm Wallace - 'Father of Scotland's Hero' - and road signs on the outskirts of the town boldly claim 'This is Wallace country.' Such enduring interest makes it all the more puzzling why the Barnweil Monument should simply have been left to languish.

The neglect of Barnweil marks the fading of one man's vision. The monument's Victorian patron was someone who recognised the value of maintaining ties with the past and who was willing to bankroll his beliefs. Fourteen years after the construction of Barnweil Tower, 'Mr Patrick of Roughwood' appears on a list of subscribers to the newly-completed National Wallace Monument in Stirling, detailing a posthumous sum of £600 that was donated in his name. His staunch commitment stands in marked contrast to today's indifference. William Patrick for one kept faith with Wallace's memory, even after death.

An Ayrshire Confederate

When *Life in the Confederate Army* was first published in 1887, the *Boston Sunday Herald* declared it 'the best story of the Southern side yet written', and went on to identify its little-known author as 'an English civil engineer'. The newspaper could have done with checking its facts a little more thoroughly. No Englishman, the book's author was in fact William Watson, a man born within earshot of the breaking waves of the Firth of Clyde.

Watson's father, it is true, had his origins south of the border. A landscape gardener to trade, Henry Watson had come to Scotland in 1820 to carry out work on the Ashcraig Estate, just south of Skelmorlie, where he would remain for the next forty years. Not long after his arrival, Henry's son, William, was born, though sadly the child's mother died while he was still in infancy. Henry subsequently remarried and went on to rear a large family in his cottage at Halketburn. It is possible, though, that he wasn't quite the unassuming family man that he might have seemed. Henry's name was linked with the trade in 'Arran water' - illicitly distilled whisky, slipped across the Firth under cover of darkness - which may go some way to explaining his son, William, embarking on a career which was a good deal more adventurous than landscape gardening.

The proprietor of Ashcraig, Andrew Donaldson Campbell, had formerly been a sugar-planter in the West Indies and this is likely to have influenced young William's decision to emigrate to the islands around 1845. He found employment in the Caribbean as a civil engineer and occasional ship's captain before moving on again some years later, this time to Louisiana where he became part-owner of a sawmill and steamboat company in Baton Rouge. When the American Civil War broke out in 1861, at first glance Watson might not have seemed the most likely backer of the Confederate cause. For a start he was opposed to secession from the United States and, on top of that, no advocate for slavery, his West Indian years having convinced him that free men made perfectly satisfactory workers. Although he had never taken American citizenship, Watson volunteered nonetheless for service with the local Pelican Rifles, not only through a natural sympathy for the underdog but also because he felt that his honour as a Scotsman was at stake. Like so many others at the time, it is possible that he was also motivated by a thirst for adventure.

In late April 1861 the Pelicans left Baton Rouge for training at Camp Walker near New Orleans where the division was rebranded as Company K, 3rd Louisiana Infantry, with Watson as first sergeant. In his published account of the war years, he would later recall that, of the 86 men in his company, fewer than half had any connection with slavery. After a month's training, Company K was posted north to Arkansas where there was believed to be a threat of Northern invasion. Although some of the men were disappointed not to be heading for the front line in Virginia, most were at least relieved to leave Camp Walker behind, with its heat, humidity and clouds of voracious mosquitoes. In Arkansas Watson's company became part of Brigadier General Benjamin McCulloch's Army of the West and the Louisiana men quickly developed a fierce loyalty to their veteran commander.

During an engagement at Oakhill, Missouri, McCulloch's troops combined with the Missouri State Guard to win a notable victory over the North, with the volunteers of the 3rd Louisiana Infantry distinguishing themselves when they routed a hard-bitten battalion of US regulars. While attempting to take possession of an enemy flag, Watson received a sword-cut to his wrist but he simply bound his wound with a makeshift bandage and carried on fighting. Later in the same engagement he sustained a rather more serious injury. 'A ball took me in the pit of the stomach,' he wrote later, 'and for a few minutes I remembered no more.' Before entering his body, it was found that the bullet had passed through Watson's water-canteen and dented a brass plate on his belt.

The severity of his injury was not enough to end Watson's involvement in the war. By March 1862 he was sufficiently recovered to take part in the Battle of Pea Ridge, a disastrous day when Confederate forces virtually collapsed and General McCulloch was fatally shot. Watson was one of those who survived and travelled on to Tennessee, arriving too late to participate in the blood-soaked two-day encounter at Pittsburg Landing. In May he was involved in a final skirmish at Farmington, Mississippi, before completing his year's military service and obtaining his discharge papers in July. Noted thereon was the observation that he was 'indebted to the Confederate States $3.25 on account of shoes.' There is reason to believe that any debt owed by Watson to his adopted homeland had been more than settled in full.

Discharge from the army, however, didn't mark the end of Watson's efforts on behalf of the Confederacy. With much of the south now under enemy control, he travelled by riverboat from Baton Rouge to New Orleans where he obtained, from the acting British consul, George Coppell, confirmation of his British citizenship though, as things turned out, it didn't do him much good. Back in Baton Rouge, he saw his livelihood go up in smoke when Northern troops set the city alight, leaving him no option but to re-join the army, this time as a private. Within a day of his arrival at the front, however, he sustained a leg-wound and was taken captive by enemy forces. Following treatment in a Northern field hospital, he was fortunate to be paroled fairly quickly, thanks to the intervention of a sympathetic Scots major who happened to be fighting on the opposite side. Once again Watson left the military and for a time procured a living through carrying out engineering works on local sugarcane plantations. When unusually high water levels flooded the sugarfields and put an end to his activities, he was forced to make his way back to New Orleans in order to seek work.

Oakhill, Skelmorlie

It was the following phase of Watson's life that prompted many to identify him as the inspiration behind the swashbuckling Captain Rhett Butler in Margaret Mitchell's epic novel of the Civil War, *Gone with the Wind*. Unable to settle down to a humdrum, civilian existence, Watson spied an opportunity. During the war years exports from the Confederate States had been severely disrupted by the stranglehold imposed by a Northern naval blockade with the result that American cotton was trading in Europe at sky-high prices. Watson resolved to make use of the seafaring experience which he had acquired, both in Scotland and the West Indies, by becoming part-owner in June 1863 of a small schooner, the aptly-named *Rob Roy*, which he went on to captain in a number of risky voyages across the Gulf of Mexico, sneaking out consignments of cotton bales right from under the noses of US gunboats, then returning with the ship's hold jam-packed with arms and ammunition, blankets and clothing, plus a few additional morale-boosting luxuries such as tea and coffee.

Of course, running the naval blockade was no easy task and the crew of the Rob Roy had many a close shave. In his second book, *The Adventures of a Blockade-Runner*, Watson tells of a curious instance where the threat unexpectedly came from within. Observing strictest silence and navigating by the stars alone, the *Rob Roy* was in the process of slipping past an enemy gunboat after dark when all of a sudden - 'Cock-a-leery-lou!' - the crow of a cock, one of a number of fowls kept on board, rang out through the night. 'Confound that brute,' hissed Watson. 'Twist its neck.' The bird was silenced without delay.

Mercifully the cock's public broadcast went unnoticed by the enemy, but Watson records a curious consequence of the creature's moment of indiscretion. Some of his more superstitious crew-members attributed its untimely crowing to the malign influence of a cat which had recently materialised on board ship, no-one could say where from. Others, however, favoured the theory that the cock's eccentric behaviour was prompted by the presence of a clergyman, Father Ryan, who happened to be taking passage aboard the *Rob Roy*. Whatever its motivation, as Watson wryly observed, the poor bird's disagreeable fate was to be 'sentenced to death as a traitor.'

Watson captained the schooner for the best part of two years during the course of which he undertook three successful runs across the Gulf. Early in 1865 he parted company with his co-owner in fairly acrimonious circumstances, but when the *Rob Roy* duly came up for auction Watson was disappointed to find himself outbid - by his former partner, as became clear later. After a short spell of job-seeking, he went on to assume captaincy of the *Eagle*, a paddle-steamer whose logbook revealed familiar origins. In a previous, more peaceful existence, the *Eagle* had plied the waters between Glasgow, Rothesay and Brodick, until she was purchased by Confederates for the express purpose of running the Northern blockade.

Sometime later, while Watson was temporarily laid up in Tampico, Mexico, recovering from what he described as 'rather a mild case of smallpox', he was shocked to hear news of General Lee's surrender at Appomattox, Virginia, something he instantly recognised as a crushing blow to the Confederate cause. Travelling to Havana for confirmation, he learned of the near-total collapse of the Confederacy and realised that his days as a blockade-runner were over. When he put pen to paper a quarter-century later, Watson would describe the time he spent running the Northern blockade as 'on the whole rather an enjoyable occupation with something of the zest of yacht-racing.' Such was the coolness that had enabled him to shrug off terrors on the high seas, including enemy gunboats and tropical storms - not to mention, of course, subversive poultry.

Blockade-running had not, apparently, proved profitable. Watson claimed that when he studied his finances at the end of the Civil War he found that he had barely broken even. Be that as it may, when he returned home to Scotland a little later he found himself in a position to acquire a substantial house in Glasgow's Argyle Street and set himself up as a ship-builder in Greenock. Around the same time he purchased the paddle-steamer, *Lady Mary*, which he put to work on the busy Ardrossan to Brodick run. Life appeared to have turned full-circle when he returned to his native Skelmorlie and built three impressive villas, overlooking the Clyde, whose names - *Oakhill, Beechgrove* and *Pea Ridge* - would serve as a constant reminder of his Civil War experiences.

The last of these, *Pea Ridge*, was Watson's wedding-gift in 1871 to his new bride, Helen Milligan, a baker's daughter from Glasgow who was just over a decade his junior. In the comfort of their marital home, he set his memories to one side and settled down to the life of a prosperous Victorian industrialist and contented family-man. But the past refused to die and finally, as old age loomed, he surrendered himself to the task of committing his wartime experiences to paper. While Clyde puffers passed back and forth outside his window, Watson travelled, in imagination, back to the battlefields of the Civil War where he relived for his readers the smoke and thunder of a lost cause.

The Irvine Valley Egg-Collectors

In the days before they were married, my maternal grandmother and her chums would occasionally walk for pleasure to Eaglesham, twenty-odd miles there and back across the moor from their homes in Newmilns. Lace workers themselves, the chances are that the girls knew well enough that they were treading in the footsteps of Irvine valley weavers of times past who used this self-same route to convey the produce of their hand-looms to the merchants of Paisley and Glasgow. Were those old-time weavers to return to the moor today - or even the valley folk of my grandmother's generation - such is the transformation that the landscape has undergone that I suspect they would recognise little of their present-day surroundings.

Making for the Glasgow markets, the Ayrshire weavers were obliged to cross the easternmost stretch of the Fenwick Moor that lay between their homes in the Irvine valley and the village of Eaglesham, further north in Renfrewshire. Spilling into both Renfrewshire and Lanarkshire, the moor was bleak and virtually treeless, much of the land spongy and saturated and consequently presenting something of a hazard to the unwary traveller. On ground rising to more than 1,200 feet, winters were long and frequently severe and snow would commonly lie without melting well into spring. Formerly part of the Loudoun Estate, the peaty moorland farms were given over almost entirely to the rearing of blackface sheep with maybe a handful of hardy hill cattle alongside.

Yet in spite the moor's apparent hostility, it provided homes for a rich variety of wildlife. Heathery country offered suitable cover for small birds like the skylark and meadow-pipit, as well as for larger species such as grouse, both black and red. In the grassier areas the brown hare and his upland cousin, the white mountain hare, were found in abundance, while ducks and other waterfowl occupied the marshy zones and rush-ringed lochans. Kestrels and hen harriers patrolled the skies overhead.

With such natural abundance on their doorstep, it is hardly surprising that long country walks were favoured during their leisure hours by many of the local mill-workers who found themselves confined for long hours amid the clamour of the looms. Not everyone, mind you, who spent their free time combing the countryside had a strictly recreational motive. There were those who viewed the moors in their backyard as a large-scale, open-air larder and, despite the best efforts of local gamekeepers, it was no rare occurrence for a hare or a rabbit - perhaps even the odd gamebird - to find its way into a family cooking-pot in one of the valley towns.

But the real bonanza came around each spring when groups of men and boys from the valley took to the hills, normally on a fine Sunday in May, in order to take advantage of a remarkable seasonal windfall. Reliably each year, large numbers of black-headed gulls congregated on the moor where they formed vast, densely-packed colonies at traditional nesting-grounds. In the valley towns the ritual of springtime egg-collecting was a time-honoured tradition, and in times when food was less plentiful than today the birds' eggs were viewed as a welcome gift of nature.

A total of seven major gull nesting-areas existed on the moor, four of them within the boundaries of Ayrshire, as well as a number of other smaller sites. The birds were known to favour two distinct types of terrain. As might be expected, some colonies formed close to a body of water, such as the small, man-made tarn known at Brocklees Loch where a few pairs each year took advantage of the safety afforded by a small island. The circumstances at Gateside Loch, a few miles away, were similar. What was reckoned to be the largest colony was located at Lochfield Loch, a marshy pool a few miles north-east of Darvel where hundreds of pairs of gulls built their tightly-packed nests on the reedy margins of the water.

Other colonies had become established on stretches of moor known as 'quaking bogs' where the birds' security was assured not by open water, but rather by soft, waterlogged peat, notorious in local lore for having allegedly swallowed up entire sheep and cattle - even, it was said, horses and carts. Frequently fenced off, these boggy areas were known locally as 'the gulls' hags' - a 'hag' in the Scots language denoting a boggy moorland morass. The birds, of course, selected these spots for very good reasons and a degree of nerve, not to say ingenuity, was required of would-be egg-collectors.

To assist them in their task, the egg-collectors brought along certain equipment - some of it improvised for the occasion. Mobbed by a cloud of squawking gulls, men and boys would strip to their underwear before stepping out on to the hags, carrying with them large laundry-baskets or pails in which to deposit the eggs. Some of the collectors attached tablespoons to long wooden poles, such as broom handles, in order to extend their reach into more inaccessible areas. Perhaps the oddest piece of gear that was used consisted of two simple wooden boards which were secured to the wearer's feet. Operating along similar lines to a pair of snowshoes, the boards enabled an intrepid egg-collector to venture on to soft ground that under normal circumstances would be incapable of bearing his weight. Once a sufficient quantity of eggs had been gathered, they were carefully packed into the baskets and buckets, each layer of eggs padded by a cushion of moorland mosses in an effort to minimise breakages.

Of course, not every egg survived intact. A minor slip or a careless nudge might easily result in casualties, and it wasn't unheard of for the men's holiday mood to lead to the odd playful egg-fight. Eggs were plentiful, and one or two could easily be spared for the sake of a laugh or a practical joke. But for that great majority of eggs that did make it down to the valley in one piece, a number of possible fates awaited.

Predictably a fair proportion of the eggs ended up on the collectors' and their families' own tea-tables, boiled perhaps or made into an omelette or alternatively used as an ingredient in baking. Older valley folk remember their bright orange yolks, and recall that bakery goods would come out tinted by the richness of their colour. Strongly flavoured, they were not possibly to everyone's taste but, be that as it may, a lively trade in gulls' eggs was carried on nonetheless. While a certain percentage were supplied to local bakers, others found their way to Kilmarnock Market, and during the years of the Second World War yet more, it seems, made the 400-mile journey by train to London to be used in city bakeries. At a time of wartime rationing, such food from the wild provided the nation's stocks with a most acceptable boost.

Even after the war ended in 1945, the tradition of egg-collecting continued and, in spite of the huge quantity of eggs lifted each year, perhaps surprisingly the gulls never chose to abandon their traditional territory and the total number of birds did not visibly diminish, possibly kept stable by the second clutch of eggs which the species routinely layed. Change did not come to the gull-hags until the 1960s.

In June 1961 the Forestry Commission purchased 1,000 acres of moorland at Whiteleehill, an isolated sheep farm on the southern rim of the moor. As it turned out, this change of ownership was only the beginning. Within a quarter-century the Commission had increased its land-holding in the area to some 15,000 acres on which it established a forest of an estimated ten million commercial conifers. With the completion in 2009 of one of Europe's largest wind farms, the transformation of the moorland landscape was complete.

Of course, the consequences of afforestation weren't wholly negative. Bird species such as crossbill and redpoll, previously unknown in the area, moved in and secured a niche in the new ecosystem while, unconcerned by the proximity of giant turbines, foxes and roe-deer were found to thrive in their new surroundings. But the classic creatures of the moorland - peewit, mountain hare, red grouse and blackgame - either dropped dramatically in numbers or else they simply disappeared. Among the serried ranks of Sitka spruce the haunting cry of the curlew was no longer heard.

But what of the black-headed gull, the bird whose appearance each spring had prompted the valley egg-collectors into activity for more years than anyone cared to remember? Sadly, like the majority of its moorland companions, the black-headed gull proved incapable of surviving the Forestry Commission's ploughing and planting, and the speed with which it forsook its established haunts was nothing short of dramatic. For some years afterwards, odd pairs turned up, attempting to nest at scattered locations across the moor, but in time the gulls simply gave up, vanishing entirely from the locality and taking with them as they went a unique fragment of the Irvine valley's social history.

Hugh's Pirlie-Pig

When Hugh Kennedy Sloan turned the tractor ignition-key, his working day started much like any other. It was fine, summer weather, ideal for continuing the task of ploughing a stretch of Balligmorrie Hill, above the Stinchar valley, in preparation for reseeding. But as Hugh nosed his tractor uphill that sunny morning, he could scarcely have predicted that Friday, 3 June 1955 was a day that would become lodged in his memory for the rest of his life.

Hugh's uncle - also Hugh Kennedy Sloan - had bought Balligmorrie Farm from Pinmore Estate in 1927, leaving home soon after to assist in the running of his family's dairy business in Glasgow - and making his name and fortune in the process when he invented and patented a pioneering bottle-washing machine. Meanwhile, his younger brother, Alexander, continued to farm at Balligmorrie where he lived quietly with his sisters, Jessie Agnes and Margaret Jane. All three never married.

Born in March 1930, young Hugh spent his early years at Pinclanty, less than a mile up the Stinchar valley from Balligmorrie. Like many boys of his generation, he left school at 15 and went straight to Glasgow where he lived in lodgings for three years while he carried out a variety of duties at the Merkland Street creamery. Called up for national service in the late '40s, he was obliged to return to Ayrshire, against his wishes, to work on the land with Uncle Alec and, despite his disappointment at not seeing more active service, he was to remain at Balligmorrie for the following nine years. In the summer of 1955, Hugh was 25 years old.

At just over 700 feet above sea level, the land to be ploughed that June morning was some of the highest on the farm: a gently sloping, grassy oasis surrounded by spongy ground that sprouted rushes and occasional clumps of heather and bog myrtle. Used for grazing sheep and cattle, this 'green grun' on the hill', as Hugh described it, had not been ploughed in living memory, possibly never. He got down to business promptly, picking up from where he had left off the previous afternoon, but when he turned the tractor at the end of his first furrow, something unusual caught his eye.

What appeared to be a round stone – too round, Hugh thought – was lying beside a clump of rushes on the grass, something odd enough to make him decide to take a closer look. Stepping down from the tractor cab, he discovered not a stone but rather a small clay container, roughly spherical in shape and slotted as if to admit coins. A mere three inches or so in height, the little pot was russet-brown in colour though traces of greenish-yellow glaze could still be seen on its surface.

The top of the pot had been broken – not recently, Hugh thought – but its contents, whatever they might be, had been prevented from spilling by compacted soil and a shard of broken clay that acted as a stopper. Curious about what was inside, Hugh used his pocket-knife to prise the pot open and as soon as he was able to dislodge the fragment of broken clay, a small avalanche of coins spilled out, virtually paper-thin and apparently of great antiquity.

Hugh's Pirlie-Pig

It isn't every day that a treasure pot materialises out of nowhere. Hugh's theory is that it had been unearthed during his previous day's final furrow and had rolled a short distance downhill before coming to rest. If his guess is right, then the pot survived by luck alone: it would have been so very easy for the plough to have crushed the tiny object - and its existence never to have been known. However - red letter day or not, Hugh still had a job to do. Ever a practical man, he climbed back into his tractor cab, popped the pot and its contents into the toolbox and simply carried on ploughing.

Hugh's discovery wasn't the only unexpected article ever to emerge from the earth at Balligmorrie. In the aftermath of the Second World War a number of less welcome objects came to light, the legacy of army training exercises conducted in the area. On one notable occasion, Hugh recalled a local shepherd who stumbled across a live shell on the hill. Mercifully army personnel arrived in time to defuse it safely with no casualties reported.

When Hugh descended from Balligmorrie Hill with his day's work done and his remarkable find safely stowed in the toolbox, it so happened that Uncle George was visiting from Glasgow and when he returned to the city he took some of the coins with him, hoping to find out more about them. This was the point when things appear to have got a little out of hand. Somehow or other the Glasgow press got wind of the story of Hugh's marvellous find, in turn arousing the interest of the local police. In what looked like coordinated action, officers from the Ayrshire force turned up that same day on the doorstep at Balligmorrie.

Hugh well remembers the scene at Girvan Police Station when he was asked to make a sworn statement before the sheriff. Advised of the law relating to treasure trove, he suggested – a little mischievously, he admits - that his find technically didn't count as such on the grounds that the coins hadn't actually been buried when he first spotted them. The sheriff, he recalls, remained unimpressed.

The coins were accordingly transferred to Edinburgh where staff at the National Museum of Antiquities identified their earthenware container as a 'pirlie-pig', or money-box, similar in style and function to a modern-day piggy-bank. It was found to contain no fewer than 578 coins – pennies and placks (a small denomination roughly equivalent to a farthing) dating from the late medieval period, specifically the reigns of James III, IV and V of Scotland. Coins depicting James IV formed the majority, suggesting that the pig had been lost – or perhaps hidden - early in the reign of his son, James V, possibly, the experts inferred, between 1515 and 1520. Minted from billon, a silver-based alloy in common use at the time, the coins were exclusively of Scottish provenance, something fairly unusual in comparable hoards.

More than one fifth of the coins turned out to be varieties not previously recorded. Two placks in particular proved to be of special interest, having old English lettering and the head of James IV on one side, but contrasting Roman script on the reverse, more in the style of James V. Just over 200 items were deemed to be of sufficient interest to be added to the National Museum collection, varieties either previously unknown or pieces in better condition than those already held. The remaining coins, over 300 in all, were returned to Uncle Hugh as landowner, while young Hugh received a modest cash reward: 'the handsome sum of £30,' he comments wryly. Worth around £600 in today's money, certainly it doesn't seem generous.

Probably it shouldn't be too much of a surprise that the Balligmorrie hoard surfaced in what might seem like a lonely spot. People had been living out their lives among these south Ayrshire hills since long before the era of Hugh's pirlie-pig. In earlier times the Stinchar valley sustained a pastoral population whose ancient fail-dykes are still traceable today as low, green mounds, thrown into dramatic relief by the setting sun. Hugh told me of an occasion when out of curiosity he had dug down into what he called a 'turf house on the hill' and found traces of charcoal, almost certainly the remains of a domestic hearth. A short distance over the hill, the standing stone at Glake, some six feet tall and imprinted with a number of cup-marks, bears witness to the labours of our distant ancestors.

And perhaps it was the feet of those early farming folk that shaped the first forerunner of the old cart-track that today winds half-forgotten from Pinmore Mains, up over the shoulder of Balligmorrie Hill and on down to the Water of Muck before crossing the old county march and losing itself in what is one of the loneliest stretches of Galloway – now largely commercial forestry, formerly scrub woodland and bare moor. Hugh's pirlie-pig surfaced not far from the old track's highest point, just east of the place where it fords a shallow burn.

But as to the pirlie-pig's story, we have nothing to go on other than guesswork. Was it deliberately buried? Or maybe stolen and then secreted - as Hugh suspects - in a convenient rabbit-hole? Most puzzling of all – not to say sinister – is why its valuable contents were never recovered. Whatever the reason, it is not hard to sense a dark deed at the heart of the mystery. All we can say for sure is that for four centuries and more the pirlie-pig lay undisturbed on Balligmorrie Hill until a summer morning in 1955 when a young man and his plough brought its long sleep finally to an end.

Muirkirk's Darkest Hour

Tom Mackin was 21 in 1947, the year he started work as a coal-miner, following in his father and grandfather's footsteps. He had recently returned home to Muirkirk after completing national service, serving in the Royal Navy in locations as far apart as Kristiansand, Norway and Bombay, India. 'I never saw a shot fired in anger,' he told me, 'I was one of the lucky ones.' Ten years later, on a night when luck deserted many in the Kames Colliery, Tom's good fortune held out – if only by the thinnest of margins.

On Tuesday, 19 November 1957, Tom was 700 feet underground, working on a narrow coal-seam with his workmate, John Frew, a miner in his twenties, and John Dempster, a shot-firer (in charge of explosives) in his sixties. It was at some point during the evening that the three men first sensed something amiss. The air in their lamplight appeared hazy, and an unfamiliar smell, impossible to ignore, had welled up via the return-airway. It wasn't long before the men's suspicions were confirmed when they received an urgent instruction to down tools and proceed at once to the pit-bottom, some half a mile or so from the area where they were working.

It was during the journey to the pit-bottom that things started to go awry. Tom became conscious of what he describes as a scratching sensation in his throat, the effect, he knew, of inhaling bad air. As the men continued, their breathing became increasingly laboured until Tom's workmate, John Frew, finally lost consciousness, having first to be carried, then wheeled in an empty hutch, or coal wagon. Tom himself was next to succumb, collapsing soon after in the gauton - or drainage channel - leaving the oldest man, John Dempster, with the sole responsibility for reaching the pit-bottom to summon assistance.

Looking back, Tom is sure that he remained more or less conscious while he lay on his back, powerless to lift himself out of the gauton, but he also remembers that the gas affected his mind in a rather strange way. He felt certain, he recalls, that he was unlikely ever to see his wife again - 'Oor Margaret will miss me the nicht' were words, he remembers, that ran through his mind. Yet, despite the gravity of the situation, somehow or other he felt a curious detachment from his predicament.

John Dempster made it through. By Tom's reckoning, it took some ten to fifteen minutes – it must surely have felt like a lifetime - before help finally arrived in the form of two, or maybe three, rescuers. I was surprised when he told me that they brought no form of breathing apparatus. Tom and his workmate were simply placed in an empty hutch and wheeled as quickly as possible to the pit-bottom. As they drew closer to the shaft, the air-quality began to improve and Tom's mind gradually cleared. He remembers being informed at the pit-head that an explosion had taken place in the West Mine, though details of injuries and fatalities only reached him the following day. Facts at this stage were still hard to come by.

Heading for the baths, Tom made his way through a gathering of local people – hundreds strong, it was later reported – silently waiting in the rain, some the entire night through. He remembers feeling a powerful need to return home as quickly as possible - perhaps the reason why, when offered an ambulance place, he admits that he declined with uncharacteristic brusqueness, something he felt sorry for later. By nature a mannerly man, the chances are that Tom's behaviour was still affected by his recent brush with death.

In time the news emerged that the explosion had originated just northwest of an area known as Casagranda's Level, a part of the West Mine where 28 miners had been working that evening. Survivors reported a deafening blast followed by a powerful rush of air which threw several men to the ground. The lights were immediately extinguished, the air quickly filled with a choking cloud of dust. During the hours that followed, specialist rescuers, rushed to the scene from as far away as Coatbridge and even Alloa, found their efforts hampered by roof-falls, pockets of gas and the debris of wrecked machinery but, despite such hazards, by two o'clock the following afternoon they had succeeded in accounting for all 28 men. Sadly not everyone had been brought out alive and word soon filtered out that a total of seventeen miners had lost their lives, the greatest ever loss of life in a single incident in the history of the Ayrshire coalfield. Profound shock travelled through Muirkirk - the victims were without exception local men, the youngest still in their teens, the oldest approaching 70 years of age. Within hours an announcement was made that a public inquiry would be set up, to be headed by Sir Harold Roberts, Chief Inspector of Mines, in an attempt to identify the cause of the blast.

Friday 22 and Saturday 23 November were dark days for the local community as Muirkirk saw an unbroken succession of funerals, attended by over a thousand people including the local MP, Emrys Hughes, as well as representatives of the Coal Board and the National Union of Miners. As the mourners paid their respects in chilly November sunshine, many must surely have felt burdened by a weight of unanswered questions. It would take some seven months before the Roberts inquiry would at last be in a position to make its findings public.

The report, when it came in July 1958, helped lay to rest the long-cherished myth that Kames was a 'safe pit.' Over the years, the perceived risk from gas explosion had been deemed so slight that no restrictions had been placed on the use of naked lights, and miners habitually smoked at the coalface. During questioning, the pit safety officer stated that he had considered the colliery 'gey near as safe as outside,' a widely-shared belief which appeared to have led to a rather slipshod testing regime. When coupled with failure to ensure adequate ventilation - the area around Casagranda's Level had been neither inspected nor ventilated for four days prior to the blast – the result had been an undetected build-up of firedamp. According to Richard Evans, Ayrshire Inspector of Mines, given the combination of circumstances, all it would have taken to prompt an explosion was 'someone in the area innocently lighting his pipe' - an everyday event in Kames.

The destructive force of the initial blast, the report continued, had been further exacerbated by a cloud of highly explosive coal-dust which had been subsequently ignited, another scenario previously thought doubtful due to the pit's pervasive dampness. Roberts' report concluded that management had failed over time to take effective measures to combat the dangers posed by coal-dust, and during the course of the inquiry the practice of using this material for 'packing shots' during the detonation of explosives came in for particular criticism. Tom Mackin remembers wryly that once the pit reopened for production, for the first time small clay bricks were supplied for just this purpose.

And reopen, of course, it did - within a few short weeks of the disaster. In spite of clear failings identified in the Roberts report – failings which in the view of the miners' union amounted to a serious breach of the Coal

Mines Act – it was the determination of the government minister responsible, Lord Mills, that no mine official need face legal proceedings. When the gates swung open once again, almost without exception the Kames miners trooped back to their colliery and prepared to go underground. For men like Tom Mackin and John Frew and John Dempster, it was simple. Whatever the dangers, Muirkirk meant mining.

The Middlefield Barn Owls

At first glance the old lime-kiln at High Aldons, south of Girvan, might easily be mistaken for the remains of an ancient fortalice, dug squarely into the rising slope of the hill. High on the front wall there are narrow slots where a family of barn owls once lived, pale and chalky, their saucer-shaped faces bobbing from side to side as they peered out. Today, half a century on, a spectacular geometric crack has riven the front wall of the old lime-kiln and the structure is barely holding together. As far as I know, the barn owls are long departed.

And it transpires that the story is the same throughout much of rural Britain. Recent decades have seen barn owl populations fall victim to changes in farming methods which in many districts led to the loss of hedgerows and their associated field margins, thus destroying valuable habitat both for barn owls and also the small creatures that they prey upon. At the same time, the impact of a rise in the use of agricultural insecticides was felt all the way up to the predators at the top of the food chain including, of course, the barn owl. And if that wasn't serious enough, the bird's plight was further exacerbated by a growing vogue for renovating and converting traditional farm outbuildings, reducing in the process the availability of nesting sites.

In spite of their overall decline, barn owls were still happily in residence at Middlefield farm when Hugh Hendry, his wife Netta, and their two children, Jan and Steven, moved in during the early 1980s. Situated more than 900 feet above sea-level, the farm occupied an imposing position high above the Irvine valley, its south-facing windows overlooking the steep-sided glen of the Burn Anne to the expanse of rumpled moorland that lay beyond, and seemed to stretch - on clear days - as far as the distant peaks of Galloway. As Hugh and his family settled into their new home, he quickly became aware that its picturesque surroundings were just as attractive to barn owls as they were to humans.

Born and brought up in nearby Darvel, Hugh had always felt drawn to the local countryside, spending much of his boyhood exploring the hills and moorlands that fringed the Irvine valley, and acquainting himself with their varied flora and fauna. When Lanfine Estate put Middlefield up for sale in 1982, its timing could hardly have been better. For a number of years Hugh had been rearing pheasants on behalf of local shooting syndicates and the farm's accompanying ten acres would provide him with ample scope to expand.

Well-versed in building maintenance, one of Hugh's early priorities was to bring the fabric of his new property up to scratch. As he set to work on the outbuildings, mending ill-fitting doors where woodwork was damaged or had simply perished over time, it struck him that an unintended consequence of his repairs would be to exclude the farm's resident barn owls from their regular haunts. With this in mind, he deliberately made sure that the birds could still gain access to the hayshed, a building he had noticed that they regularly frequented. The plan was successful. The barn owls stayed.

If anything, Hugh's attachment to his local wildlife grew even deeper as the years went by. During his time at Middlefield he witnessed with sadness a sharp decline in the numbers of several once-familiar moorland species: the curlew and the peewit, and both the red and black grouse. Happily, barn owls fared rather better, bucking the trend and thriving at Middlefield. Living cheek by jowl with his family, the owls came to occupy a special place in Hugh's affections. Conscious that he couldn't be Middlefield's guardian for ever, and keenly aware that the fate of a growing number of farm steadings were to be converted to up-market residences, he resolved in 2008 to take practical steps to secure the barn owls' future.

Hugh's vision of creating a purpose-built, permanent owl-house, constructed as far as possible using local and traditional materials, was one that required a builder, and this was where his cousin, Pearson Park, stepped in. Having spent his entire working-life in the building trade, if anyone knew how to put together a sturdy, durable structure then it would be him. When Pearson heard the details of Hugh's proposed 'owlcote', without a moment's hesitation he agreed to be part of the project.

What Hugh envisaged was a tower, round in shape, whose inner core of brickwork would be faced with an external layer of hard-wearing stone. True to his principle of utilising local materials, he acquired a batch of second-hand bricks (fired originally at the former Maxwood brickworks at Galston) from a demolished lace factory in Darvel which also proved a useful source of roof-slates. A nearby former Co-operative building supplied wooden spars and sarking which would be used during construction of the owl-house roof. Purchased from a quarry near Troon, whinstone for the external wall qualified nonetheless as a local material, having been excavated in times past at Law Quarry near Darvel.

High Aldons Limekilns

The spot chosen was a short walk east of the farm steading, on the boundary between open grassland and an adjacent belt of trees. The initial turf was cut in the New Year of 2008 and signalled the start of building in earnest. First, a base had to be completed with the tower's circular shape, some eight feet across, laid out on top. Hugh mixed and barrowed cement while Pearson started laying the first courses of bricks, encasing them within a rugged outer shell of whinstone. Work inched forward throughout the year, the two men devoting as much of their spare time to the project as they could afford. When the walls reached an appropriate height, protruding stones were put in place for use as perches by the building's future tenants. Autumn brought a dip in temperatures, and large wooden boards and tarpaulins were required to protect the cement mortar from frost damage at night-time.

In spite of bad weather and shrinking daylight, Hugh and Pearson simply wrapped up warmly and kept on building. When it was no longer possible to work from ground-level, the men erected homemade wooden scaffolding which they used to position an entrance-hole for owls, high on the west face of the tower. By March 2009, at a height of just over twelve feet, the walls were complete and, in preparation for a peaked roof, spars and sarking were nailed into place. In a nod to modern times, PVC bargeboards were fitted snugly round the eaves. Finally the roof-slates were secured on top of roofing-felt and lead-flashings, and at last the owlcote was fully wind and watertight and ready to receive its first guests.

A few cosmetic touches, however, had still to be added. Donated by a Kilmarnock blacksmith, a decorative iron gate was installed at the entrance-way, complete with an attached nameplate - 'The Owlcote' - put together by a Galston engineering works. Last but by no means least, a wooden nesting-box was placed inside the tower, high above head-height, in an effort to tempt the local barn owls to take up residence. That done, all that remained for the builders to do was to step back and admire their handiwork, then walk away and leave nature to take its course.

Things happened more quickly than expected. By early autumn there was evidence of occupation when stray barn owl feathers appeared on the floor alongside the pellets of indigestible food that the birds habitually regurgitate. So far so good, but no-one could have the predicted the testing times that were just around the corner. That winter of 2009-10 proved one of the harshest for many years with prolonged snowfall and untypically keen frosts, conditions that are well known to take their toll on barn owl populations. High above sea-level, Middlefield was still under snow at the start of April 2010, and as many as three barn owls were known to have perished locally during the freezing weather.

Spring, of course, finally made it through and fortunately the surviving barn owls were strong enough to stage a remarkable come-back. A pair of the birds began to show an interest in the owlcote and by August the nesting-box was found to contain no fewer than five growing owlets, all of which went on to fledge successfully. And the good news didn't end there. The owlcote's tenants have continued to breed each spring, rearing a new generation of barn owls which have dispersed when mature to colonise the surrounding countryside.

So, thanks to the vision and forethought of one man and the expert craftsmanship of another the future of the Middlefield barn owls is assured. Well, maybe. Despite the success of the project, Hugh Hendry has grave concerns about the spread of afforestation in the area, not sadly our native woodlands that give shelter to a plethora of small creatures but rather a monoculture of commercial conifers which robs the owls of their preferred habitat and offers nothing by way of return. Recent years have seen another local predator, the hen harrier, vanish entirely from the forested moorlands. What the future holds for the barn owl time alone will tell, but what is certain is that the efforts of two dedicated men have made its survival a good deal more likely.

What Ayrshire Lost

Up until 1987, if voters on the upper reaches of the Main Water of Luce wished to exercise their democratic right then they were faced with rather an unenviable prospect. Those sufficiently sound in wind and limb - and who had the best part of a day to spare - might have donned warm clothing and a stout pair of walking-boots and trekked up the old cart-track that climbs north from Lagafater Lodge, up over the 1,400 foot shoulder of Beneraird before dropping down to Kilwhannel and the last weary miles to Ballantrae - a distance to the polling station of well over five miles. Even for those with access to wheeled transport, the act of voting involved a circuitous 30-mile drive, passing by necessity through a stretch of Wigtownshire, re-entering Ayrshire at the foot of Glen App and finally heading north to Ballantrae before you could so much as catch a glimpse of your ballot-paper.

Of course, in the past the majority of country people had no option other than to walk, though the secluded Beneraird track didn't always make for a safe or easy crossing as a tragic case in the late nineteenth century demonstrated only too clearly. March of 1891 had been a cold, dry month but the first day of April brought a dramatic change when the weather turned to snow. It is possible that James Henry, a gamekeeper at Lagafater, was returning from the annual Colmonell cattle show when he found himself in difficulties during a snowstorm on Beneraird. When he failed to arrive home, it took three days for his absence to be reported to the authorities - quite possibly Lagafater was snowbound - but, once alerted, the police responded speedily. During the search that followed, PC Donald Henderson was combing the hill-top of Beneraird when he came upon the missing man's body, lying face down in the snow, some 50 yards adrift of the trail. A regular attender at Ballantrae Church, the gamekeeper was known for his habitual sobriety and was undoubtedly well acquainted with the local area, yet it was concluded nonetheless that the snowstorm had caused him to wander from the path until finally, disorientated and exhausted, he had succumbed to the cold a mere two miles from his home. The dead man left behind a widow, Elizabeth, though - perhaps mercifully - no children. At the spot where his body was recovered a mossy cairn now stands with a small metal plaque attached whose legend reads simply: 'James Henry Overcome by Blizzard 1891.'

When the Lagafater Estate, complete with its recently-completed lodge, went on the market in 1910, the successful buyer was a prosperous Liverpool merchant, Cedric Boult, who had acquainted himself with the area during previous visits as a shooting-tenant. Like others of its kind, the estate was geared largely towards the late summer grouse-shoot, with some exceptional bags recorded in the local area over the years. On one notable occasion - in 1877 - no fewer than 470 brace of birds had been shot in what must have amounted to a four-day slaughter on the Glenapp hills. Such was the sport's popularity among the late Victorian well-to-do that an isolated railway station was established at Glenwhilly for the specific use of well-heeled sportsmen seeking ready access to the grouse-moors. An old cart-track that climbs north-west from the railway station and descends from the hill near Barnvannoch was upgraded at Cedric Boult's behest and, before the rise of the motor-car, it formed the estate's principal supply route.

Lagafater Lodge

At the time of his purchase, Cedric's son, Adrian, was an undergraduate at Christ Church College, Oxford, a young man whose penchant for music was such that he was elected president of the University Musical Club that same year, numbering among his college friends the distinguished composer, Ralph Vaughan Williams. During his holiday visits to Lagafater, perhaps it comes as no great surprise that the scholarly young musician made for rather a reluctant sportsman and was reputedly a rather wayward shot on the grouse-moor. Mercifully, he was quite aware that his calling lay elsewhere, proceeding in due course to wield his conductor's baton to better effect than he ever had the sporting gun. No doubt the gamekeepers and grouse-beaters of Lagafater were delighted - not to say relieved - at Adrian's (later Sir Adrian's) continuing musical success with the eminent orchestras of his day.

On the other hand, his older sister, Olive, was a regular and devoted visitor to the family's Scottish estate. So thorough was her knowledge of the property and its history that when, during the 1960s, a number of Glasgow and South-Western Railway 'chairs' (cast-iron brackets used to affix rails to sleepers) turned up inexplicably in a far-flung corner of the moor - a good six or seven miles from the nearest stretch of track - it was Olive who came up with an explanation. Prior to her father's acquisition of Lagafater, the previous owner had been an official of Glasgow and South-Western Railways. Following Cedric's purchase of the estate, Olive recalled, he had for several successive summers engaged a seasonal worker, an Irishman named Landor from Donegal, whose job it was to undertake drainage work around the estate. To avoid the need for tramping daily in and out of remote areas, the ditcher would construct for himself a simple sod hut where, equipped with provisions, he would live in situ for the duration of the job in hand. In all probability, Olive suggested, the railway chairs had been lying unused until they were transported across the moor by pony in the years immediately prior to the First World War where they were used to bolster the perimeter of the spring that provided the Irishman's drinking-water. The fact that the lonely spring went by the name of Landor's Well only served to lend credence to her explanation.

While she was in the habit of spending her winters in the south of England, nonetheless Miss Boult returned faithfully to Lagafater each summer until well into old age. If she happened to be in residence at election time, she would make a point of being driven round to Ballantrae in order to cast her vote, possibly the only elector south of Beneraird who bothered to do so, and invariably she would make a day of her outing by lunching out. Such was her affection for her Scottish home that, following her death, aged 98, in July 1980 at Tunbridge Wells, the old lady's ashes were subsequently brought north for burial in the grounds of the lodge. Miss Boult's death notice in *The London Gazette* placed her beloved Lagafater 'in the counties of Ayr and Wigtown.'

Regrettably the gamekeeper, James Henry's, death in the late nineteenth century was not the only loss of life, or indeed the greatest, to occur on the Lagafater moors. In June 1945 another gamekeeper, James Wright, presumably got something of a shock when he found a seriously injured American on his doorstep who gasped out news of an air-crash in the surrounding hills. A search party was promptly assembled which duly located the aircraft on Pildinny, a 1,200 foot hill-top situated a half-mile or so to the south of Beneraird.

The crashed aeroplane, it transpired, was an American Liberator bomber which had departed from RAF Seething in Norfolk bound for Prestwick and had subsequently been reported missing some 36 hours before the injured man, Staff Sergeant John May, struggled off the hill. Of the plane's twenty passengers and crew, sadly only Sergeant May and two others survived and were transferred as quickly as possible to the RAF hospital at Lochnaw Castle near Stranraer. Although weather conditions at the time of the accident were believed to have been misty with light rain falling, ultimately it proved impossible to establish categorically the exact cause of the catastrophe. A theory was advanced that perhaps the crew had made the tragic error of mistaking Loch Ryan for the waters of Ayr Bay which, signalling the Liberator's approach to Prestwick, would have prompted the pilot to descend.

By a cruel irony, the passengers were all American servicemen, *en route* to the USA following the cessation of wartime hostilities in Europe. Seven of their number, including the pilot, James Blank of Lehighton, Pennsylvania, were laid to rest in the American Cemetery in Cambridge, while the bodies of the remaining men were flown back to their homeland. Of the three survivors, Staff Sergeant May, who in spite of his own grievous injuries had struggled from Pildinny to raise the alarm, was decorated in his home country when he received the Soldier's Medal.

In the post-war years Lagafater slipped from the public eye until the 1980s when it awoke with a start to find itself the surprising subject of political debate. In February 1986 a boundary amendment was proposed by the then Kyle and Carrick District Council whereby the isolated residences on the upper Main Water of Luce, along with more than 6,000 acres of associated hill and moor, would be removed from the Council's jurisdiction and pass instead to the Wigtown District of Dumfries and Galloway. During the consultation process that followed no objection was raised from any of the nine members of the electorate who would be affected by the proposed move.

Barnvannoch School

Perhaps their silence isn't so surprising. As far back as the 1940s, the primary school at Barnvannoch, a couple of miles south of Lagafater, had been closed - contrary to the wishes of the local people - in a bid to save Ayr County Council the cost of a teacher's salary: £500 per annum at the time. It wasn't as though the council had ever splashed out much on Barnvannoch School, originally a prefabricated hut which had seen service during the First World War in a munitions factory near Gretna. As a result of the school's closure, four children of school age were conveyed daily to be educated in neighbouring Wigtownshire at a cost of 35 shillings (£1.75) per child per day, payable to the Wigtownshire authorities, thus trimming

Ayrshire's annual saving to a paltry £150. If that wasn't bad enough, shortly after the school's closure Ayr County Council declined to make a contribution towards the upkeep of the Lagafater road along which the children passed each day to and from school. All things considered, it would be no more than understandable if the people of the Main Water of Luce felt a little cool towards their local authority when over a period of decades it looked very much as though Ayrshire's main priority had been to get them off its hands. At any event, the transfer duly went ahead on 1 October 1987 when the upper reaches of the Main Water of Luce were severed from Ayrshire and repositioned instead within Galloway.

To reach Lagafater today, you must drive south from Barrhill over the moors around the Cross Water of Luce. Crossing into Galloway, a winding minor road turns north at New Luce which soon offers views of the Main Water of Luce. At the farmhouse of Shennas, older maps indicate that you have crossed into what was once Ayrshire, the former boundary no longer signposted.

As you proceed, the sense of remoteness seems to intensify, scarcely marred by the distant presence of wind-turbines, manning the far horizon. Beyond Barnvannoch - site of the former school - a grassy embankment, lying at right angles to the Water of Luce and divided mid-way by the flow of the stream, is all that remains of Cedric Boult's efforts at creating a man-made loch for use in activities such as boating and duck-shooting. The project wasn't wholly successful. The dam gave way during the 1950s and, when Olive Boult's attempts to bolster it eventually ran into difficulties, it was judged best to allow it to remain breached, a decision likely to have been applauded downstream. Ducks, in any case, had evidently been savvy enough to give Cedric's loch a fairly wide berth.

Shortly after, the road takes a sudden dip and you find yourself descending into a wooded hollow, the kind of place where it isn't difficult to imagine the steady gaze of a wolf, or a wildcat perhaps, penetrating the tangled thickets of times past. From the bridge spanning the Laggie Burn you catch your first glimpse of the lodge - an elegant Edwardian mansion, tastefully painted in pastel-shades and ringed by ornamental trees and tidy lawns.

Lagafater feels very much like what it is - the end of the road - though it wasn't always thus. In the past families tramped in and out of Strabracken, an isolated shepherd's house now ruined - and on perhaps, for whatever private purpose, to what was known as the 'the Whisky Glen' beyond. Others, of course, would have crossed to Ballantrae and the coast via Beneraird. But today most traffic is brought to a halt at Lagafater whose tranquil beauty serves as a poignant reminder of what was lost in 1987 when the lodge, its personalities and its history were excised from Ayrshire by a few brief strokes of a bureaucrat's pen.

When Times Were Tough

On 28 November 1913, Robert McMaster McIntosh Kellie emerged, kicking and girning, into daylight, fifth of the six children born to William Kellie, a south Ayrshire shepherd, and his wife, Annie Boddan. The couple's fourth child, wee Annie, had died at eighteen months when the doctor didn't make it through the snowdrifts. David, their sixth and last, didn't appear till his father was on active service overseas. William and Annie Kellie were my grandparents, their son, Robert, my father. Within a year of his birth, shockwaves from distant events would carry into his family's quiet backwater and change their world forever.

Home in those early days was Blanneyscaw, south-east of Pinwherry, an isolated shepherd's cottage without power, running water or even a proper access road. Robert Kellie maintained that his earliest memories stretched back to this time: of sitting, for example, on the knee of a uniformed man with a moustache – his father, most likely, home on leave from the front. For William Kellie died at the Somme on 21 March 1918, the very date of his second son, Willie's, ninth birthday.

Postmen, it seems, wouldn't make the climb to Blanneyscaw, so an arrangement had been made with an obliging farmer's wife by the roadside that whenever there was mail she would hang a bed sheet on the line. I often picture my grandmother that bitter morning in 1918, the white sheet flapping in a blashy March wind and the fateful telegram in her hand. It is hard to imagine her thoughts as she cooked and cleaned and scrubbed and mended as on any other day, forced to conceal her anguish. She must surely have wondered how she would face the years to come.

After my grandfather's death, his family were obliged to vacate their tied-house and a horse-drawn cart trundled their meagre belongings a dozen or so miles up the winding Water of Assel. Their destination was Tormitchell, at that time an industrious small community of quarrymen and their families, persistently choked in quarry dust and rocked at frequent intervals by the blasting of dynamite.

My dad had vivid memories of community events at Tormitchell, such as the grand occasion when the first wireless set arrived, installed amid great ceremony in a hayshed with sufficient space for the whole community to attend. Much twiddling of knobs ensued before finally the radio crackled into life, linking Tormitchell for the first time with the wider world. So startled was my grandmother by the quavering voice from the ether that she suffered bad dreams as a result for weeks to come.

Every spring the Tormitchell boys made an annual pilgrimage to Pinclanty Loch, tramping across the hills in holiday mood with high jinks and capers the order of the day. They took with them a supply of empty pillowcases to be stuffed with the eggs of the seagulls that nested in large numbers by the loch shore. Jubilantly the boys would carry home their spoils, to be sold by weight to a carter who turned up at this time every year. The earnings they brought in provided a modest boost to the Tormitchell economy. The eggs, it was believed, were to be used in the production of glue.

On a hillside west of the quarry, at the end of a puddly track, sits the old farmhouse of Barbae. No more than a shell today, its outbuildings are ruinous and open to the sky. Things were different in my dad's day, and Barbae featured in his store of boyhood memories. Sent to the farm for a dozen eggs, somewhere along the way a half-crown slipped unnoticed from his pocket. The loss of two and sixpence was no laughing matter but, despite a desperate hunt, the money never turned up. When I was a boy myself, my dad would still start rooting around whenever we passed Barbae, poking into clumps of dockens and nettles with his walking-stick, eyes glued to the ground. That was just him. Even after half a century, he hated giving up.

Money, of course, remained the perennial problem. Working class Scots of that generation didn't expect life to be easy, particularly for a war widow raising her family on a meagre income. My grandmother rose early each morning to bake and get the children ready for school. Then, several days a week, she would trudge the three miles to Pinmore Station in time to catch the early train. Her days were spent in Girvan, cleaning and baking for the Mitchell family who owned the Tormitchell quarry. Late in the afternoon, she would make the return journey, arriving home in time to feed her family and make a start on her own housework.

Tragedy very nearly struck one winter morning, in the wake of a night of high winds and torrential rain. Making for the train, my grandmother headed in darkness for the narrow wooden bridge that spanned the Assel along a path that I am certain she could have followed blindfold. Suddenly she felt herself step into nothing, swept away by powerful waters. She must surely have been frantic as she snatched at twigs and branches, choking and spluttering in icy spate-water, before finally she succeeded in hauling herself on to the bank. When she recovered sufficiently to see that the footbridge had been washed away, my grandmother's blood must have run cold. What thoughts ran through her mind as she fought and struggled that morning in the grip of surging waters? In one fleeting moment, her children might easily have been orphaned.

My dad never grumbled about his three-mile walk to the wee school at Pinmore – that generation didn't. Every stretch and bend was known and named, and every step of the way possessed its reservoir of memories: the Keeper's Gairden, long overgrown now and swallowed up in trees; the Tinkers' Turn, a widening of the road presumably sufficient in times past to take a horse and caravan; the Dalfask road-end, where yellow globe-flowers bloomed every June, and still do. My dad held his primary teacher, 'Miss Broon', in high regard, speaking of her affectionately throughout his life. But promising scholar or not, like most schoolboys, he wasn't averse to a day off if the opportunity arose.

In the years that followed the First World War, farmers still made use of schoolchildren as a convenient pool of casual labour. So when a local farmer appeared in the classroom at Pinmore offering a day's turnip-thinning, my dad wouldn't have passed up the chance of a sixpence. In dry weather it wasn't such a bad job – you worked your way up and down the drills on all fours, removing by hand all but the sturdiest young plants, though for a schoolboy in short trousers it was undeniably sore on the knees. So improvised knee-pads were issued, cut out of rough sackcloth, but by the time my dad reached the front of the queue there were none left.

His knees, of course, grew red and raw as the morning wore on, scratched by the small, sharp stones among the soil. To ease the pressure, he took to sitting to one side as he worked, eager not to forego the wages that had been promised. But the farmer, watching like a hawk for signs of slacking, lost no time in bellowing - 'Ye'll no' dae much work sittin' on yer erse, boy.' Stung by injustice, my dad rose to his feet and left the turnip field without a word. He walked home, bleeding and affronted, the precious sixpence forgotten.

Under Miss Broon's guidance, my dad progressed in due course to Girvan High School. Although the County Council had agreed to reimburse the cost of a bicycle, so deeply ingrained was my grandmother's habit of thrift that she bought a second-hand bike. On glorious summer mornings my dad relished his eight-mile ride to school, swooping and freewheeling downhill with fine views ahead as Ailsa Craig edged around the shoulder of the Byne Hill. But on a blustery January afternoon, near-dark at four o'clock, the homeward journey would have been a lot less appealing. Within a few miles of the shore, the Pinmore road climbs to a height of 500 feet where it curls around Dinvin, a commanding prehistoric hill-fort. But the rigours of the road didn't seem to trouble my dad. There is a snapshot, faded now and cracked with age, in which he poses proudly on his bicycle with a well-loved fox-terrier, Jimmy, on his knee. It dates, I suppose, from the mid-1920s.

The rector at Girvan was Mr Finlayson, a scholarly man who had edited a collection of Ayrshire poetry that found a place on many a local bookshelf. Under his tutelage my dad continued to prosper, excelling particularly in English and foreign languages. With an impressive clutch of Highers and Lowers under his belt, he was offered a place at Durham University, the tuition fees to be waived if he agreed to take on the duties of games instructor in an associated boys' school. But the specialist sports clothing that the position required - known as 'whites' - was beyond my grandmother's means and the opportunity slipped away. It seems strange now, but the thought of taking on even a modest loan was simply not in her orbit.

Employment was hard to come by during those years of depression. Mr Aird of Asselfoot, a kindly local farmer whose circle of acquaintance was wider than most in the locality, consulted the Chief Constable of Ayr who advised that my dad apply to a Scottish burgh police force, while posting off a second form as back-up to an English county. As things turned out, Essex pipped Kilmarnock Burgh and, with a heavy heart, my dad packed his bag to head south.

Romford in the early '30s was effectively an extension to the grim eastern suburbs of London, its sprawling streets and smoky terraces a foreign land to a young man from the Scottish countryside. One of the first jobs my dad faced was being instructed to cut down a suicide victim who had died by hanging – a serious test of a young recruit's mettle. He was accommodated in spartan police barracks where the other recruits' idea of fun was to call him 'Jock' and to stomp around the dormitory, carrying him shoulder high and skirling in raucous imitation of a pipe band. Reared on plain, home-cooking, my dad found institutional food disagreeable, though the cook prepared him a regular ashet of baked rice in place of the pickles which his English counterparts unaccountably enjoyed, spread thickly on slices of bread. When he became unwell, his skin erupting in boils, an Essex doctor's best guess was an allergy to the local water and suggested that a transfer closer to home might be the answer.

My dad related a curious incident which conveyed vividly the homesickness that had haunted him during his time south of the border. For a spell his nightshift partner was an older officer, a sergeant who had originated in rural Aberdeenshire. As they pounded the gloomy Romford streets, checking on door-handles and the locks of shop premises, an unexpected sound one night stopped both men in their tracks. High above the roofs and streetlamps, curlews were calling as they passed overhead. To my dad, the birds' familiar warbling cries conjured up the hills and moors and lonely places of home, in sharp contrast to his present surroundings. 'They're faur frae hame,' was the older man's comment. That was the poignant moment, my dad would later recall, when it struck him forcibly what he must do.

And so came the move to Kilmarnock, an easy bus ride up the coast from home and a more familiar world than the dismal streets of Romford. During the war years he met my mother – in a police cell, as it happened – a pretty young police shorthand typist with dark hair and fine, regular features. 'What were your initial impressions?' I remember asking. Never one to give much away, his reply was characteristically guarded. 'It occurred to me,' he finally admitted, 'that I'd need to keep my eye on this one.'

And the rest, as they say, is history.

Index